ARCHIE MACPHERSON was born and raised i
end of Glasgow. He was headteacher of Swin
before he began his broadcasting career at
here that he became the principal commentator and presenter on
Sportscene. He has since worked with STV, Eurosport, Talksport,
Radio Clyde and Setanta. He has commentated on various key sporting events including 3 Olympic Games and 6 FIFA World Cups. In
2005 he received a Scottish BAFTA for special contribution to Scottish broadcasting and was inducted into Scottish football's Hall of
Fame in 2017.

Touching the Heights

Personal Portraits of Scottish Sporting Greats

ARCHIE MACPHERSON

Luath Press Limited
EDINBURGH
www.luath.co.uk

First published 2022

ISBN: 978-1-80425-018-1

The author's right to be identified as author of this book under the Copyright, Designs and Patents Act 1988 has been asserted.

The paper used in this book is recyclable. It is made from low chlorine pulps produced in a low energy, low emission manner from renewable forests.

Printed and bound by Robertson Printers, Forfar

Typeset in 11 point Sabon by Lapiz

To Pat Woods, my researcher, who through the decades has been a constant source of inspiration.

Contents

Acknowledgements

I WOULD LIKE to thank Dr Gerry Hassan for his overall critique of my manuscript and I am grateful to the BBC's Tom English and John Beattie for their evaluations of segments of the book. Tommy Gilmour, former boxing promoter, guided me carefully as I ventured into his sport, as did former Ryder Cup player Bernard Gallagher in pursuance of Eric Brown on to the links. I am indebted to Lara Scott, assistant editor of the *Daily Record* picture desk for her assistance in providing the photographs from the newspaper's archives. I was rightly kept in line throughout by the meticulous care of my editor Kira Dowie. As the book is also a product of the time of the Coronavirus lockdown, I hold AstraZeneca in awe for keeping the wolf from the door.

Prologue

FRIDAY AFTERNOON WAS that magical time I have always associated with the emergence of the Scottish hero. Just after two o'clock, on those days, our teacher in the primary school in the east end of Glasgow, Miss Paton, would tell us to sit back, put everything away and just listen. She would leave her desk and sit in a chair in the middle of the floor in front of us, to remould herself as storyteller, distinct from the strict martinet she damn well was. One day she told us a tale from this russet-coloured book about Eric Liddell and the Olympic Games in Paris in 1924. It thrilled and puzzled me. His strict Christian beliefs prevented him from running in the 100 metres heat on a Sunday, for which he was favourite, and instead he won the 400 metres gold on a weekday. It was difficult to grasp. I could understand the likes of shunning football in the backcourt to attend bible class on the Sabbath, but tossing away the chance to win the coveted Blue Riband event and the honour associated with it, was a sacrifice that was beyond the comprehension of a ten-year-old.

It was not until decades later in 1970 that I fully grasped the effect Miss Paton's story was to have on me. It was during the Commonwealth Games in Edinburgh. Fortune had smiled benevolently on me. For in the BBC's Games office, in the media centre in Edinburgh, my desk was only feet away from that of the great Harold Abrahams, then a BBC athletics pundit. As anybody who has seen *Chariots of Fire* will know, Abrahams won the 100 metres gold in 1924, principally because the British record holder for that distance, Eric Liddell, had refused to compete.

Thinking back to the day I first heard Liddell's story in that classroom, I was in awe of this old man sitting near me. Then aged 71, he commanded respect from everyone and from his desk he intoned, like a cardinal, about athletics; his statistics sounding as if they had been plucked from the Old Testament. But, in fact, he also turned out to be a cantankerous old bugger, breaking hardly a smile in all the time I was in his presence and clearly not suffering fools gladly with his waspish delivery to all and sundry. And as a result, for a fledgling like myself in broadcasting then, he had become virtually unapproachable. When I recounted my disappointment to the superb BBC radio commentator Welshman Peter Jones, he was at pains to alert me to the disappointments the great runner had suffered in later years and that at heart, Abrahams was a romantic, as portrayed by Ben Cross in the film. For hadn't he taken a sliver of gold from the medal he had won, almost certainly because of Liddell's absence and converted it into a wedding ring for his betrothed? And then had not both medal and ring subsequently been stolen from his home? It was a kind of precis of the collapse of his fortunes. It didn't ease my discomfort though at being so close to his hovering truculence and I assumed that had I brought Liddell into the conversation Abrahams would have barked my head off. Admittedly, I was something of a faint heart then, so I learned nothing of that tumultuous time of Paris 1924 from that iconic figure. And, in any case, weighing heavily on me was the feeling that it was not the occasion for reflection and analysis of the past, amidst the helter-skelter of reporting on the Games, so eventually I was swallowed up in pursuit of other events. I still regret that.

But it was then I realised I was in debt to Miss Paton. For she had brought a sportsman into the classroom where previously her history stories were about kings and queens, knights and battles. She had given sports its proper place in the forefront of our appreciation of the past. So I can claim to trace my sports zealotry back to the Liddell story and of the mission I found myself following, of convincing people of how vital the battles in sports arenas were in shaping society's character, and lending us safety valves to ventilate deep-rooted feelings. It has never been easy. For instance, I used to relish coming across some hugely buttoned-up administrative BBC mandarin who would affect a disdainful air when you associated yourself with sport, clearly regarding it as waste of anybody's time. Then suddenly, from the depths of their subconscious they might utter, 'The ball's in their court'; or 'it's par for the course'; or, as the executive said to me just as I was leaving the BBC, 'You've had a good innings'; and as a reflection of the kind of political scene in the last decade, 'They're moving the goalposts'. All as if sport had slipped under their radar, triumphantly embedding itself in their language. They certainly were indifferent to my acceptance of George Orwell's assessment of sport as being, '...war without the shooting.' It reached a peak of callousness for me in 1971 in a discussion about the Ibrox disaster, when 66 people, including some kids, were killed in a staircase accident, and Pat Walker, a BBC executive asserted to me, '66 out of 80,000. Not all that many.' A mining disaster of that dimension would have provoked a different sort of response.

But progress was made. Not long after that I proposed to BBC Scotland's new flagship news programme, *Reporting Scotland*, that they should establish a regular Friday evening sports bulletin and weekend preview when, at that time, sport was barely mentioned in news except when some football personality transgressed the law of the land. The almost dismissive resistance to that idea was such that I became painfully aware of how a suffragette must have felt in fighting for the vote. Then along came a new tough but progressive news editor in George Sinclair who was a regular attender at Scottish football, saw the light and thus was born the Friday night sport niche, the kind of which is seen on any news channel in the land now. Of course, my main passion was football which figured heavily in that preview. But I was also occasionally unfaithful to it and strayed. I found myself courting boxing, athletics, golf and even rugby personalities, as will be seen in this narrative. They all excited and inspired me by how they fought their corners in their private lives and taught me something about how to survive in their harshly competitive world. Some well known, others less so. Certainly their stories of sporting excellence would have been fit for that Friday afternoon story-time spot, given that Eric Liddell had paved the way for them. So I want to place them all round a fantasy dinner table, not just to dine, but to relive how I saw them in action and how much they had in common. I suppose some would end up throwing bread-rolls at one another, or at me, and certainly a few would end up legless under that table. I would recount their stories to prove how much they had in common.

My first invite would be to the man who grew up near me, ate from the same fish and chip shops, swam in the same baths, clambered along similar backcourt dykes, played on the same ash pitches and, as life proved, certainly did not squander those character-building pursuits.

CHAPTER I

The Bowery Boy

THE DOC STRODE into the BBC building, in 1971, with a smile on his
face, armed with a ready quip about the lah-de-dah folk of Glasgow's
west end around Queen Margaret Drive, sat back in a chair like he
had staked it forever and then proceeded to hold the Corporation
to ransom. He had arrived for an interview. You felt instantly that
Tommy Docherty was playing a role on a stage to a wider audience
than merely the handful around him in the BBC sports office. A seis-
mic change was about to take place in the humdrum normality of
that setting which ran daily on the principle that nothing ever changes
much. It was about to. For without further ado he asked a question.

'How much am I getting for this?'

It had the nonchalance of a man asking for a cup of tea, but a
silence immediately fell over an office containing several producers, a scattering of secretaries and a television presenter, all of whom
had never heard that sentence uttered in their presence before. In that
office where money and contracts were never mentioned, it had the
effect of someone farting openly and loudly without any apology. All
this was accentuated by the fact that nobody there could answer that
question. He then made it clear that he would not be doing any interview, unless he knew what we were crossing his palm with. No hostility in his voice, no aggression. It was going to be a friendly stand-off,
because nobody really knew what to do next. Anybody in the media
business would have known that all this should have been arranged
in advance by somebody somewhere, even someone in that office,
except for the fact that the BBC was quite unlike any other business.
His request would have to go through various strata of bureaucracy,
with an added complication that the interview I was about to conduct
with him would be used by our colleagues in London on one of their
network programmes, so the cross-border political question would

have to be thrashed out as to who was actually going to pay for his presence. Of course, we were hoping the lords of the manor in London would stump up whatever the fee was likely to be. In any national issue, major or minor, we in BBC Scotland always played the subordinate role.

I knew this would take some time, as one of the producers set off to tackle this problem with a look on his face of a man asked to find the source of the Amazon. Meanwhile the Doc sat there and flicked over a newspaper, humming and whistling, awaiting the outcome of our tackling the labyrinthine BBC accountancy system. Our colleagues in London were interested, simply because the Doc was popular in England, particularly throughout the media, where he was seen as a sure antidote to bland clichés. After all, in his interview with Chelsea directors for the managerial post, he admitted afterwards to the press, in referring to Vic Buckingham, the other man in consideration, 'If I get the job you'll get a coach. With the other man you'll get a hearse!' His tongue was quicker than that of the lizard. He had been in the south since 1949 having only played senior football for two years in Scotland with Celtic, where on his debut they lost 1–0 to Rangers. Then he moved on to Preston North End. But what really caught their imagination in the south was his management of Chelsea, right in the heart of the metropolis, where they could boast of support from a wide array of public personalities, including many from the entertainment business – like the late Hollywood actor Steve McQueen, Tom Courtenay, Tommy Steele or the late Sir Richard Attenborough who became obsessed with the club after being allowed to train there for his demanding role as Pinky in the film *Brighton Rock*. Ultimately he was to become a director of the club at the time the Doc was manager. That glitzy decor suited the Doc with his ability to reach out to the media as if he were part of showbiz himself. After leaving Chelsea he had drifted to four other clubs before accepting an interim provisional two-match post as Scotland manager, in September 1971, when he was holding a minor assistant manager's job with Hull City. Throughout though, he still carried that confident swagger that was a combination of the Glesca 'fancy-your-chances-then-big-man?' confidence and the cosmopolitan ease he had soaked up on his travels. All that was irresistible to the media.

On the assumption that somebody would cough up enough to satisfy the new Scotland man I sat alone with him, the sun shining strongly through the window, in keeping with his sunny, cheery disposition of non-compliance. It was then I decided to play my trump card.

'I was born in Shettleston,' I told him. '771 Shettleston Road. Above a Tally's. Billiard hall just round the corner. *Palaceum* cinema just across the road.'

He located that immediately. He put down his newspaper and I knew that the familiarity of that geography had slipped through his guard. There was a popular belief, which I think still exists, that he had been born and brought up in the Gorbals area of Glasgow which, since its generational association with deprivation and squalor, suited the dramatisation of his rise to fame. In fact, his family left the Gorbals before he could walk and he lived in the east end right up to his teens, only half-a-mile away from where I was born in Shettleston. He certainly did not have an easy life there. He told the *Daily Telegraph* once,

> If you wanted a new pair of shoes you went down the swimming baths in bare feet and just nicked a pair. I didn't think it was morally wrong. It was the thing to do.

His lamp-lighting mother Georgina, who brought up her family in dire straits, recounted to Jack Webster the writer and journalist in 1971, on the week the Doc accepted the Scotland job, of a compassion that never left him from childhood. She had come home one night and found a strange boy sleeping in the family bed. The Doc had found him in an air-raid shelter and said to his mother, 'Ma, we cannae leave the wee sowl sleepin' out in that damp shelter.' Georgina and the Doc cared for him for the next ten years.

But all of that was not in the Gorbals. It was in that area of Shettleston streets we called the Bowery. Nobody knows why it was thus named, although the strong suspicion was that it was to mirror the rough, tough neighbourhood that was pictured in the highly popular

Hollywood series, *The Bowery Boys*. Unsurprisingly we identified a lot with American cinema. Because of that lurid reputation, we always gave the streets around his home a wide berth, since tribal affiliations could sometimes lead to combat, which was not always unarmed. The Doc though, was proud of where he was brought up and especially of our mutual love of the first club he played for, Shettleston Juniors. That day, as he sat waiting for some princely sum to come his way, he suddenly became more contemplative when I informed him that in 1947 I saw him making his debut for Shettleston, or the 'Town', as it was called in junior circles.

Standing in the crowd I heard the first sounds of 'C'mon, Doc!' being shouted from the small but packed terracing to the right-hand side of the pavilion, where stood a phalanx of blinkered men who introduced me to an appealing variety of inventive curses that I kept in store, and effectively used, in later years. They were also men who could tell the quality of a player in his first couple of touches on the ball and knew he was a class above the rest. But it was not that the Doc, playing there for the first time, was a stranger to many of them. In a close-knit community they would have known about his qualities from the days he would have been watched from the windows of the tenements playing in the backcourts, before graduating to the likes of amateur football on Shettleston Hill pitches where Corinthian values were scarce and crowd invasions were hardly rare. He was no longer a fledgling, but a bona fide Shettlestonian by wearing the white jersey of the Town which I always considered to be the shirt of neutrality, given the strong Celtic and Rangers sectarian identities which permeated the entire east end. Of course, the others who were playing for the Town around that time made him look like a young prince. One player seemed to typify the loveable peculiarities which surfaced at junior level. Doc McManus was his name. He came from the distinctive tradition of Scottish inside forward play, owing much to stunted growth, a fondness for the bevvy, a disdain of sprinting any more than six yards and a body swerve in which the heavily endowed backside and torso seemed to part company for a fraction of a second. But loveable, for all those reasons, because he could also bewilder the opposition. Others around him there had less subtlety and would have put the boot into a begging infant if required.

It is not that junior football did not excel in many ways and could produce great players in those days. It drew big crowds. In the immediate post-war years there was a hunger for the game at that level because it nurtured local identities, was relatively cheap and convenient to the workplace. I used to see men, having come straight from work in the bottle-works adjacent to the Town's ground, Greenfield Park; maybe having a quick pint; putting a bet on with the illegal bookie, hidden in a close somewhere; and then queuing up to get into the match in their dungarees. The smell of sweat and the pungent odour of their working clothes wafts towards me again even as I write this.

The Doc was not part of that scene very long. Only six games later he left to go to his beloved Celtic. The affection for that club, and his identity with the upbringing that was deeply influenced by St Mark's Catholic School just off Shettleston Road, clung to him for the rest of his life. Although, he couldn't supress his natural irreverence about anything, so long as it made people laugh. I recall sitting beside him at the top table of a dinner he was speaking at in a Glasgow hotel when, during his hilarious speech, he quipped about his religion, 'I was a Catholic until I watched *The Thorn Birds*', referring to the TV series that portrayed illicit love between a priest and his married lover. Nothing escaped his wit, which was honed around the streets of the Bowery where a quick mouth earned you respect. It was no surprise then that he could always refer back to his childhood with ease as if it were only yesterday.

With all of that in his background it is certainly true that the pull of his native land had something to do with him accepting the Scottish managerial post. Here was a feisty fighter from the Bowery who joined Chelsea as manager when they were in dire straits and heading for relegation. He could not save them from that fate, but steered them to promotion in the next season and then went on to win the League Cup in 1965. Playing attractive attacking football which earned his team the name 'Docherty's Diamonds', they went on, in the following two years, to reach two FA finals as runners-up and reached the European Fairs Cup semi-final. More than a reasonable record for a native son. But he was always restless and sometimes stubborn to a fault.

His downfall at Chelsea, for instance, can be traced back to the night in Blackpool when eight players broke a night-time curfew before the match, including the revered Terry Venables. The Doc sent them packing back to London on a train the following morning, and with his virtual reserve team resultingly defeated 6–2, their chances of the English League title had disappeared. Even some of his admirers were critical of that reaction, given that the players had been cooped up in a hotel for a solid week in advance of the League game and that he had misjudged their mood. It began a chain of events which saw increasing hostility between himself and his board, until he simply walked out on them in 1967 – to the alarm of many supporters, one of whom paid for a death notice in the *Times*, 'In memoriam. Chelsea FC, which died Oct 6 1967, after 5 proud and glorious years.'

He was assistant manager for Hull City in 1971 when the emergency call came from the SFA to become caretaker manager replacing Bobby Brown who, after a glorious start to his reign in 1967 by beating the World Champions England at Wembley in 1967, 3–2, had suffered seven defeats and one draw in his last eight games. On the Doc's temporary appointment on 12 September 1971 the *Glasgow Herald* reflected the mood of the entire media when they described the Doc as 'the 42-year-old fiercely partisan Scot'. The rest of the media immediately played up his fiery, cross nature with little scrutiny of that other restless, ambitious side of him and most certainly, his relationships with various football directors, some of whom he was not slow to call 'parasites' to their faces. On top of that some people could not stomach his breathtaking candour. When, for instance the Chelsea director Mr Pratt, who was eventually to become chairman, clearly irked by the Scot's cockiness, asked him in exasperation, 'Is there anything you're not good at?' The Doc instantly replied, 'Failure!' Pratt could not grasp the instinctive irreverence of the Bowery Boy whose quips could flatten any ego, and eventually they were to clash dramatically on the eve of his departure from Chelsea.

When the SFA decided to opt for him as interim manager and put him effectively on trial for two games, they were in desperate straits and were banking on his personal popularity to lift spirits all round. They paid scant attention to the fact that he had been a wanderer – four clubs since leaving Chelsea – and I was not alone in thinking that whatever happened back among his ain folk that this post was not his ultimate ambition. It was the immediate future though that was in everyone's mind as 58,612 hopefuls turned up for his first challenge against Portugal at Hampden on 13 October 1971. Something exceptional occurred in that game which could have made you believe it was manufactured by some mystical force to reflect the personality of the man in the dugout. Scotland had gone into the lead through John O'Hare in the 23rd minute, as the product of an overall brisk, aggressive performance that was enthusing the crowd. However, we were in cautionary mood at half-time. Then came a remarkable period of play. Portugal equalised in the 57th minute from Rodrigues. His free-kick bent round the wall, wrong-footed goalkeeper Bob Wilson – the Arsenal Anglo-Scot and my later broadcasting colleague – which produced that eerie silence of anti-climax that sadly we recently had become accustomed to, in what had previously been a buoyant crowd. It is what happened next that confirmed we were in the presence of a new dynamic. Scotland equalised in exactly 60 seconds. Not only is an instant reply, to put you back into the lead, one of the most inspiring rebuffs to the opposition, but the manner in which it was achieved was as if the Doc had come out of the dugout himself to score it. For a man even smaller than the Doc, Archie Gemmill rose to a cross with their towering goalkeeper Damas and incredibly beat him to the ball and forced it over the line for a 2–1 victory. It ignited a volcanic response from the crowd. It was as if Scotland had played out one of his quick, fiery quips to flatten some loudmouth trying to outsmart him. The Doc had arrived. And with it came the kudos.

Jim Parkinson of the *Glasgow Herald* reported that Scotland 'reclaimed some of the pride that has drained away from the Scots in international matches in recent seasons'. And the manager received the ultimate accolade from the great Eusébio who had retired injured in the game: 'It was much better for the Scots than in Lisbon. Tommy Docherty has already helped Scotland. He is a very good manager.' Davy Hay, with Celtic at the time and who played in defence that night, talked to me about the huge impact of that game on the players.

'What counted was the way he could talk to you and drive you on. You just felt a bit taller and stronger after his words. He was tactically aware of course but I think it was his ability to coax you into a performance, that was his biggest asset. And, of course, I have a kind of affection for him because when Celtic were playing Ujpest Dozsa once and he was a pundit on a television show he called me "The Silent Assassin". That name stuck to me. I think it was meant as a compliment. You know, I can put this simply. I enjoyed playing under him. And that's the biggest compliment you can give a manager.'

The press conference afterwards was like a beatification after the recurring wakes of the tail end of Bobby Brown's tenure. The Doc milked it for all its worth, as he was entitled to do, accompanied by a barn-storming session of quips to pressmen and broadcasters that we all lapped up like travellers at a desert well. The SFA did not drink at the well with us but preferred to give him his second contracted game before making any decision about his future. Scotland did triumph again against Belgium 1–0 on 10 November, after which he accepted the job, six days later, on what was called a 'permanent basis'. The fact that the SFA had now appointed no fewer than ten managers in the space of 17 years, and linked it now with a man whose volatile nature caused him to bounce around the footballing world like a Mexican jumping bean, meant they were blissfully unconcerned that permanency was not a concept well understood by them, or by the Doc.

Then came Copenhagen on 18 October 1972. It helped shape his long-term future and sucked into his orbit the Celtic manager Jock Stein in a duel that even affected Stein's health. The Doc had stabilised the squad and had lost only one competitive game in that time, against England 1–0 at Wembley in the British Championship. The Idrætsparken stadium that night was surprising to those of us who had never been in that country before. We expected the crowd to reflect something of their nation's reputation for cool, austere design given that their furniture was all the rage in the UK at that time. In fact, they were as belligerent a crowd as any I had witnessed around Europe, but made little impact on the Scots whose 4–1 victory turned out to be one of the most significant on foreign soil, with consequences that went much deeper than historical statistics and the easing of our path towards qualifying for the 1974 World Cup in Germany. For back in Scotland Stein was watching this with interest because one of his players had starred in the game. Stein, alert as always, had sniffed something was afoot.

THE TUG O' WAR

A troublesome triangle had formed. It comprised of the Doc himself; Lou Macari, a favourite player of his; and the manager of Celtic, still in command of his patch. Central to all the twisted events of the aftermath was the man who scored the opening goal in Scotland's astounding 4–1 romp, which had an even more intoxicating effect on us than some of the local Carlsberg brew we partook in celebration. Lou Macari put a gleam in the Doc's eye. Small, elusive, fleet of foot and nipper of many goals, he bonded immediately with the manager who saw in him something of himself, short in stature, but with abundant confidence and ability. But I could tell from my chats with him in his early days with Celtic that Macari was no ordinary man. It did not surprise me that when I met him in England during his managerial career down there he had set tongues wagging with his unconventional management style which bordered on the bizarre, especially when he appointed a former professional circus clown as his kit man at Stoke City. But what lifted him above the mundane was his social conscience. This became dramatically evident when during the Covid epidemic in 2020 he set up shelters for the homeless and provided them with the basic sustenance to survive. This led to his development of 'glamping', the system of pods which put roofs over the heads of many who would have gone without. All that indicates that Macari was a man of independent mind who, after that Denmark game, would become the centre of one of the great footballing tug o' wars between the two giants Matt Busby and Jock

Stein. It was firstly about Stein that Macari wanted to talk when I spoke to him from his home in Stoke.

'I played under Jock Stein who never spoke about the opposition, never talked about any of their players, and if he did he just rubbished them to give you the sense that you were better than them. Tommy was the same. He never laid out any schemes based on their players. He talked about ourselves. And he was just great company. He would make you relaxed in the dressing room. It was a laugh a minute. He was the funniest man I ever met in life, not just in football. And before you knew where you were, you were heading out to play, with his last words something like "Go on. I know what you can do. Go out and do it." Simple.'

The night in Copenhagen had turned out to be such a contrast to some previous trips abroad when you had to skulk back home. We knew we were returning to ecstatic headlines like that of Glasgow's *Evening Times* the following day, ' Our Best Team In A Long Time' with the experienced writer Hugh Taylor almost beside himself with admiration,

> So one swallow doesn't make a summer and we are a long way from the finals in Munich, but this is the best combined Scottish team I have seen – a young team geared for attack – and how they attacked.

And significantly the Doc went public with some words of gratitude to the men whom he knew might influence his future one way or the other. He told the *Evening Times* the following morning, 'Incidentally I greatly appreciate the telegram of congratulations from Scotland's football writers. These things mean a lot.'

It was obviously the start of a love affair. Sadly, it only lasted a few embraces. For another man was in the throes of admiration. That was the very evening that Sir Matt Busby, having seen the action from Copenhagen on television, was finally convinced that he had to bring the Doc to Old Trafford. He had watched an attacking performance that seemed to fit the nature of United's proclaimed vision of football – on the front foot, progressive, adventurous. At that stage

Sir Matt was simply a director of the club, but nobody disputed the fact that he still carried enormous influence there and as he had revealed with his previous interest in Jock Stein, his Scottish genes were vibrating again. Lou Macari acknowledges that.

'Sir Matt and the others sat up and took notice of the manager. Here was a fellow Scot who had gone to Denmark and won, but won handsomely in attacking style, and, of course, that's got to be the way at Manchester United as many managers have found out to their cost.'

Scotland did indeed win their second game with Denmark at Hampden 2–0, with the opening goal scored in only two minutes by a young player called Dalglish; a result that enhanced the notion that Scotland would reach the World Cup finals for the first time in 16 years. Meanwhile, United sacked their manager Frank O'Farrell on 19 December 1972, at the same time as George Best was writing a letter to the United board stating categorically, as reported in the *Glasgow Herald,* 'I have decided not to play football again. And this time no one will change my mind.' He hadn't met the Doc yet! But United were in a mess. After a 5–0 defeat by Crystal Palace they were in danger of relegation.

I have little doubt that the Doc knew, either by press gossip; or instinct; or actual contact, which in that business was hardly unheard of; and that given United's interest, he was already beyond Hadrian's Wall on the way south. Over and above that he had experienced, as a player in two World Cup finals, the instability of the national managerial post. In 1954 in Switzerland the SFA had their manager Andy Beattie walk out on them, because of interference in his player selection, after a first game defeat by Austria, 1–0. Manager-less in the following match, they were run over by Uruguay, 7–0. In the World Cup of 1958 in Sweden, with Matt Busby unable to take on the job as he was recuperating from his serious injuries of the Munich air disaster, it was left to the trainer of Clyde, Dawson Walker, to take overall control of the squad, but the team talks were led by the goalkeeper, Tommy Younger. Doc, in later years used an old Glasgow expression to describe the SFA's handling of these events: 'They couldn't run a menage!' Being witness to a succession of events that made the SFA seem like a three-wheeled waggon competing for customers in the age of aviation, made him very wary of how this would turn out for him. But it was an offer that had put him back into the limelight from relative obscurity. He had to take his chance. But United were now offering him a renewal in England.

'There is no way he could have turned down the United job,' Lou Macari told me. 'For a start he would be getting a huge increase in his wages. And there was a challenge for him because as he could see himself he still had great players there, or at least that's what he judged before he went.'

His acceptance of the United post produced an appropriate headline to Ian Archer's article in the *Glasgow Herald* the day after the news broke of his resignation. 'No Need For Wailing – Docherty Has Left A Rich Inheritance', under which he wrote, emphasising the views many of us had about his tenure, 'Those of us who followed him around the grounds and in trains and planes, always suspected that his term as Scotland's manager might be short.'

It had been 14 months. So United gave the Doc double his Scotland wages of £7,500 and from the outset he saw the need for change. The player he wanted most from Scotland was Lou Macari and Jock Stein the Celtic manager knew that now, only too painfully. He would know that the Doc would be hunting Macari. And he would know Matt Busby would be looming large over proceedings. Over and above that he would know Macari would jump at it because he was in a long-standing feud with Celtic about wages. Stein was a bad loser. There was no way he would bow the knee to the man who had taken the very United job that he had turned down after his Lisbon triumph. Pride was involved. Stein made it his mission to prevent it. But, despite the Celtic manager lending the impression that he was invulnerable, the pressure of dealing with games and the increasing demands of more emboldened players to speak up about money was seeping through his defences. Stein had an explosive temperament and his anger over Macari might have tipped his health over the edge. One day, in the final week of December 1972, driving out of Parkhead with the Macari issue still burning in his mind, he became ill and ended up in the Victoria Infirmary because of an underlying heart condition that was to lie in ambush for him a few years hence.

Certainly, he had tried everything he could to prevent Macari from moving to Old Trafford. He had gone out of his way to arrange a meeting between his player and his old mate Bill Shankly at Liverpool, with the obvious encouragement to sign for them. It is a meeting that was observed by a United visitor, assistant manager Pat Crerand, who alerted United to that. The Doc, now firmly installed at Old Trafford as manager, swooped. Stein's particular anger mostly stemmed from how he thought he had been duped by Lou in allowing him to believe that he would sign for Shankly. But in accepting the inevitable, in a final flourish he insisted that United pay £20,000 more than he would have accepted from the Liverpool manager.

As Stein lay in his bed in the infirmary on 6 January 1973, listening to the radio commentary of the Old Firm game and hearing of his team losing 1–0 to Rangers, he knew Lou was on his way south. Two days later the Doc had got his man. The player is adamant that he handled the process fairly. They had offered him a deal which simply enriched him.

But he also told me, 'I went because they were struggling so I knew I would get my chance there to play at the top. And I also went because Best, Law and Charlton were there. Little did I realise that the Doc was going to get rid of them. Indeed, they were the only three players I saw him falling out with and getting really angry over. And, of course, I just got on well with the Doc.'

Most people did. Little did I realise that the game at Hampden against Denmark on 15 November 1972 would be the last time I would watch him manage any side. He was lost to me for years as he continued to ply his trade, principally with Manchester United, and so many others, which gave rise to his famous utterance, 'I have had more clubs than Jack Nicklaus.' Or, still being able to smile adversity in the face like his reflection on his time at Rotherham, 'I promised I would take Rotherham out of the Second Division – and I took them into the Third. The old chairman said: "Doc, you're a man of your word!"'

It was when he left United in 1977 that we met up again. One night in a Stirling hotel, late on at the bar, just after both of us had spoken at a dinner to a packed audience, he revealed a bitterness that I had never witnessed before. It was shortly after he had been abused by fans in a railway station who had shouted lewd remarks to him about the exposure of his love affair with the wife of the Manchester United physiotherapist Laurie Brown. He brought it up himself, as if he wanted to unload his frustration on someone. Not a plea for sympathy, just a burst of anger, and then it passed. Perhaps it wasn't the lewdness itself that still irked him, but a stark reminder of what the terracings can do with mention of sex and of how the relationship ended his career at United. When he talked to me that night, he did not mention Sir Matt by name, but his bitterness about the club sounded like a proxy attack on the saintly figure of the great Scot whom he felt could have supported him. He actually said when he left that he was the only manager ever to be sacked for falling in love. I suppose it was difficult for many of us to associate this witty, but also pugnacious personality, with romantic inclinations and perhaps it was too obvious for his detractors to associate his relationship with the wife of physiotherapist Laurie Brown as anything other than venal. Clearly it was not. Equally clearly he had committed adultery and that collided terminally with the morality which stemmed from the figure of Sir Matt. There was no chance of survival there under the circumstances.

But, of that night when he opened up to me, he had reinvented himself as an after-dinner speaker and being on the circuit myself at times, I was meeting him frequently. Frankly, he made my efforts sound like readings from a telephone directory. It seemed easy for him. You could imagine him using that sharp wit in a street in Shettleston or in a dressing room coping with massive egos and proving nobody could top him. He could convulse a room of fat cats in the burgeoning hospitality environment of the modern game, or have them rolling in the aisles at a miners' welfare. Much of it was self-deprecatory, but even though he used the same material repeatedly, it was always like listening to him for the first time. He had never really left Shettleston behind. It echoed in every quip, and the instinct for survival honed in those streets kept him buoyant when many others would have sunk without trace. It kept him going to the age of 92.

However, that night in Stirling when, for a fleeting moment he did look like a tired and beaten man, was in stark contrast to the day at the BBC in 1971 when I had first encountered a bubbling personality in his prime. That was the Doc I care to remember – brimming with self-confidence, unperturbed by the cloistered nature of the BBC, determined in a way that reminded people of the Hollywood tough man Jimmy Cagney. Add the impish Puck of *A Midusmmer Night's Dream* to that description and you get close to what he was at his peak. And, indeed, we settled with him that day. He accepted £200 pounds. A sum which, at that time, took our breaths away. In 2021 it would have been the equivalent of £1,200. It was daylight robbery. The kind that came naturally to a Bowery Boy.

At my fantasy table I would sit boxer Jackie Paterson next to the Doc. They were both wee men who could punch above their weight. Paterson literally so.

CHAPTER 2

The Punch

ON THE 23 December 1985, Umkhonto we Siswe an operative of the banned African National Congress planted a bomb in a rubbish bin outside a shopping centre in one of the paradisial stretches of the South African coast, where golden sands and white-crested surf provided the perfect seductive poster advert, even for a country poisoned by apartheid at that time. There was nothing particularly exceptional about the statistics of five people killed and 40 seriously injured as a result, because even worse events had been occurring in the struggle against the existing political system. In that sense, when I read about the atrocity, it might have been swallowed up among the other ghastly incidents which had taken place and simply laid aside. But something stirred me, subconsciously. It was the specific name of the town where the atrocity had been committed. *Amanzimtoti*. I knew I had seen it somewhere before but couldn't quite pin down its strange echo in the mind. But then it did break through the fog, and it struck me with a force that drew its strength from the indissoluble links with boyhood. A hero of mine had died there years before. According to the report he had been murdered – a broken bottle thrust into his neck where once fists, garbed in boxing gloves, used to land. A later report described it as an accidental fall on broken glass during a drunken binge. But, whatever, it was the squalid end of Jackie Paterson.

That Zulu place-name brought back to me the sadness I felt in hearing of his death on 19 November 1966, just as Tommy Docherty was still pulling them in at Stamford Bridge. It was thousands of miles distant from the environment where Paterson developed into a world boxing champion. He had entered my early years like a legendary knight, slaying dragons and putting villains in their place with his unsheathed, famed right hook. He also gave me one of the nights of my life.

It is a truth universally acknowledged that you could get on in life in Glasgow if you were handy with your fists. If you used them spontaneously in the streets you could gain awesome neighbourhood credibility. If you worked hard at cultivating them within the constraints of the noble art and made the gym an essential part of your life, you could conquer the world. Jackie Paterson, in the boxing ring, did exactly that. His birthplace was actually in Ayrshire although his frequent presence in Glasgow rings lent the impression he had slugged his way up from the city's streets. He achieved success particularly with his famed punch, which from early on in his career had secured him a place in the demolition business. So, when I was told I was to be taken to see him in action for the first time in 1946 and, more than that, defending his World title at our great national institution Hampden Park, especially against an Englishman, I felt I was being ennobled. In retrospect I also believe that my father, whom I cannot recall ever attending a church and chose a registry office for his nuptials, must have assessed that night as the equivalent of a coming-of age ritual, somewhat akin to a first communion or a bar mitzvah.

He simply adored the little flyweight and spoke rapturously about his right hook, like an arms salesman extolling the virtues of the Kalashnikov. It was almost like listening to the incantation of boxing liturgy when he would return from a fight and describe it to me, blow-by-blow, like he was still on a high from just having seen Paterson put someone on the canvas, which he sometimes did with apparent ease. My father, a baker, was little different from many other men in our neighbourhood who could talk with authority about that sport and mix it easily with their other passion: football. Manliness, apparently, was not simply about the hair on your chest, but your ability to segue from one sport to the other and talk with authority about both, in the sure knowledge that you were confirming the proper characteristics of your class. And your sex. At that time women in my neighbourhood were in purdah, rarely seen inside a football or boxing stadium, or heaven forbid, drinking in pubs. A blinkered patriarchy existed. And, yes, men who showed no interest in the testosterone-induced passion for the two sports were considered odd. About that time I was to become aware of the exclusionary word, 'poof'. Contrast that with the liberated 1984 Olympian Sandra Whittaker, whom I present in a later chapter.

But it was a fighter who came before Paterson that spurred my interest in the southpaw. In 1982 I wrote and narrated a short film for BBC *Grandstand* on John Burrow's excellent book *Benny: The Life And Times Of A Boxing Legend*. Paterson, who trod in the footsteps of Lynch had to come up in discussion. So that short film drove him into my vision again and revived thoughts of how 'twinned' football and boxing were in my city.

This was expressed well by Tommy Gilmour, a contemporary of mine, who maintained the highly successful family traditions of boxing promotion, stretching back to his grandfather who could claim to be an amateur champion of Great Britain himself, when he wrote in his autobiography, *A Boxing Dynasty: The Tommy Gilmour Story*, 'At every corner there was football and boxing. We Glaswegians were famous, for boxing, football and shipyards.' The simplicity of that description ought not to mask the fact that he was identifying this blending of cultures to perfection. It was also inevitable that Lynch and Paterson competed for men's affections as if they were in a contest to be confirmed as 'the greatest'. A fruitless pursuit you might think, in retrospect, but in a city fond of an argument or two and where bragging was a street sport, it was almost a necessary self-indulgence to argue over the merits of two Glaswegian World Champions. Lynch, pre-war, had ploughed that furrow where Paterson now reaped a harvest of wins in post-war austerity.

For this was the era of Glasgow's wee fighting men who gave great credence to the phrase, 'punching above their weight'. One after the other, over a decade, they personified the 'guid conceit' the city had of itself in believing that it could withstand anything thrown at it, like a world war.

As I moved into long trousers Paterson was drawing the crowds in. It was really only in later years that I began to appreciate what sport meant to a city. Indeed, attendances at the plentiful bouts in and around the city fitted into the overall energetic response of a Glasgow determined to liberate itself from the suffocating rigours of the world war just ended. Rations books were passports to bare minimum survival for many and there was much evidence that although the bombs had stopped falling, the pre-war conditions of social deprivation would still scar the city as much as any damage done by the Luftwaffe. In the year before the Paterson fight at Hampden, a Glasgow councillor Jean Mann, who was to be elected to Parliament in the Labour landslide of 1945, reported, 'There are instances of Glasgow householders having to burn the gas all night to keep rats off their beds.' And was recommending parents to make 'full use' of the city's children's clothing and footwear exchange in Kilmarnock Road where garments were disinfected before re-issue. Her colleague on the council, David Gibson, offered evidence of 200 cases in Shettleston alone in which more than ten people were living in one single-end.

Brutalised by a war, scarred by the historic negligence of successive governments, it is little wonder that post-war Glasgow folk sought communal release in variety of ways. To be sure boxing was principally a male preserve, and I suspect many a man, like my father, recompensed the family by taking them to the flourishing and plentiful cinemas, if only for a fleeting hour or two. And tales of what could happen in the back-row of the stalls stirred my imagination as much as the action on the silver screen. However, if this bonded a family, other pursuits could rip them apart. For 'going to the dogs' had no real metaphorical relevance around our neighbourhood, since it literally meant going to Carntyne greyhound racetrack, where many a pay packet was squandered, apparently with the gay abandon of a Champagne Charlie at Ascot. This was the very addiction that was to strip Paterson of practically all of his hard-earned capital.

But then, I sensed that virtually all men gambled. Since my father seemed never to be away from the bookies I could hardly have held Paterson in disdain for his particular urges, if indeed I had known about them at the time. For it all seemed so natural, so Glaswegian, even though street gambling was completely illegal. After all, the bookies looked after their flock, dispensing charity in an almost farcical way. Thus, I felt no shame in witnessing the accepted ritual of my father and his friends being carted away in a police Black Maria once, after they raided his own particular bookie's patch. They were released immediately at Chester Street (the famed name of the local police office), where the bookie paid their fines and they all trundled back to the same patch and continued gambling. It was like a scene from a *Carry On* film.

What I certainly did appreciate is that boxing interest was global. For the brown box in the middle of the kitchen was our ear to the world. On that radio we listened to boxing from around the UK and from the USA. Radio was a friend, an ally, a promoter, an educator, a stimulator and a platform for voices which still ring in my ear to this day. The boxing voice I listened to with most respect, pontificating from the ringside with his inter-round summaries, was that of W Barrington Dalby, a name that I always expected to come across in a PG Wodehouse novel. Very English. Very BBC. He was the outstanding authority for us and loved the city of Glasgow, because of the number of times he watched both Lynch and Paterson in action. For in his *Desert Island Discs* appearance on 1 February 1960, with the originator of the series Roy Plomley talking over his 50 year career in broadcasting, his final choice was a rendition of the 'Dashing White Sergeant', sung by the splendid Glasgow Orpheus Choir. It perhaps reminded him of the whirls he had seen in the Glasgow rings. It was a musical appreciation of his times in the city where he often revealed his fondness for these wee men, weighing just on eight stone, who had the ability to move their feet with the elegance of Fred Astaire, but could deal with opponents like hired assassins. But, as a ring historian as well, Barrington Dalby appreciated the growth of boxing in the city which had produced as knowledgeable a public as you would find anywhere in the world.

He saw with his own eyes the gyms which flourished all over Glasgow, particularly in the harshest of pre-war social conditions. They were evidence of a refinement from the primitive days of the boxing booths, especially those linked with travelling fairgrounds, where the Marquess of Queensberry rules were creatively reinterpreted. They were not for those who were squeamish at the sight of blood. But they attracted a special breed. 'Go three rounds and win a pound' was the staple challenge of the booth owners. This was not only for those with a sense of bravado to step out of the crowd and face up to one of the hardened ex-pros who frequented these places, but for those with empty pockets. Tommy Gilmour's father, the city's foremost boxing promoter of legitimate contests, appreciated the existence of the booths, as his son explained:

'He knew why even some of his boxers would go back and fight in the booths in the summer when times were slack for them. It was about survival. They had to feed their families. That's why they volunteered to climb through the ropes. The money.'

Further back, his grandfather, typifying both the allure of the sport and its means of sustenance, actually fought three ten-round contests in a single day. He would end one fight, put on his over-coat, get in a tramcar, reach the next venue, take his coat off and get stuck in again and follow that up for the third fight after which he had earned himself a pay packet and, furthermore, added to his prestige by winning all three fights on points.

It is little wonder that earning a bob or two at the cost of facial disfigurement had been going on for decades. Lynch and Paterson were the products of that instinct for the fight. And it could make them money. Indeed, you cannot look at one of them without think-ing of the other. In a way they were superimposed on one another. Lynch led the way at a time of dire straits. When he was aiming for the welter-weight World title himself, and coming to the fore in 1935, unemployment had reached 100,000, equivalent to the population of Aberdeenshire at the time. It was so bad that young men who called themselves 'Nomads' – out of work and denied benefits under the hated Means Test – lived rough in woods and glens in the countryside near Glasgow and described themselves as 'belly thieves', because they stole to eat. And it was the year when a book was published that was both lauded by social commentators but denounced by others as a 'gross libel on Glasgow' for its par-ticular depiction of life in the Gorbals area, where Lynch was born and brought up. *No Mean City* was a fictional account of hard-ship in family life and gang violence in the streets, centred on the violent exploits of a self-proclaimed 'razor king'. Its biblical title, taken from the apostle Paul's description of Tarsus as 'no mean city', offered graphic descriptions of social conditions that shocked people to the core, particularly the city fathers who felt such images distorted the overall picture of Glasgow. No local bookshop would sell it, the libraries were not allowed to stock it and the *Glasgow Herald* refused to review it. Nevertheless, the title and the images it conveyed, hung round the neck of the city for decades, like a label with a territorial warning that you would ignore at your peril.

These Glasgow boxers seemed to represent our battle against the sheer drudgery of daily life that was heaped on so many in deprivation. You might even have seen them as social workers, in the sense that when they put a man flat on the canvas they boosted morale to a great extent, created a sense of community and simply lent comfort to many who saw in them working-class success in times when much in their world seemed negative. Apart from that, the sheer skill and success of Lynch, and then Paterson, increased the respectability of their sport. Anybody could roll up and be entertained without thinking they were slumming. One such was Scotland's famous troubadour Sir Harry Lauder, when he was just a plain commoner. Most Friday nights he would turn up in main street Bridgeton at the Premierland boxing venue, which housed some of the great fights and where Lynch made his professional debut in 1931. It was noted though that Sir Harry did enjoy his home comforts and would send somebody out to the nearest licensed grocers to come back with a gill of whisky to wet his thrapple between bouts. For a man who comically played up the alleged stinginess of the Scots for his stage act, it was against his image that he rewarded the messenger with a sixpence which at that time was like a gold ingot to young men. Boxing was revealing the authentic Harry Lauder.

So he watched both of these men fight at Premierland and was anxious to identify his affection for them. This fed into the growing respectability for those wee men who went into a ring with the brazing self-confidence of those who deliberately put themselves in harm's way. Although anybody making comparisons between the pair would have to admit that Lynch had blazed the trail. In that *Grandstand* film on Benny, my interview with Joe Aitchison stood out amongst the pack. He was a Glasgow boxing trainer of renown who sounded as if he had been able to look deep into Lynch's soul. A silver-haired, gnomic little man, he spoke with measured solemnity, as if searching for thoughts from a deep well within himself and making me feel conscious of how respectful I really ought to be about the wee boxer from the Gorbals. For when I asked him eventually for a few words to sum up Lynch, he paused, thought and then answered.

'He had moral courage.'

Not just 'guts', which is what I was expecting, but something more noble, more transcendental, as if boxing itself carried with it spiritual demands that went beyond the mere inflicting of pain. What emerged strongly for me, was the portrait of a man who particularly inspired the large Irish-Catholic community in the Gorbals area of Glasgow – a community which had experienced historical discrimination and rejoiced that the World Champion was lending them more visibility and providing them with something they could boast about in a city where many still openly regarded them as outsiders.

However, they were not the only ones who greeted Lynch back to Glasgow after he had won the flyweight title for the first time. Much of the city was aroused. His opponent in Manchester on 9 September 1935 was Jackie Brown, who was pummelled remorselessly into submission, the fight being stopped in the second round after Lynch had put him on the canvas eight times. That explosive shock and awe in itself augmented the response to his dramatic seizure of the British, European and World flyweight titles all in one. It so excited his followers that it was estimated 20,000 greeted his return to the city's Central Station, with thousands more in the surrounding streets. So it's little wonder that for one brief, shining moment this new World Champion had inspired his followers and rerouted them dramatically away from the harsh realities of their lives. *No Mean City* was no fantasy world to many of them.

However, from the pinnacle of that day what followed was Lynch's remorseless collapse into alcoholism which reduced him to standing in a Glasgow pub years later, offering anybody a free punch at his face if only they would buy him a drink. This is why his life story has attracted so much attention from writers, playwrights, documentary film-makers, artists – all fascinated by his rise from the slums, his battles in and out the ring, the degradation and death at the early age of 33 exactly four weeks after my trip to Hampden to see another World Champion in action. But I never saw him fight. Paterson, I certainly did.

THE SUCCESSOR

Jackie Paterson took over his boxing mantle but as an entirely different personality. He had been born in Ayrshire on 5 September 1920. When he was eight his family left for Scranton in the USA and when he returned to Scotland in his teens he worked in John Brown's shipyards in Clydebank and thereafter had a spell as a butcher. He began to train at a renowned gym in the Anderston area of Glasgow and became a professional boxer at the age of 17. There is nothing in his pedigree that suggests he had to tussle with impoverishment, like that of many in Lynch's environment in the Gorbals, although neither had he been born with a silver spoon in his mouth. Nor did he seem to represent any particular segment of the city with a core urge to prove a special identity. For me he was simply a guiding star in the complexities of the boxing world and a hero of mine through the ministrations of my father. He made sense of boxing for me simply because I could focus on his career and come to understand why a southpaw, like him, could outbox so many and win 41 of his 119 fights by a KO. I reacted to his defeats – and he did lose 25 of his fights – with the kind of anguish of a thwarted lover.

So on the morning of Wednesday 7 July 1946, Hampden loomed for me. Paterson was to defend his World flyweight title against Joe Curran from Liverpool, who had already beaten him twice out of their three previous bouts. The front and back papers were full of news of the fight. Elky Clark in the *Daily Record,* the renowned boxing journalist, issued a cautionary warning to us all:

> For the first time in many years the title-holder is not a safe bet.
> His 'boiling down' to make the flyweight poundage of eight stone
> is bound to sap some of his strength.

And then went on to add,

> The Scot looked drawn compared with the healthily tanned Curran, who has never had any difficulty in making the weight and conceded Paterson nine pounds the last time they met.

Clark was reminding us of the agonies that Paterson had to inflict on himself to sweat off even an ounce of weight to make the grade. At most of his and Lynch's weigh-ins, standing on the scales had the tension of a courtroom drama when all eyes are focussed on the chairman of the jury about to deliver the verdict. The needle on the scales rotating towards the 8st limit held as much terror for these two flyweights, and their acolytes, as having to face a firing squad, hoping they might just possibly miss their mark. Anybody harbouring doubts about that should consider this scene from how Lynch lost a title.

June 1938. The offices of the *Daily Record*. The weigh-in for the World flyweight title between Lynch and Californian Jackie Jurich was taking place there. The pseudonymous 'Waverley' wrote about the event.

> As soon as I looked at Lynch I knew he was overweight. If I hadn't seen him I could still have told by the haggard look on the face of Puggy Moran, his trainer. He was called to the scales by Mr Charles Donmall, secretary of the British Boxing Board of control, about two o'clock in the afternoon. Lynch stood on the scales with his hands clasped behind his back, a defiant sort of expression on his face. Secretary Donmall moved the measure up and down. 'Step off,' he said. Lynch moved off the scales and immediately there was a round of applause. Those in the hall thought he was 'under'. Donmall raised his hand for silence. Then, unemotionally, he announced Lynch's weight, six and a half pounds over the stipulated 8 stone. I watched promoter George Dingley. He was stunned. He looked as if he had taken a left hook on the solar from Lynch. Crowds milled outside the office. And, inside, the dethroned champion's wife was on the verge of collapse. Lynch, meanwhile, was in a restaurant having his first solid meal in days. And in tears.

He had lost his title by default although he was to go on and knock his opponent out in the twelfth round of the fight at Love Street,

Paisley. Paterson, several times in his career, had to climb on scales like Lynch, having slaved up to the last second to make the weight. So Clark's words in the *Daily Record* of that July morning about Paterson's physical condition perplexed us. It was on my mind as we boarded the tramcar. It was one of the longest journeys I had ever taken around the city and felt like a potentate on the humming, swaying, clattering ride without realising that before returning home I would be given an insight into how my city was about to change and that the tramcar was on its way to the knacker's yard.

THE BOUT

Hampden seemed sedate when we arrived. The seating had been arranged around the ring placed near the centre-circle, with both the north terracing and the south-stand packed with a standing crowd of over 60 thousand. It was certainly plentiful enough for the Dundonian promoter of the title fight, George Grant, who had gambled on paying Paterson his biggest ever purse of £4,500 to prevent the fight from going to Liverpool and as a bonus had been blessed with a sunny evening, when it certainly could have been a wash-out in our city of quixotic weather.

I have vivid but fragmented memories of that night. Thankfully, there are moments that stick in the mind like stepping stones taking me carefully through the narrative that otherwise is blurred by time. My first impression was the immensity of Hampden, the size of the crowd and the good-natured banter including a man who said to my father, 'If the boy cannae see I'll haud him up.' It is true we were low down in the north enclosure with the ring further away than I had expected. And certainly the entrance of the boxers is glued to memory because they seemed so small and slight. Seeing them in the flesh for the first time was almost disillusioning. In the stories I had heard about Paterson and Lynch's achievements I had built up superheroes in the mind's eye; men of stature who could take on the world's heavyweight champion Joe Louis if required. Now, as they bobbed up and down in their respective corners awaiting the first bell they looked like wee boys merely there to sing for their supper. Then there was the clenching of my fist. It was there ready to throw a right hook at Curran as I skulked after him from the start.

What stands out immediately was the sight of Paterson putting both arms down by his side and circling, inviting Curran to strike in the very first round. And nothing happening. They circled and did much holding and rolling around the ropes that puzzled me. The press were to conjecture later that Curran was trying to play the long game and take advantage of Paterson's reputed lack of stamina because of his weight problems. Although, the Liverpudlian was obviously wary of what Paterson had in his right glove. And that was why my fist remained clenched throughout. That was the pent-up tension underlying everything. I could feel some deep longing within me that I think was being shared by the thousands there. Yes, Paterson was striking Curran, but we were all awaiting THE PUNCH. In a way our flyweight champion had been hoist by his own petard. He had won his title at Hampden on 19 June 1943, by one of the most spectacular knock-outs in World Championship history when he put Peter Kane on the canvas after only 61 seconds in the first round. Hugh McIlvanney, one of the great writers on boxing, was to write in his assessment of fighters through the years, 'pound for pound Paterson had the best punch in the business'.

So where was it now? Where was the terminator? Yes, I saw Curran on the canvas three times through the fight, but he was to get up again. They looked merely like shoves to me. I had the blood lust. I wanted to see a swaying, drunken-like figure with ghostly expression collapsing to the canvas, felled as Miss Paton had told us how Robert the Bruce had flattened that other Englishman De Bohun at Bannockburn, with one fierce blow. I hadn't come all the way there on a tramcar just to see a points victory. Nevertheless. I felt no anxiety around me as it was increasingly apparent that although THE PUNCH was apparently on furlough, Paterson was himself in no real danger and that he was coasting to victory.

There was no restraint in the cheering crowd therefore when the referee raised Paterson's hand at the end of 15 rounds, to register that he had retained his World title. Euan Wellwood in the *Evening Times* wrote;

Paterson won so handsomely that it would be churlish to criticise his performance unless it be of a constructive nature. There is an old adage that it takes two to make a fight and Curran did little more than lend weight to that.

And I took some consolation in Elky Clark's interpretation in the *Daily Record* when he told us,

Paterson was so much on top that the crowd expected the end to come at any moment. In the sixth round for instance, Curran actually had no idea where he was.

But, he had survived, and then the Liverpudlian himself gave us an interesting hint of Paterson's possible decline when he told Wellwood after, 'Paterson is not punching as hard as he did when I met him before the war.' I paid little heed to that at the time.

Indeed, it was the last fight I attended for decades but still followed Paterson's career with somersaulting emotions which saw me suffering days of depression one year later, when before a World title fight with Dado Marino, he collapsed at the weigh-in due to weight-losing exertions, so they took the title away from him. He resorted to court action to get it reinstated, which was only allowed on the condition he fight Rinty Monaghan in Belfast for the flyweight title, which he did on 23 March 1948.

He was so ill-prepared though in trying to make the weight, that he was counted out in the seventh round, 'one leg folded up under him like a sheet of paper, physically conscious but so weak as to be utterly incapable of rising' as Fleet Street's most famous boxing correspondent Peter Wilson wrote. Monaghan always sang the almost spiritual song of the Northern Irish, 'The Londonderry Air', or 'Danny Boy', as it was popularly called, before his fights and as he performed that evening before dispensing with Paterson. To me, overnight that air became a funeral dirge.

The fact that he won only three of his last 12 professional fights, did nothing to diminish the memory of that Hampden night. I knew nothing of his gradual decline through the years, caused by incessant gambling on greyhounds that virtually cleaned him out of the reported £100,000 he had earned in his sport and aggravated by mixing with the lowlife that can flourish in the habitat of the gambling world. Then, there was that day in November 1966, when I heard on radio the deeply saddening news that Paterson had been murdered in a brawl outside a bar in Amanzimtoti, stabbed in the neck with a broken bottle. I hadn't even known he had emigrated to South Africa. The details of what provoked it are still murky, and indeed, a later report claimed there had been a fight, but that his death had been accidental. Whatever, his legacy for me was a continuing love of boxing even in the face of the realities of what we now know about the hazards of the fight game.

Yet, the passing of time has not lessened the tragedy of how two working-class boys were allowed to squander their respective and deserved fortunes. The circumstances they were born into meant they had been fighting the cause of survival since leaving the cradle. They transposed that triumphantly to the ring. When they were in free-fall nobody stepped in to help, even in a city renowned for its compassion. It still had that. But what it lacked was understanding. Back then alcoholism and indiscriminate gambling seemed part of the matrix of working-class life. Buy Lynch a drink? Of course. Why not? He's famous even though he's now a begging alcoholic. Lend the skint Paterson a fiver when you know it will go on the nose of a dog running at Carntyne? Certainly. Didn't he entertain us all? That seemed simple and benevolent, when in fact it was toxic. My regret for the manner of their downfalls only heightens my respect for them and how life would have been much poorer if boxing had not existed and had I not been taken to see a World Champion in action that July night.

Not that we were about to denounce the evil of the bookie as we left the stadium, for I knew that my father had won money on Paterson. So we stepped into the darkening night in a jaunty mood along with the jubilant crowd to queue up for the late-night tramcar. It never arrived. Along instead came a bus, to the utter bewilderment of the disorientated crowd whose agitated Glasgwegian protests could be summed up as, 'Are you effin' kiddin''. The clippie shouted back at them like a comedian dealing with hecklers, 'Use ye'r bloody imaginations and just think ye'r on a caur! It's gaun the same bloody route!' Thus, there I was, boarding this new mode of transport, a corporation bus, for the first time in my life. I now realise that on a single night, not having witnessed THE PUNCH, I had been given a forewarning of the imminent demise of a great boxer and of my equally beloved tramcar.

Seated next to Paterson would be a man who could share stories about the footwork they both excelled in and about their love of the fast lane. Jim Baxter – as elusive as the boxer, even though nature had mismatched his legs.

CHAPTER 3

The Left Foot

AN EXCLUSIVE NEWS story is one of the gold nuggets of journalism. Some might arise accidentally, but most come through hard work and perseverance, like the panners in the Klondkye days who would beaver away in the belief that one day, flowing downstream would come that nugget which would be theirs and theirs alone. It is little wonder they call them 'scoops'. As Robert Service wrote of the gold rush, 'There are strange things done in the midnight sun / By the men who moil for gold.' And no stranger thing was done than on 21 June 1960 when a man walked into his workplace, the *Daily Record* newsroom in Glasgow, and alerted everybody that he had an exclusive story in his sights and demanded a car be put at his disposable as soon as possible, but refused to say to anybody what was afoot. Nobody questioned his air of urgency, for they all knew that as panners go, he was the Dangerous Dan McGrew of them all and seemed to own a mother lode of stories, some of which it was suspected he had a legitimate hand in creating himself. So, true to form, he insisted that nobody should let it be known to anybody outside that office that he was off on a mission. The car was provided and off he sped.

He was a sports journalist called Jim Rodger. He might not have been known widely to the public like the big-hitters in his trade, who commanded columns and wrote forthright opinions on football. In fact, Rodger's written pieces did not exactly leap out of the page at you, but seemed aimed at those who read slowly. More importantly he could make headlines. But from hamper boy to club chairman, everybody in Scottish football knew him and had brushed against him, or been phoned in the middle of the night by him, or collared in a dark corner by him, or been offered jobs by him. He became so readily available as a goffer to the great and mighty in football, to do their bidding, that I now rate him as the *Alexa* of his generation.

His greatest impact on me was in 1978 when he phoned one day to ask if I would call Jock Stein who had just become manager of Leeds United. I obeyed. Stein had only been in that post for about 50 days, so when the former Celtic manager asked me if I would go on television and promote the idea that he would be interested in returning to Scotland as the national manager with Ally MacLeod on the way out, I was both intrigued and excited. So I did make that announcement to a UK audience on BBC's *Sportsnight*. As expected, it created a media fuss. Although the following morning on radio I heard an interview in which Jock Stein poured water on my report, saying it was pure conjecture that I was indulging in. I knew I wasn't, but was eagerly playing my part in a ruse, thought up by Stein, to lend air to his obvious desire to get that job, but put into operation by his go-between, the 'Jolly' Rodger. Stein, of course became Scotland's manager about a week later.

So when Rodger announced that he was off on a quest that day, nobody in the office blinked. For they also knew this ex-pit-boy from the mining community in Shotts in Lanarkshire, was of a different breed from many others in the trade and could claim, with considerable justification, that he was on first name terms with those who trod the corridors of power. As a Labour loyalist he was always one of the first to welcome both Prime Minister's Harold Wilson and James Callaghan, whenever they stepped off the train at Central Station in Glasgow in their time. Added to which he was a full cousin to Sir William Armstrong, private secretary to three Chancellors of the Exchequer, encouraging us to believe, as well, that a mandarin of Britain's civil service was at the other end of a phone line to him when required. And truly, on 17 March 1976 in that grey and drab city of Karl-Marx-Stadt (now Chemnitz) in East Germany where Celtic were playing a European tie, I witnessed him advancing on the receptionist of our hotel with the barked command, 'Get me Downing Street!' The news had just broken that Harold Wilson was retiring as Prime Minister. Of course, by this time we all knew that he was not merely an affectatious name-dropper, but was an extremely useful ear to the ground for a variety of politicians. All of which meant that his colleagues in the office would keep their heads down and let him get on with matters his way, as much of what he dug up aided the *Daily Record* in their attempts to oust the *Daily Express* as the biggest-selling newspaper in Scotland, and to which he would desert in a future year.

So, eventually when he sat in the car, he told his driver to travel south-west out of Glasgow.

'Head for Kilmarnock. And tell me if you think anybody is on our trail.'

However, they did not reach the Ayrshire town but stopped, on command, in the middle of Fenwick Moor. According to the driver, Rodger then stepped out of the car and looked around at the bleak scene, which being so close to Glasgow can induce a feeling of leaving civilisation behind. Only a few sheep and seagulls were in view. A single car passed them. He waited until it was out of sight.

'Don't think anybody has followed us,' he told the driver and waddled his way back in. 'Right. Turn round. Drive as fast as you can. We're heading for Fife. Hill o' Beath.'

Now travelling to Fife via the Fenwick Moor would not, even by the wildest of interpretations, be considered the 'tourist' route – Hill o' Beath being something like 60 miles away in the opposite direction towards the east coast. Dutifully the driver did a U-turn and put his foot down. So why was this rotund journalist – whose spiritual needs were fortified in the Tron Church in the centre of Glasgow every Sunday – acting as if the 'deil' was on his tail, like Tam O' Shanter's mare? It should be pointed out that Rodger lived all his professional life obsessed by the notion that his phone was continually being tapped and feared his initiatives could be nipped in the bud by any of his competitors. That was embedded in his psyche. Then you add to it three other factors – the claustrophobic nature of the press's relationship with football in Glasgow, the rivalry of the Old Firm and the harsh climate of the fierce circulation wars between newspapers in the early sixties when the print industry was at its zenith. For these were the heady days of journalism, when the buccaneering spirit dominated and cheque books clashed like cutlasses in the daily skirmishing between papers. In that culture Rodger was in his element and such was his obsession with the 'scoop' that it was generally believed that he 'arranged' some himself.

Here I issue a spoiler-alert. The nature of secrecy might have led some, even in his office, to think extra-terrestrials had chosen Hill of Beath for a dramatic landing and that the ubiquitous Rodger would be there to greet them, before any other paper sniffed it. In fact he was about to meet a young man with a left foot that had come gift-wrapped by nature and was used to mesmerise other terrestrials who faced him on a football field. On the surface, perfectly mundane. But not in the context of the frenzied pursuit that sometimes affected a target in the football transfer market. And, of course, it depended on who was involved. Rangers were. They were the dominant force in Scottish football at the time. And their target was a lad from Hill o' Beath called Jim Baxter, riper for picking than any other young player in the country. Rodger knew that Baxter had promised to move to Rangers a couple of months previously, on the eve of a Scottish Cup final against Kilmarnock, on 22 April. But the deal had never been clinched because of disputes about the fee demanded by his club Raith Rovers. It wasn't completed until two months later, when eventually £17,500 passed hands as a new Scottish transfer record. But it was a long hiatus. Baxter still had to sign on the dotted line. Newspapers wanted to know exactly when, since it would be a major happening. Rodger knew – apparently exclusively – and this was now within his grasp. So, nugget in sight, he was off his mark, his subsequent actions like they had been scripted by John Le Carre as he personally shepherded Jim Baxter to Ibrox. However, as the news eventually broke, there were some among the Ibrox faithful who were slightly dubious about the transaction.

There is a phrase that has great street credibility in the environs of the Old Firm and which I have heard repeated constantly through the years, like being given the stamp of 'A1 at Lloyds'. It's when you heard someone opine, 'He's no' Rangers class'. Or is – as the case may be. The definition was hardly scientific and lay simply in the eye of the beholder. However, generally speaking Rangers, particularly at that juncture, still stood in the reflected light of their great manager Bill Struth who had built up the Iron Curtain defence – a team of strong, virile players which carried few weaklings. So, when I saw Jim Baxter for the first time, I can hardly say that I foresaw

any kind of future for him and certainly not at Ibrox. It was on
29 November 1959. He played midfield in the Raith team which
beat Rangers 3–2 that day. All I can recall is that he was conspicuous
by his physique which, compared to some of the Rangers players
thundering around him, made him look like an undernourished waif.
And he treated his right foot like it was a pariah, shunning it at every
opportunity, with his left leg in an exclusive pact with his brain. Even
some in the press box were not convinced he was 'Rangers class', in
the sense that physically he did not match the Ibrox prototype. Oh,
yes; clever, tricky, elegant and utterly self-confident in his swagger at
times. But that in itself could have meant nothing, as many a young
player could come to Ibrox or Celtic Park and give the performance
of a lifetime, enthused by the great theatre they were in, and dis-
appear from sight thereafter. However, Scot Symon saw something
much more influential in him that day and after weeks of delibera-
tion made his move to bring him to Ibrox. As Rodger neared Hill of
Beath, he could not possibly have had the foresight to know that he
was involved in one of the most significant signings in the history of
the Scottish game and of bringing to the wider public the evidence of
a single foot which could mesmerise so many.

For he was the source of unleashing a talent in which brilliance
and self-destruction were so intertwined that you might be forgiven
for concluding that the one could not have existed without the other.
Valorous deeds on the park were to be matched by infamous deeds
off it. His fragile personality, succumbing too easily to worldly temptations, would make him appear to rival the Sultan of Brunei in his
regard for money. Indeed, it saw him turn the sedate St Enoch Hotel
in the middle of Glasgow into a palace of self-indulgence, where
booze flowed and lavish meals were enjoyed – all at Rangers expense.
Indeed, sometimes he would sign another player's name in the bill
that would be sent for payment to Ibrox. Scot Symon's response,
even aware of what was happening, would simply be to sign the
bills with the devotion of a sugar-daddy to a favourite danseuse.
And in between times, card games would be played there that would
have done justice to Caesar's Palace in Vegas, encouraged on by his
admirers, many of whom, attracted by his handsome profile were

unsurprisingly of the opposite sex. His mastery on the field lent him immunity from any reprisal from club, or from the fan base, which became almost reverentially alive with gossip about his lifestyle, simply because he had brought an indispensable new art form to Ibrox with that left foot. Swiftly he had become immortalised as 'Slim Jim'.

For there was that other more beneficial self-indulgence. This is what gave him his universal acceptance. It was his plea from the heart, which spelled menace for the opposition, when he would shout, 'Gie me the ba!' He felt he had to be the fulcrum of the side, the real perpetrator. They would gift him it gratefully. Indeed, some Rangers players would claim that Scot Symon's only known coaching advice could be summed up in a sentence, 'Give the ball to Jim'. In doing so Rangers were running up success, and the elegance and the ease by which Baxter skewered defences with that left foot led to the inevitable comparison with the skill of the Brazilians. Indeed, one of his outstanding performances was against Brazil on 25 June 1966, in a pre-World Cup friendly which was drawn 1–1. I was criticised that day for saying he had outshone Pelé, but the great man himself, after that game said, 'I wish Jim would have been born a Brazilian.'

By the time I interviewed him for the first time he was probably the most talked about footballer in the land, and as a fledgling broadcaster then, I did feel slightly overawed by a man adored by so many and being gossiped about the way Casanova had been in 18th century Venice, with distinct Glaswegian variations. That interview was just after the Scottish Cup final replay against Celtic on 15 May 1963. Rangers not only won 3–0, but Baxter had turned the game into a cabaret act that essentially was an attempt to humiliate the Celtic players and which even incurred the unusual wrath of Scot Symon who, as the Rangers Captain Bobby Shearer once told me, would have come down from his office to wipe Jim's arse for him if required. So, in front of the mic for the first time with me, he was unabashed about his attitude in the replay and blissfully unconcerned about upsetting his manager, tossing all suggestion of controversy aside with his musical Fife accent that sucked you heartily into his bosom. Although he offered me no more than clichés in that first interview, I recall it vividly now for I judged him, at that moment, to be destined for global greatness. Unfortunately, at that same time, he had fallen deeply in love with Bacardi.

Almost 40 years later in 2000, my wife and I sat with Jim and his partner in the middle of a Variety Club Christmas Ball in Glasgow. He was slightly hunched, pale, soft-spoken. The story of his recent and dramatic illness had been splashed over all the Scottish newspapers. He had been diagnosed with liver failure in 1994. There followed two transplants and given the publicity of his lapse into drinking again, criticism was heaped on him by the public, angered by the apparent insensitivity of someone misusing the almost sacred and scarce procedure of transplanting. Certainly no alcohol passed his lips that night, that we could discern, and although that was a positive sign, little did we realise that pancreatic cancer was eating into him and would take him away the following April. He never moved from his seat all night despite his natural milieu of revelry going on all around him. Nature had clapped him in irons now. So, here I was sitting beside a man who had aged before his time – wasted and done – and I had used the word 'genius' about him almost 40 years previously. The bottle, and the wallet that couldn't resist a bet, had taken its full toll. It was a waste that could easily anger anybody looking back, because in the final analysis, despite the glory he attained relatively briefly, Jim Baxter fell well short of what he could really have achieved. The phrase, 'what might have been', is actually too timid to apply to his career.

WEMBLEY

The paradox was that this would be the longest time I would ever have spent chatting to him, and given his frail condition I certainly did not want to pester him. But he was in a quietly receptive mood and I couldn't resist asking him about Wembley, above all else. I told him I had been a Wembley babe being held up to a window to see the gathering of the Shettleston neighbourhood, as they waved and cheered their men setting off for London in their special bus; for which they had been saving up their shillings and pence over the previous two years. The special Wembley club was a great agent for social cohesion, in the centre of which was the treasurer, as important a figure as anybody in the local clergy. Over the years, as I grew up I witnessed this ceremonial departure of men, almost as if they were off to the trenches to defend our very survival. We counted them all out and we counted them all back again, with the absentees accounted for through traditional Wembley self-indulgence that was associated with temporary memory loss and the likely onset of liver problems. But, too often, very sad men would troop off the bus after defeat sending me into black despair, as I had a visceral hatred of Englishmen in white shirts, particularly four named Stan Matthews, Raich Carter, Tommy Lawton and Tom Finney, wonderfully skilful players whose sole mission in life was to humiliate Scotland on a football field.

Then Jim Baxter came along. He came at a time when I had just been introduced to the microphone, and Scottish football looked as if it were slipping into terminal decline. It was so bad that you felt that there were matters that ought not to be discussed in front of the bairns, like Scotland on 15 April 1961 being thrashed 9–3 by England at Wembley on a 'day of infamy', as Roosevelt had said of Pearl Harbour. Exactly one year later, almost to the day, Jim was part of the team at Hampden which beat England 2–0 – the first Scottish win at Hampden in a quarter of a century. It is difficult to convey the great outpouring of relief and gratitude that was felt around the stadium that day. It was as if we had found our identity again. But, another Wembley was on the horizon and another group in Shettleston was saving up for the bus, with a sense of bravado, suggesting that no pain the English could inflict on us would dampen our enthusiasm for the trip. Thousands were of a similar mind.

However, decades later when I sat with Jim in that festive Glasgow hotel, we talked about one of the oddest features of his career and that mood of revival which he had helped whip up at Hampden. For mention Baxter and that stadium in London in the same breath to any Scot around the world and you will see the faces brighten up like they were recalling some gleeful, treasured family moment they would take to their graves. Of course, it is the 'keepy-uppy' image of 1967 that is probably as iconic a moment as any in the history of the Auld Enemy fixture. How could it be otherwise? There I was watching Baxter flipping the ball upwards from his left boot, like a schoolboy with a 'tanner ba' (his right foot only there to help him balance) in front of thousands of Scots – forming the majority of the crowd – ecstatic at the sight of torment being heaped on the existing World Champions, England, as they faced defeat from Scotland in 1967. After the previous Wembley humiliations Scotland had suffered, this was like a joyful exorcism. It was almost the sole topic of conversation in London that night, as 'keepy-uppy' was being talked about like a new dance had been born to oust the Twist, which by then was running out of steam. Although, seeing a group of supporters attempting 'keepy-uppy' with a bobby's helmet hinted of a rowdier Wembley of the future.

That night of long conversation with Jim in the hotel revealed a much more sanguine attitude to that 15 April 1967 day. Certainly age and weariness of having talked about it so much over the years would have mellowed him, but he dismissed those pleasurably provocative seconds of taunting the English in one short sentence, 'It was for the punters.' Not that we ever had any doubts that his feet were semaphoring to the tartan battalions, as if he was riding a bike for the first time, 'Look. No hands!' He certainly did not express any regret to me about his showboating, but he was simply identifying it for what it really was, as his manager at the time fully and regretfully understood.

For during one of the anniversaries of that event I had the occasion to talk to Scotland's manager of that day, the venerable and tanned-looking Bobby Brown, the former Rangers goalkeeper, who at 92 was bearing his age so well you had to resist the temptation to ask him what his secret was. He had been far from happy with Baxter, as I clearly recall.

'No, no. He shouldn't have done that. We could have won that game something like 5–2 instead of 3–2. I wanted to rub it in. Wouldn't you?'

There was no need to reply to that. Indeed, he went so far as to tell me he thought Jim McCalliog, the 21-year-old Sheffield Wednesday player making his debut for Scotland that day, had been more influential than Jim Baxter. But, what was becoming clear to me in my conversation with Jim himself, is that in a historic and very personal sense he had done himself a slight disservice, because the Wembley game that he really thought showed him at his best has almost been side-lined in the great oral tradition that keeps memories of Scottish football flooding back to us. Everybody talks about 1967. Hardly anybody looks back on 1963 where I would agree with his own verdict that it was his finest Wembley, where we witnessed the more 'team-player' Baxter. Of course he had given interviews in which he played up the cabaret aspect of his 'keepy-uppy' as if to further endear himself to the fans.

That 1963 game was my first Wembley, which in itself coloured my impression of the whole occasion. There was firstly the cultural shock of witnessing London being engulfed in tartan and the English being greatly outnumbered in the stadium itself. It was all a healthy, colourful and tuneful patriotism, that sadly within a decade was to become sourer and more destructive, with London on the receiving end of some mindless vandalism rooted in burgeoning anarchic anti-English sentiment. But, in that year, if such a future scenario had been predicted for us we would have regarded it as preposterous. All was well with the world. And although I still felt the stomach churning walking up Wembley Way, there was the previous year to look back on at Hampden when Jim had been part of the side which beat England, 2–0, and the thought of which did smooth the nerves slightly. After all, the mastery of his performance in that victory inspired the *Daily Mirror's* Peter Wilson, who was never enamoured of Scottish football, to write,

> Frankly the game was so one-sided at times that the English fans should have got their money back. It was staggering to see the bemused expressions grow on the faces of these much-lauded English stars as they watched Jim Baxter execute a progressive twist marathon, smoothing down the divots with velvet feet before sliding into the area marked 'Danger'.

Then there was the whole 1963 team itself. I spoke to Willie Henderson, Rangers winger, who was making his Wembley debut that day, and in vivid recollection he spoke with both emotion and pride of the men he walked out with that afternoon.

'What a team, when you think about it. Best Scottish team I played in. We had Bill Brown of Spurs in goal when he was at his best. The full-backs were my mates at Ibrox, Eric Caldow on the left and Hammy (Alex Hamilton) from Dundee on the right. And what a midfield! Dave Mackay, Ian Ure and Baxter. Think about that. Dave was still the mainstay of Spurs, Ian was one of the best headers of a ball playing in Scotland with Dundee and Baxter was, well Baxter, Slim Jim. Nobody like him. Unique. Then there was me on the right wing and Davy Wilson from my own club on the left, about the best winger on the left they ever had. And John White. Remember him? The White Ghost. Revered at White Hart Lane. Poor boy killed by lightning on a golf course. Right up front there was Ian St John, ramming them in at Liverpool and Denis, who else but Denis against the English?'

Willie's voice, simply mulling over these names, was like a lullaby from the past. Although two of the men he talked about, Denis Law and Dave Mackay, about to walk up the wide ramp on to the pitch, were in no mellow mood but in a high state of tension with a burning desire to get their teeth back into the English again after both having been humiliated in the 9–3 massacre. It had hurt them beyond measure. As Denis Law was to tell me some years later, 'I felt like going into hiding. I got it in the neck from some of my mates for some time.' So they sought revenge. Jim Baxter, on the other hand, was putting on his best bib and tucker for the event, as if he was about to appear as a Footlights entertainer. He told his now very good friend Jim Rodger, just before the game, 'This is the London Palladium. If I don't turn it on here then you can kick me up the backside after the game.'

Kick-off at Wembley in the Auld Enemy game had a special quality. The two-year wait was over. All that cash the thousands had saved up in that period to get there and which might have been spent on a week at Saltcoats, or a new carpet for the living room, or a bike for the wean, now seemed worth every penny scraped together.

They did so with a roar of acclamation as the ball first moved, overwhelming English voices and stirring the emotions to the point where the critical faculties were numbed and for one brief shining moment it only mattered that we were all there together, kith and kin, in a manner that excluded the possibility of defeat. Then, of course, reality would seep in.

On that day, it did so in a horrendous fashion.

In only five minutes the nature of the game completely changed. One tackle sufficed. It looked brutal, and even when it happened, like those around me, I shuddered. You can tell when somebody at the receiving end is not going to get back on his feet again. On his back, writhing, lay the Scottish captain, Eric Caldow. He had been tackled wildly by the English centre-forward Bobby Smith of Spurs. The English journalist, Norman Giller, once described Smith as someone 'who mixed cruiser-weight strength with subtlety on the ball', almost as a warning to all-comers. Perhaps more revealing was the title of Smith's autobiography, *My Life of Birds, Booze and Betting*, suggesting he was skilled at putting other people on their backs, in other more clandestine settings. Caldow's leg was broken in two places and the sight of him being stretchered off stiffened Slim Jim's resolve. There was to be no self-indulgence. This was to be a pure team performance now, with Davy Wilson the winger filling in at left-back and Baxter patrolling in front of him, still elegant, but committed and determined, and arousing Gair Henderson of the *Glasgow Evening Times* to report that Baxter, 'tackled, like I never thought he could tackle'. That change of character has been rather lost in the publicity and praise he received for his two left-footed goals inside two minutes. Willie Henderson was behind both of them.

'Although I say it myself, I was giving the full-back Byrne of Liverpool a right roasting. I think he only got one other England Cap after that game. Well, I got some space to whip the ball across and there was Jimmy Armfield fumbling it and in steps Jim, controls it with the left foot and sweeps it past Peter Shilton in goal. As cool as a striker. And you could scarcely believe it, two minutes later, Byrne right on top of me brings me down in the box. Penalty. Stonewaller. You wouldn't credit it. Baxter had never taken a penalty in his life, never. But Dave McKay threw Jim the ball as if it was the natural thing to do. Up he steps, no argument, no discussion, he wanted that ball and now it was up to him, with what must have been the weight of the Empire State Building weighing on his shoulders in front of 100,000 people. Well, as calm as you like, as if he was playing in the public park, he wrong-foots big Shilton and slips it past him to the left. And he just says to me, casually, "Well, that's got that out the way." But we're two up! We're flying!'

If Jim had decided to retire on the spot and had headed down to Monte Carlo and a lifestyle for which he was apparently born, tartan pilgrimages would have followed for his unique achievement of scoring a double against England, his first ever at that level. And yet, all that seems to have been relegated to a kind of afterthought in the shadow of those few seconds in 1967 and the defeat of the World Champions. But that game had nothing of the drama of the broken leg and the Baxter double. A Scottish captain leaves the field with a broken leg, Smith, the Englishman, injuring himself in that fateful tackle, nevertheless returns to the fray just before the interval so effectively creating 11 against ten for the remaining 50 minutes. Perhaps the criticism of the English side, even by Scots, might have diluted the appreciation of victory. Gair Henderson of the *Glasgow Evening Times* on 8 April of that year, summed up the opposition thus, 'But for England, the most humiliating fact of all, was that the hobbling Smith was their most effective forward.' And as for the nature of the game which turned volatile and bad tempered after the fateful tackle, Cyril Horne of the *Glasgow Herald* wrote, 'I have seen as much dignity in an average game in Glasgow Green of the old days, as I saw at Wembley' and added about Scotland, 'They will seldom be faced by such an incompetent set of opponents' – who in fact scored through by Brian Douglas ten minutes from the end, and in the Auld Enemy fixture a 2–1 defeat was painful for them, as there is no such thing as a consolation goal on these days.

But the pale figure beside me at the Variety Club Christmas Ball, all these years later, resolutely, but quietly, insisted that the Wembley of 1963 was the international that really did resonate with him. His captain's injury had been a sobering influence. There were to be no fripperies. All this was turned turtle in Vienna on 8 December 1964 against Rapid where, according to his teammates, he exceeded that Wembley performance and played the game of his life in a Rangers 2–0 victory which put them through to the next round of the European Cup. Just before the final whistle he decided to torment his perpetual marker, by going round him once, twice and then on the third attempt was brutally tackled by an incensed opponent. He was on his back with a broken leg as the whistle went. For all his greatness that night – his natural inclination, his arrogance, his superb skill, all combined to put an end to the cavalier Jim who had entranced supporters and opponents alike up till that incident. For he was never the same again. For all that he played on for other clubs in England and returned to Rangers four years later, his body was weaker, his left foot/brain collaboration slower.

But he will always remain among the pantheon of great left-footed players. Messi and Maradona were certainly left foot inclined, but their right foot was never wholly isolated. Davy Cooper's lent him occasional mastery. The really lop-sided variety like Arjen Robben or Gareth Bale used speed, rather than Baxter's evasiveness to succeed. Only one other, in terms of style and manner came close in one-footed manipulation of opponents – Wim van Hanegem of Feyenoord. Jock Stein recognised that in May 1970 just before the European Cup final in Milan when he described him in the team-talk before the game as 'a slower Jim Baxter with a right foot for standing on'. But, he was crucially underestimating him, as was recognised by Lisbon Lion Tommy Gemmell, who adamantly told me years later, 'The man van Hanegem, who was supposed to be a one-footed weakness, was still running stronger than anybody in extra-time and pinging beautiful passes all over the field.' For me, in the San Siro, it was like watching a disciple of the master from Hill o' Beath.

That left leg of Slim Jim is now on permanent display in a statue for him in his own village where for the sake of support they had to include a right leg as well, just as nature had done in the 61 years before his death on 14 April 2001. His funeral drew thousands of mourners to the streets of Glasgow and the following day Celtic supporters, at Hampden for a Scottish Cup final, held up a banner proclaiming, 'Slim Jim. Simply The Best'.

Jim Rodger was not there to see his good friend put to rest. The journalist had died four years earlier. He would have been dismayed at how steep the decline had been for the boy from Hill o' Beath. To the end he still regarded his triumph in panning the competitive waters for the Baxter nugget and scooping the rest of Scottish journalism, as like discovering the Koh – I – Noor diamond in a pit-bing in Fife.

Baxter, like many footballers, was fond of the occasional round of golf. So beside him I sit Eric Brown where they could not only share views on the links, but about how they fought their personal demons.

CHAPTER 4

The Bomber

IN APRIL 2020 Dr Anthony Fauci the highly respected scientist at the heart of America's response to the Covid pandemic, then sweeping the globe, told the *Wall Street Journal*,

> As a society just forget about shaking hands. We don't need to shake hands. We've got to break that custom. Because, as a matter of fact, that is really one of the major ways that you can transmit a respiratory illness.

His words sounded so radical that it felt like he was heralding the end of human discourse altogether. Shaking hands always seemed to sit beside the importance of eating meals, breathing in and out, opening your eyes in the morning, recognising your loved ones, justifying your own existence in the world, recognising achievement and very often an acceptance of your status in life. It also brought to mind that phrase which springs directly from competitiveness, 'the sporting handshake'.

But some are memorable. One such, in those bygone days, left me with the feeling that the pressure on my hand would have registered on the Richter scale. It was the day when a man who could lay claim to being one of Scotland's greatest golfers strode into my life.

Eric Brown, his intense eyes focussing on me like he wanted to bore a hole in my head to find out what was in my mind, reached out and gripped my hand in a fleshy vice that forced me to resist looking down to see how many fingers had survived the experience. It was like he was passing silent information about his personality – forthright, aggressive, intense, confrontational; all the things I had heard about him previously – all condensed into a single handshake. We were putting the seal on an arrangement with a brewery company to travel around Scotland and deliver talks to audiences in hotels, with myself as chairman. I knew these evenings would hardly be sedate. After all, his nickname was The Bomber. Of course, being a man who had twice captained Britain's Ryder Cup team, never lost a singles against any American in the four times he competed and won tournaments handsomely around Europe, with a power that was awesome to watch at times, I could hardly have expected his grip to be that of a maiden aunt. Nevertheless, it was as if he was making sure that in this new relationship that we were about to establish, I was clearly going to perform the function of caddy.

After the bone-crushing handshake, I noticed how those mighty hands which had nursed him round spectacular rounds of golf and brought an ex-railway fireman fame and fortune, were red and scaly, like he had eczema. Even though you could hardly miss his condition it was not something that I felt I could raise, even solicitously. But, of course, I was eventually to find out that the state of his hands stemmed from a daily act of self-sacrifice that reflected on the difficulties he was encountering in life and which, sadly, were biting deeply into his morale.

I was slightly in awe of him though, both for the scale of his achievements and for his reputation for shooting from the hip, regardless of the circumstances, and for the apparent ease with which he could row with the lowly and the mighty. But I certainly knew there would be a healthy public reaction to his presence because, as his good friend and Ryder Cup colleague Peter Alliss would say to me whenever I mentioned Eric's name, in admiration of him, 'What a fighter!' It was that which seemed to endear him to the Scottish public. In his duels with the Americans in the Ryder Cups, where in singles he was untouchable, at a time when the USA generally dominated that series, he lent the impression that when he chose his awesome driver on the tee in the matches against them, he was pulling it, not from a golf bag but from a scabbard. Something stirred in him when he heard the American accent. Their abundance of great players seemed to antagonise him. But technically he was equipped to take on anybody, for Bernard Gallacher said this to me about Eric's prowess.

'John Jacobs always said to me that Eric was the best driver of a ball, long and straight with high draws, a great putter and tremendous out of a bunker. He had all the attributes to make up a great golfer.'

As one of the great students of the game Jacobs's judgements were rarely ignored.

That power and accuracy was grounded at Bathgate Golf Club. This town is near the watershed in the narrow waistline of central Scotland and to the majority of travellers between our two major cities, it simply exists to be bypassed. But taking the trouble to go *off-piste,* away from the main drag of motorway, you can come into a town which has much to boast about in golf. For at this club you will be on hallowed ground. This small and almost inconspicuous institution can boast of producing two Ryder Cup captains – three Ryder Cup players. Perhaps historically just as significant, is that it represents the egalitarian nature of the development of Scottish golf and why local men without any trace of privilege, Eric, Bernard Gallacher and Stephen Gallacher, made it through the ranks to the Ryder Cup. Stephen Gallacher, who played in the 2014 competition, and who grew up on the course, talked to me about those 18 holes which produced such quality.

'It's a demanding track. The greens are tiny. You have to have a good short game and be a good iron player. It didn't suit one kind of shot. There were doglegs both ways. But, you know, I cannot work out precisely why Bathgate reached these heights.'

Nor, I suppose, could anybody. Except that Stephen's uncle Bernard does point in the right direction.

'Eric was the reason. We all wanted to be another Eric Brown. He inspired us. We would see his portrait up there with the treasured jacket on. That's what we all wanted to be.'

With great potential Eric was entering a sporting world with a highly stratified culture. 'Manners maketh man' might have been coined for the institution of the golf club, with its normally strict household etiquette, which has very little to do with knocking a ball into a hole in as few shots as you can muster. Around the start of Eric's professional career, in general the sport was seen as for the favoured few. Women were not welcome in many clubs and certain institutions like R and A or the Honourable Company of Edinburgh Golfers, aka Muirfield, created atmospheres more akin to monasticism than sporting endeavour. My own experience of the Honourable Company was of walking in there one day with the distinguished BBC senior announcer Alastair McIntyre who had a cultured voice made in heaven, and a crusty gentleman looked over the newspaper he was reading in a lounge, so hushed you could hear the paper rustle and remarked to him, 'Have you had the leg over this week, McIntyre?' which suggested they were not entirely monastic. So how would the pushy artisan fit into all of that? When I talked to Bathgate Councillor Harry Cartmill, who had been a member of the club there for years he did direct me towards a wary relationship between Eric and golf club conventions.

'He had this reputation for being rough and ready, a little bit gruff, maybe not the most personable of gentlemen, but to me, as a lad after I got to know him, he couldn't have been more helpful. But we all knew he could be blunt with people and he didn't suffer fools gladly. And since he was so brash at times some people would just avoid him.'

Eric himself recounted to the audiences the times he would try to arrange games against some of the best players at the club, but they would shun him. He could never decide whether they were scared of being beaten by someone who was only a fireman on the railways, which he had become after leaving school, or because, as he openly admitted to me, he was a cocky youngster who got up peoples' noses.

To the general public he was a refreshing contrast to the almost aristocratic image of the great Henry Cotton who had dominated British golf for years, pre and post-war, and seemed to personify the age of plus fours and mashie-niblicks. For Eric was still stoking coal into trains when he won the Scottish Amateur Championship in 1946 at the age of 21, and after which golf released him from the grime and sweat of manual labour into a profession where his hands and arms were put to more lucrative use. For he was now to shovel honours into his household, topping the European Tour of Merit in 1957, winning the Scottish PGA Championship seven times between 1956 and 1968, and representing Great Britain in the Ryder Cup in

1953, 1955, 1957 and 1959. And, in 1969 and 1971 he certainly looked as if he were to the manor born as non-playing captain of the GB team, but he attached to it a demeanour that suggested he took inspiration paradoxically from an American – baseball coach Vince Lombardi who once stated, 'Winning isn't everything, it's the only thing.' This is why as a youth I was so attracted to him. At that stage in life you are fonder of the irrregulars, of the rebels, of the challengers to the status quo, the mavericks.

It was not just that he would go on to win 26 professional tournaments in his career in the UK and around Europe, but the combustible personality which emerged in that time had caught the imagination of the Scottish public. They were aroused by the spectacle of a man who had got his hands well and truly grimy before he transferred to the lucrative feel of the golf glove. Even when at times he was technically 'unattached' with no club job, you felt he was yet attached to the ordinary man in the street.

At first his nervousness in front of our audiences was apparent, as he explained how he had emerged from his early days as a golfing prodigy, picking up titles like they were daisies in the field and then on moving to his professional career. It was when someone eventually asked him about the American golfer, Tommy Bolt, that the Madame Tussaud Brown became the Bathgate one. However, Eric's version of that day differed in some ways from the popular media interpretation of events.

His clash with Bolt at Lindrick in South Yorkshire in the Ryder Cup in 1957 has by now veered into legend. It came on the second day of the tournament when the GB side had started badly in the foursomes, with Eric and his partner Christie O'Connor going down heavily, 7 and 5. Eric's response, on the rebound the following day, has since been considered a historic turning point in the history of the competition. As leader of the pack, he had to take on Bolt, whose throwing of clubs in anger had become so prevalent that it might have persuaded the IOC to turn it into an Olympic event. It is said when he took his young son onto a course one day to demonstrate to an audience how well he had taught him how to use a 5-iron and asked him to perform, the youngster simply lifted it and threw it down the fairway.

At the start of their singles encounter Bolt, boosted by his easy foursomes victory, behaved impeccably and cheerily, like a *magna cum laude* out of an American charm school. But by the 15th hole the pleasantries had ceased when he was three down to Eric and a Mr Hyde emerged. He griped, shouted at the crowds and scowled at the Scot who, from the turn, had kept telling Bolt to stop his moaning about what the American thought was a partisan crowd. When Eric put an iron shot close to the hole, with Bolt still yards from it and no chance of saving the match, instead of gently conceding and shaking hands, he took his putter and swiped Eric's ball off the green in a fit of petulance backed up by a fusillade of obscenities. Eric told him, in imaginative terms, where he could insert his putter.

But the marker had been laid down. The public recognised The Bomber facing down a loudmouthed American bully which seemed to inspire his colleagues to go on and win the Ryder Cup for the first time in 21 years. It also made Eric seem almost heroic and, adding to his previous Cup singles wins, that his dislike of American arrogance brought out the best in him. But, in fact, it was much more nuanced than that. Allan Herron, one of Scotland's great sports journalists who 'ghosted' Eric's widely read column, in the now defunct *Glasgow Evening Citizen*, amplifies that.

> Eric told me that during that round Bolt threw a club down the middle in pique. So Eric did the same, much to the amusement of Bolt and the surrounding crowd. After which Bolt turned to him and said, drolly, 'If you're ever going to throw a club, throw it forward so you can pick it up on the way down the fairway!' But although they had words at the end, let me tell you that Bolt eventually turned to Eric and said, 'You know Eric, you are one helluva man!'

According to Herron they actually liked each other. Bolt had come up the hard way, from being a carpenter and then on to caddying for a living, before joining the American PGA tour only at the late age of 34 because he simply couldn't afford it any earlier. Despite the theatrics which certainly made attractive headlines there had been a deeper bonding. Temperamental, argumentative and having both toiled to make a living before golf took command, Eric recognised a man out of his own mould.

His captaincy of the Ryder Cup team, eventually, was an inspirational choice as Bernard Gallacher who played under him explained to me.

'He was marvellous as a captain. In the previous Cup in 1967 the GB team had been trashed with the biggest defeat ever. 9–2. He revived us all. He made us all angry thinking back to that defeat. And, I tell you, we were unlucky not to win.'

It had ended in a 16 point tie, the climax of which is also recalled as a supreme example of sportsmanship when Jack Nicklaus, on the final green, conceded an entirely missable three-foot putt to Tony Jacklin. Eric had made them believe they were all Tommy Bolts they were facing and it had worked.

Because of his recurring success in the Ryder Cup in singles matches, his audiences on the tour pursued him for memories of those battles, to reinforce their image of him as Bomber Brown, the man who took no prisoners. But it is a measure of the decency of the man that he kept referring back to his great rival and good friend, Ryder Cup colleague John Panton who during my early days in broadcasting seemed to be on the fairways with Eric so often that they looked like the Ying and Yang of Scottish golf. They represented Scotland together 13 times in the World Cup. But that was an aside. As our evenings progressed, it became clear that there was a major obsession in his life.

THE CLARET JUG

It towered over every other challenge. He had entered his first Open in 1947 and his fortunes thereafter would have suggested that the only way he could place his hands on the trophy was by armed robbery. Then he won the European Masters at Crans-sur-Sierre in 1951. That fuelled his ambition. But when he talked about what was then to occur, in his pursuit of what he considered the greatest of all the prizes, it began to sound like the biblical story of Job and the tale of unmerited suffering. I particularly recalled the events surrounding the Carnoustie Open of 1953.

I had just started working in a summer job as a student with the parcel office of British Railways at Glasgow Central Station but my mind was elsewhere. In that dungeon of a place, where parcels were thrown around with gay abandon, we were all listening to the radio reports from the course at Carnoustie – not because of interest in the general progress of the tournament but particularly of one man's fate. I had just been to the cinema to watch the film *Follow The Sun,* the story of the Texan golfer Ben Hogan, played by Glen Ford, one of Hollywood's box-office favourites. It was the story of indomitable courage.

Yes, in recent times Tiger Woods, recovering from serious back problems to win the Masters in 2019 could easily be considered to have achieved one of the greatest comebacks in sport, but it has tended to make us overlook what happened in the 1940s. Hogan at that time had been the leading money maker on the PGA tour in five out of eight seasons, from 1940 to one catastrophic evening in 1949. On a densely foggy night, on a bridge, his car smashed headlong into a bus. If he had not dived to the side to protect his wife, the steering column would have penetrated his chest and killed him. As it was, he suffered a double fracture of the pelvis, a fractured collar bone, a left ankle fracture, a chipped rib and near-fatal blood clots. By a superhuman effort of recuperation and constant practice on the golf range, for which he was renowned, he started to play competitively again. Now popularised by what was admittedly a highly sentimental portrayal of events by Hollywood, he had come to play in one of the most challenging Open courses and the outpouring of sympathy for him in Scotland was as if he were an exile returning to his native land. Before anybody teed off at Carnoustie I failed to meet a single person who did not want him to lift the Claret Jug because of his compelling story. Here was something akin to a fairy tale about to fall into our laps on Scottish soil and I sensed we were reluctant to turn our backs on it. But where did that place Eric who was riding high in popularity as a favourite son? He told me he knew he could not compete with the popular admiration for a brave man, anticipating what the conditions would be like for other players with a global star in their midst. This was a significant factor identified by the *Glasgow Herald's* report on 9 July 1953.

The championship proper was given a fine send off, as crowds drawn from all parts of Britain by the Hogan magnet. Programmes and tickets ran out early in the day, and the caterers could not cope with demands for lunch. It was fitting therefore that the 'stars' should provide entertainment of such high quality, but the crowds, concentrating principally on Locke and Hogan, slowed the play down tremendously.

It's that which angered Eric. The unruliness of the crowd. It slowed play to his great annoyance. Anybody who was challenged by Eric on the course, for having annoyed him, would remember it for the rest of their lives. Despite all that he was well pleased by shooting a 71 in that first round, only one shot behind the young American amateur Frank Stranahan who led the field. Eric ended up his second round by sharing the lead with the Welshman Dai Rees. Hogan was in a group two shots behind. And so arose this odd feeling of a division of loyalties. Not long before Carnoustie Eric had relinquished his post as the professional at Hartsbourne in England. He had driven to the Labour Exchange in his vastly expensive Ford v8, signed on, drew his dole money and then headed north completely unattached and looking for a job. Now, here he was, on those daunting links, still unattached, obviously in the mood to go on and actually win this tournament for Scotland, for the first time since George Duncan accomplished that at Royal Cinque in 1920. And at the age of 28 he was a virtual youngster compared to the company he was keeping at the top of the scoreboard. All that sounded heroic and had the makings of an epic achievement that would excite the Scottish public. But, he was also intending to spoil the miraculous tale that most of us had built up in our minds, of a mangled body being pulled from a car on a foggy night in the States, going on to defy medical predictions and then travelling all the way to north-east Scotland where he would lift the trophy in glorious technicolour – despite it being Carnoustie. That's the way my imagination was working, and I was not alone. Hogan was intruding on my native loyalty, in a very uncomfortable way. Also, I had the Texan on the parcel office sweep.

This clash of emotions intensified in the third round when we heard through radio that at the tenth hole Eric was four strokes up on Hogan and he admitted to his audiences that he felt he was on the verge of something great, having been doubly incentivised by his critics who had written him off as something of a maverick, who lacked consistency on the course and stability off it. But it was at this hole, where the Barry Burn lays a corridor of treacherous water about 40 yards off the green, that fate intervened.

Play had been notoriously slow given the size and perpetual intrusions of the crowd. He told us that after some waiting he had played a decent drive but because the green had not cleared of the play ahead and the crowd were slow to disperse from watching Peter Thomson, the great Australian golfer who was to go on and win the next three Opens in succession, Eric felt he had waited about quarter of a hour before he picked up his 3-iron. Unfortunately, it took another few minutes for his caddy to go down the fairway and shout at a white-jacketed steward who was standing in his line for the hole. The man stepped aside and crouched. But, as Eric was in the first motions of a backswing, the man suddenly stood up and bolted across the course. His swing, as this figure caught his eye, went off its hinges and the Barry Burn accepted his ball with the typical silent derision of a water trap.

The championship had ended there and then for him, as he put it. He never recovered his early flow. His 75, followed by a final round of 75 put him in 9th equal position on 292 with his friend Peter Alliss. Hogan, almost to a heavenly chorus in the background in my imagination, lifted the trophy by four shots with a remarkable final round of 68, even though he was battling flu. A ticker-tape celebration awaited him on Broadway on his return. In front of his audience, Brown, relating the story of his late collapse, told it like it was one of the most disillusioning days in his life. That was to pale into insignificance compared to another day on famous links.

It was at St Andrews on the Old Course, where his striving to consummate his lifetime desire took on something of the characteristics of Greek tragedy, in which the main character falls to a disaster that seems beyond all comprehension. It was the Open Championship of 1957. He spoke about the circumstances of that tournament several times in our tour round the country and never once did it seem he was parroting the same tale mechanically. It was still hurting him too much for that. However, Allan Herron puts into perspective Eric's unsettled approach to the Old Course in the first place.

'He disliked it immensely. He felt it was basically unfair. That after you hit a good shot you could end up in an awkward position on the fairways because of all the knolls that litter them. So pure luck was involved. And he felt there were up to ten holes where you had to play blind shots to the green. He simply did not like it despite its world-wide renowned reputation.'

In fact he was doubly disappointed because the Open had been scheduled to be played at Muirfield that year, but because of petrol rationing caused by the oil shortage, which could be traced back to the Suez Canal crisis of autumn 1956, the R and A had decided that most people travelling to St Andrews by railway would be in the better national interest.

On 5 July 1957, the unemotional *Glasgow Herald* reported thus:

> E.C. Brown (Buchanan Castle) will start the final day's play in the Open Golf Championship on the Old course here tomorrow the leader of the 46 competitors who will take part in the last two rounds. With a 36-hole aggregate lead of 139 (67,72). Brown is one stroke ahead of F van Donck (Belgium).

That bare communique conveyed nothing of the surging national excitement surrounding the distinct possibility of a Scot, two ahead also of the talented Bobby Locke of South Africa, winning on the very territory which had helped gift the game to the world.

It would be something like a homecoming if he were to succeed. The title had been exiled since James Braid had won it there for Scotland in 1910. I suggest, that to the Scottish golfing public, Eric bringing it back home would have had more spiritual meaning than the Stone of Destiny which had been lifted back to Scotland from England only seven years before. The public were stirring to this prospect and crowds of support flocked into 'the auld grey toon'. This was despite the fact that the BBC were televising live the final stages of the Open for the first time.

Unfortunately, many of the public were behaving on this sacred territory like they were at the Boxing Day sales and even the *Glasgow Herald* itself seemed stunned by the invasion.

> As on the previous day the least knowledgeable and the most undisciplined of the thousands of spectators attached themselves to Brown's following, and on more than one occasion he had to attempt to maintain reasonable order.

Note that 'most undisciplined' term. That was to matter. But, on that Friday morning of 5 July 1957, the final day of the competition but with two rounds to complete, expectations of Brown's ultimate ascendancy soared around the country. When I listened to him telling his audiences what was to happen next, even though I was to hear it several times, it never varied in tense emotion. He seemed to be appealing for some kind of understanding, that for all his skills, the one thing he couldn't control were the quirks of fate.

He teed off for the first of the final two rounds and when he had reconnoitred the Swilcan safely and putted out confidently on the first green, the crowd erupted as if they were on the terracings of Hampden Park. It was an emotional outburst that ironically contained the ingredient of his downfall. He could see that play immediately in front had come to a halt because golfers of a lower order were experiencing difficulties, especially in the apparently magnetic gorse bushes.

Standing on the tee, edgily waiting his turn, felt like an eternity. The crowds accumulated into a dense throng just behind and to the side of him. Then eventually, it was time. A reverential silence fell as he addressed the ball. Alan Herron recalls it vividly.

'Suddenly the hubbub subsided and the hush fell. I can't recall just how long we had waited but given Eric's leading position I think we felt as if some power was torturing us. All the press out there wanted him to swing and get on with it. It was infuriating. Then order prevailed and I recall him even now taking up his stance as he must have done thousands of times in his professional career. We all knew this was different though.'

Eric began his backswing, but from somewhere among that mass of humanity a voice suddenly screamed, with the power and effect of a low-flying jet passing overhead, 'Hit it down the bloody middle Eric!'

Whenever Eric repeated these words to an audience it was like hearing a man utter his own epitaph for a life unfulfilled. He was utterly convinced that that single moment cost him the Open, as all the co-ordination that he had worked on all his days was put slightly off kilter and in a massive misjudgement, he put his ball straight into a gorse bush where it was deemed unplayable. He called it simply 'an angry swing' and never did discover who had shouted, but admits that had he done so blood might have flowed. For he finished with a six at the hole. From believing strongly that he could win the title, that intrusion had unsettled him and he finished with a 73 as opposed to Bobby Locke with a 68. In the afternoon final round of the championship he steadied himself and shot a 71 but four shots behind the Open winner Bobby Locke. I could understand the passion and historic frustration that surfaced when he told us of that particular day, but even though that simply joined other incidents he told us about which might have prevented him from winning other Opens, there was no self-pitying whine about him. He was simply recounting 'what might have been'. And after all, the St Andrews incident would have turned even his mild-mannered friend, John Panton, into an assassin had it happened to him.

However, as Bernard Gallacher wisely remarked to me, 'All the best golfers look for excuses when things go wrong.' What made matters worse for Eric is that Locke had lifted the Claret Jug, something that soured him, as Allan Herron explained to me.

'He hated Bobby Locke. There might have been something personal in it. But I think it was mostly about golf. For he thought Locke didn't play the Old Course the right way. He never used a driver off the tee, only a 3-wood. He thought that just wasn't manly. And as you'll recall Locke did not replace his ball on the correct spot after marking it a putter-head away from his opponent's line on the final green, but the R and A accepted his explanation and let him off. For Eric, it all counted against Locke.'

That he was quite open in his distaste of an Open winner was typical of the unapologetic candour that never deserted him throughout his career. By the time of this tour with me though, that great career was well behind him. Life was presenting different challenges over and above his frustration at the diminishing of his ability on the fairways. His beloved wife was in dialysis and he explained to me the scurvy look of his hands was caused by his having to deal with that complicated medical process. I could tell how intensely this was affecting him in ways much deeper than his skin. For he was drinking heavily. It seemed to be part taste, part refuge. He was never without a glass of sustenance to hand during our tour, much of it supplied by a grateful sponsor. I felt profoundly sad for him and, as I was hardly an abstainer myself, I refrained from mentioning his weakness until one evening when it was so pronounced that he became involved in an alcohol-induced argument with one of the audience, I had to bring proceedings to an end for his own sake, as things looked to be getting out of hand. All this was intensely uncomfortable because I was honoured to be sitting beside this man who had done so much to draw the world's attention to Scottish golf and deserved rescuing from self-destructive lapses like that. But, sadly, there were people in his sport who applied almost mechanical intransigence to someone they identified merely as an outspoken, opinionated golfer, not a man fighting his personal demons who needed help.

For because of his severe financial straits, about which he was too proud to admit to anybody, not least the PGA, he was banned from its membership, the very organisation that had made him Ryder Cup captain and PGA captain, for non-payment of dues. It all seems in retrospect so unnecessary and unedifying, although it does also tell us something of how this man inspired harshly contrasting views on his volatile nature. However, those who really did understand him, never lost sight of what he meant to them and the image of Scottish golf. Such a one was Bernard Gallacher who cannot forget a significant day in his young life. It was 1971 at Lundin Links in Fife when he was 22. He had to go into a play-off to win his first Scottish Pro tournament. His opponent was Eric Brown.

'He was great', Bernard told me. 'He couldn't have been nicer to me, genuinely. And, I suppose, with 24 years between us he must have realised that he was coming to the end of his great career. That was the Eric Brown I care to remember. A great man. A great talent.'

Eric was a complex character who had so many qualities that brought him not only admiration but, in the kindness he could show others, lifelong friends, like Bernard. That other belligerent side of his personality which could startle people, was like a primal scream from someone who perhaps thought he never was fully appreciated by some of the mandarins in his sport. And yet you have to think that had he not borne these competing traits in his character which produced the dynamic thrust of his nature, he would still have been shovelling coals on engines at the very moment when, in fact, he was standing on the second tee on the Old Course on that fateful day. The Scottish public found it easy to endorse a man who so often shunned convention and spoke from the heart with scant regard for the consequences. So we grieved when we heard he had died of a stroke on 6 March 1986 at the age of 61.

I last saw him in the early hours of one morning at my home, not long before his death, after we had finished our tour. We chatted cosily, mostly about football and about his love of Hearts which he had supported since boyhood. He said he would take me out one day on a practise range and cure my hook. We never got round to it. The hook is still there defiantly reminding me of the man who was within a shout of attaining the goal of his life.

His love of Hearts did not blind him to rare talent in other fields. He adored Jimmy Johnstone. So naturally he would be at his elbow in the next seat.

CHAPTER 5

Il Topolino

IMAGINE YOU HAVE been put inside a prison cell for life. There is to be no parole. Then the walls begin to shrink, getting closer to you by the week, inching in remorselessly until you realise they are about to crush you to death and there is nothing you can do about it. Your fate is sealed and all you can contemplate is the manner in which you will face the end.

That is how the famed historian Tony Judt described his situation as he lay in his New York apartment waiting for motor neurone disease to put an end to a distinguished life. As I read what Judt had written, on the morning I was to make a visit to a North Lanark-shire house to meet someone suffering a similar fate, I was at odds with myself as to how to engage with this. How easily would I talk and chat to someone for whom I knew there would be no salvation and with the cell walls already on the move inwards for him? My unease was accentuated by the fact that I was thinking of a wee man who had endeared himself to millions with vivacious performances around European football fields that, in the mind's eye, still sparkled like Roman candles, inextinguishably. Largely it would depend on what the mood would be like within the household. Within seconds of crossing the threshold I could tell that Jimmy Johnstone and his wife Agnes had never heard of the Grim Reaper.

With a broad welcoming smile the former Celtic player greeted me heartily, sitting comfortably in an armchair, his arms close by his side, his hands neatly folded in his lap, his legs outstretched – a man at ease with life it seemed. Within seconds, bantering with Aggie about getting a cup of tea organised and peppering each other with mock insults and cheery repartee that looked as if it had been developed over the years, it was as if nothing was amiss, as if nothing had changed. It was a scene of determined levity and was infectious enough to put me at ease. But it was not until the tea came that reality slipped into view. The cup was placed on a table beside him. He had to reach out with both wrists and press them against the cup, his fingers unable to function, then lift it gently, awkwardly and with just a hint of shake, to his lips.

It was like he was beginning to mime his problem to me. Words were unnecessary. At that stage I did not know how far advanced his motor neurone condition had progressed and as if he wanted to distract me from having witnessed such an effort to manoeuvre a cup to his mouth, he burst into a cheery anecdote about how his close friend Bobby Lennox, his fellow Lisbon Lion, had visited before me to reminisce about their early days at Celtic Park. It was infectious. The tea drinking was put behind us and, with great gusto, he talked about his intense personal duel with Burgnich, the Italian defender, who had clung to him like a leech in the Estadio Nacional in Lisbon in May 1967 in the European Cup final. There was nothing wrong with his memory – not then, although having researched the symptoms of the disease before I visited, I knew that a gradual decline of all his faculties was inevitable. I would have to return at some later stage but, even so, I began to dread what I might witness. Because he was not simply Jinky the footballer to me. He was almost a neighbour – a Lanarkshire boy, born and bred and enduring. Perhaps his fear of flying, which stemmed from his experience of a sudden drop in altitude on a transatlantic flight he was once on, was also associated with his grounding in the industrial area of his neighbourhood, for which he had a deep fondness. He was essentially a homer. His reputation eventually vaulted over the parochial. The great Inter defender Giacinto Facchetti, called him *Il Topolino* after the Mickey Mouse cartoon character, because of the uncatchable antics Jimmy could get up to with the ball at his feet – a name that underscored the impact he had made well beyond his own borders. It was the continental form of 'Jinky'.

In many ways I was fortunate to have lived near him at the time when his stock was rising, but his resistance to the temptations of the flesh was faltering. We had mutual friends – one in particular was Joe Reilly, a former player with Albion Rovers who now, sadly, like many others from the leaden leather-ball era, was to be diagnosed in later life with dementia – so we socialised often and had more than a fair knowledge of some of the best howffs in the district. You had to feel that Jimmy hated to be on his own and the more people surrounded him he was like the excited moth to the flame.

On the evening of 5 May 1973, after his side had lost 3–2 to Rangers that afternoon in the Centenary Scottish Cup final, he came to our house with Joe and other friends, where I was hosting a 21st birthday partner for my sister and entranced the company with his singing, as if nothing of note had happened earlier in the day. It looked as if he had buried the pain of that defeat somewhere in a Lanarkshire layby. However, it was not that we were about to embark on an intimate relationship. But, because I would meet him probably more often, socially, than any other player I can recall, we could talk comfortably together in the mutual understanding that nothing would escape and reach the ears of his mentor, his nemesis, his surrogate faither – all in the one – the manager Jock Stein whom he both loved and feared in equal measure. We knew that both of us would be blown away if anything indiscreet was ever traced to us. For Jimmy's entire professional career was shaped by the strength of character of Stein.

Perhaps Jimmy had a foretaste of stern stewardship in football, long before he came into Stein's purview. It was under a man called John Crines, schoolteacher at St Columba's School, who ran his school team with a passion for winning and with such a distaste for defeat that pupils would see him punch the walls in anger on losing anytime. As a schoolteacher myself with my team playing regularly in Lanarkshire football, I had heard about, but not seen, this wee red-haired boy who played for Crines' team and was such a wizard with the ball that nobody could take it off him, unless they booted him. So I wasn't surprised when I learned that Jimmy was such an asset that Crines kept him on at primary school until he was 14 – well past the time he could have gone to secondary school. And his eventual signing by Celtic was spurred on by the news that Matt Busby in Manchester had seen him play in a Boys Guild game in Salford and had expressed an interest – but inevitably to Parkhead he went.

Now, never having seen him as a schoolboy, but having heard so much about him, I was intrigued when, just after joining the BBC and attending the Old Firm Scottish Cup final of 4 May 1963, I heard the Celtic team selection. And there was the name. J Johnstone. Could it possibly be that same wee red-haired boy who was the Garrincha of Lanarkshire Schools football? As soon as he touched the ball early on in the game, pirouetted on the slippy, damp surface and turned the Rangers full-back Provan inside-out, I knew it must be the same lad. That game ended in a 1–1 draw but Jimmy, looking more like a ball-boy who had strayed by accident on to the pitch, made such a huge impact with his jinking performance on a wet pitch that the famous Fleet Street journalist Peter Wilson was to describe him as:

> The red-haired featherweight imp who ranged up and down the wing and cat-footed it around the penalty box, his clown-white face a-pump with excitement, as he chased the ball in a manner reminiscent of Harpo Marx chasing blondes in his palmy days!

Celtic promptly dropped him for the Wednesday replay, which they lost to their great rivals, 3–0 – a modest result given Rangers' superiority. So when Stein arrived in March 1965 he knew he had a unique talent at his disposal. Although even Jimmy himself admitted to me that he wasn't quite sure what the new manager would make of him. But when he was fielded by Stein in a League Cup quarter-final against Raith Rovers on 15 September 1965 and ran riot in Celtic's 8–1 victory, there was no way the new manager was going to release him. Instead he gave him a contract worth £35 a week.

It was the start of something big, and a relationship between manager and player which remains one of the most volatile, but productive, in the history of the Scottish game. Immediately you have to consider a string of phenomenal performances, particularly in that astonishingly short period of two and a half years between Stein's arrival at a moribund club and lifting the European Cup. In such a monumental achievement Jimmy knew he was indispensable to the club and he knew Stein was fully aware of that himself. It was that exceptional leverage he had with his manager that provided him with the insulation that saved him on countless audacious mishaps in his frequent nocturnal adventures. That bond was constructed on the park. For instance, Jimmy's left foot shot from 25 yards in the mud of Ibrox a couple of weeks before Lisbon of 1967, which effectively secured the title for Celtic and almost derigged the net, remains one of the iconic goals in the club's history. What particularly endeared him to Stein was his astonishing Old Firm record of having scored ten goals against Rangers, four of which were amazingly by headers, despite his size, and five of these goals at Ibrox. Then there was Lisbon itself. Although he made it clear to me that he was not satisfied with his own performance that day, he was being unduly modest, for his very presence and reputation caused the astute Inter manager Helenio Herrera to construct his defensive ideas around stemming him in particular. And then, beyond Lisbon, as Celtic pounded on he was weekly providing ammunition for the prolifically-scoring strikers. His stock was soaring so much that the supporters could argue for hours amongst themselves as to which was his best performance. High up on their reckoning was the night at Parkhead against Red Star Belgrade on 13 November 1968. Out of it came myth.

It was said that with the score 1–1 at half-time Stein had chatted with Jimmy in the toilet and told him that if he produced something special in the second-half, he would not require him in Belgrade for the return match, fully aware of Jimmy's fear of flying. In fact, Stein had disclosed that ploy publicly in his weekly article ghosted by journalist Rodger Baillie in the *Sunday Mirror,* several days before the match. It would have been strange if any Celtic player had not read the manager's comments before such an important match and knew about Stein's intentions, thus the toilet story was a fanciful embellishment. But, the story of two men peeing and at the same time reaching a deal that would produce one of the greatest individual performances seen at Parkhead, took traction and as the newspaper editor in John Ford's classic film *The Man Who Shot Liberty Valance* declared, 'When the legend becomes fact, print the legend!'

After glowing performances like that he would go out and enjoy himself. He did so often around our own area where tales of his escapades, which largely revolved around drink, would circulate like wildfire. One night in Da Luciano's, a posh restaurant in Bothwell, he came in, sat down at a table, then hailed me loudly from across the room. Clearly, he had already had a few. We chatted vociferously about football, above the head of the diners, and then he began to sing, melodiously, which in an Italian restaurant you would not have thought was wholly inappropriate. But you could see the middle-class clientele becoming fidgety and distressed, as they wished not to be interrupted in their Mediterranean reveries as they downed their Chianti, and as if they wished to deny the existence of an unruly street-urchin nearby, who clearly had no manners. I viewed that scene simply as watching a working-class boy ascending to a new social level, minus the decorum that was expected to accompany that. This was a tiny and mild example of what was happening in his social life and why Stein would personally seek him out in North Lanarkshire, like a bounty hunter, when he heard – through his almost Stasi-like spy network – that Jimmy was on the tiles. But there was nothing aggressive about him that night in the restaurant. He was a jovial drunk who was blissfully unaware of the consequences of such, which were sometimes grossly exaggerated in the local tittle-tattle in the days before social media. And, even as he tried to avoid the ire of his manager – sometimes with spectacular failures – underneath it all he had true grit. One day it produced a flash point.

On 5 October 1968 commentating from the platform suspended over the 'Jungle' enclosure at Celtic Park I watched an incident that spoke much of Jimmy's independence of mind, in the face of a manager who could immobilise you with just one stare. Jimmy was having one of those dithering days that even the best of mercurial ball-players endure. Stein decided to substitute him. As he left the field, to the astonishment of everybody in the 46,000 crowd, Jimmy took off his jersey and threw it, in disgust, into the dugout, where it just happened to strike the manager in the face. The little man then raced up the tunnel, like a Pamplona street-runner having bated one of the bulls, and knowing he was on more than the horns of a dilemma, realised it was time to bolt. Stein leapt from his seat and hirpled, with that distinct limp, faster than I had ever seen him travel, in pursuit of his little red-haired winger. Jimmy told me what then happened, with a glint in his eye and the smile that only a treasured memory can produce.

'As soon as I did that, I thought, "My God, what have I done?" and I belted up that tunnel as fast as I could. I got into the dressing room, slammed the door shut, then locked it. I heard him kicking the door and then battering it with his fist. I knew then I was in deep shit. I shouted out, "I'll let you in if you promise not to hit me!" Then the battering suddenly stopped and would you believe he burst out laughing and I heard him walking away. I was suspended for seven days after that. If he had got his hands on me I might never have lived to have a suspension.'

That one story encapsulates one of the most endearing and yet puzzling relationships ever between a manager and player. Stein never talked publicly about Jimmy with anything other than affection, except on one noted exception, although he did admit to me that he drove him to distraction from time to time. The truth is Jimmy piled pressure on himself with almost gay abandon. In May 1969 when he failed to turn up to join his international colleagues before setting off to play England at Wembley, without informing the Scotland manager Bobby Brown, Stein uttered the first ever public disapproval of his little winger, when he described him to the press as 'undependable'. However, only four weeks later, Jimmy was eventually stopped by the police in the wee sma' hours, after a long chase through the streets of Hamilton and Motherwell as he had failed to stop on their command at Clyde Bridge and was charged with being drunk in charge of a vehicle. Privately Stein was fuming, but equally privately he worked with lawyers to help the wee man, by having the court date changed so that it fooled the media, who turned up a day too late to publicise the event. He didn't escape a fine of £50 though and a ban for a year. So, there was this strange contrast between the enraged, moralistic Stein and the solicitous one, willing to come to the aid of an errant son. Why? Because Jimmy was a priceless asset. Stein, after all, was a supreme pragmatist and worked round the indiscretions skilfully. But there was another equally valid reason. For all of the player's misdemeanours, the bond between them was a very masculine one. That was based on Stein's profound admiration for Jimmy's genuine courage on the field.

Game after game he would watch his winger being chopped down regularly by opponents, who realised that brutality was the only weapon they had at their disposal to put pay to this will o' the wisp. All this was on more dramatic display to the wider European public, when on 10 April 1974, in the first leg of the semi-final of the European Cup, Atletico Madrid came to town with the swagger and intent of a Mafia hit squad. They set about Jimmy in particular like a pack of hounds on a stag. At every brutal collision he simply got back on his feet and went after them for more. After a goalless game and in preparing for the return leg, a threat to assassinate Jimmy was revealed by the Spanish media. Stein sought to comfort him by saying, 'You can jink about the field as you usually do. They'll never get you in their sights. Think of me. I'm on the bench. I'm a sitting duck.' Jimmy survived while Celtic went out of the tournament, 2–0.

By 1974, when I travelled with him and the rest of the Scottish squad to the World Cup in Germany, his talents were becoming less visible, less consistent, less menacing, but certainly not completely shorn from him. And he had presaged more trouble ahead by taking a rowing boat from the shore at Largs, in the early hours again, where Scotland were in preparation for the tournament, but japing about, ended up oarless as he drifted helplessly towards Arran, in an escapade which landed him on the front pages. Willie Ormond, the Scotland manager, mentally dismissed Jimmy then and never played him in Germany, particularly as he and Billy Bremner in Norway prior to the World Cup had broken a curfew in a drunken spree. However, Johnstone ought to have been fielded in the last game against Yugoslavia where even a few seconds of his latent brilliance could have broken the 1–1 draw that put Scotland out of the tournament.

But, in all the time I was there, with Jock Stein as my co-commentator, not once did I hear the Celtic manager speak a word of support for Jimmy's selection for any of the games. I think he was starting to give up on him and that the publicity of the Norway fracas tipped the scales against his player. This was the beginning of the end for him at Celtic. But, the ending when it came, always remains for me something of a puzzle. I have emphasised the special relationship between the two of them, which Stein claimed kept Jimmy in the game much longer than he would have under any other manager, unable to understand how to balance the conflict between the genius on the park and the recurring vagabond off it. Stein's frustration was that of a beleaguered father who would not give up on a favourite son. It had paid off handsomely. That is why Jimmy's last months with Celtic intrigue me to this day.

On the evening of 3 May 1975 we broadcast *Sportscene* live from the New Orleans restaurant in Rutherglen where the Celtic team were celebrating their 3–1 win in the Scottish Cup final against Airdrie and where Billy McNeill announced his retirement from football. Off-camera I asked him why Jimmy Johnstone had not been selected for the game. He was very circumspect about a man he adored and despite my prompting, would not provide an answer about Jimmy's future, which was the subject of much chat amongst the media who generally believed that Jimmy was on his way out. Seven days later Celtic faced Rangers in the Glasgow Cup final on a rain-sodden pitch. Jimmy was in the squad and indeed Hugh Taylor of the *Daily Record,* in nostalgic mode and fully aware of the conjecture surrounding the player, wrote, 'I'm betting the wee winger, one of my favourite players – and the favourite of anyone who likes entertaining players – will be on at some time.'

He never appeared. He did warm up to the generous reception of the Celtic crowd. But he was never brought on. It indicated initially that Stein was no sentimentalist. He must have known that he was going to release Jimmy in another four weeks. Not for him a fond farewell, the final bow, the lowering of the curtain on a distinguished career. Jimmy was out. That was all. At first I thought that was insensitive, then it gradually dawned on me that Stein was playing against his great rivals, which he always faced up to like his life depended on it, Glasgow Cup or no, and as the game was poised at 2–2 right to the end, sentiment was only for Valentine cards. So his last wearing of a Celtic jersey was almost tragically uneventful as, 'unused sub'.

Curiously, Stein did not tell him he was no longer needed at the club. He left that surely emotional moment to the hardened accountant Desmond White, the chairman. The late Sean Fallon, Stein's assistant manager told me years later, 'To be honest Jock and I couldn't face up to it. Whatever passed between them through the years, Jock loved and respected the wee man, and he just couldn't bring himself to tell him that he was finished with Celtic. I know that Jimmy just broke down and wept. The tears were rolling down his face.'

The following years were of a man trying to find some kind of peace in the wilderness. He wandered from San Jose Earthquakes in the States, to Sheffield United, Dundee, Shelbourne in Ireland and ultimately to the Scottish Highland League club, Elgin City, where his career came to an end in 1979. He was lost. Again, because he lived near me, we would enjoy an occasional night out together with our mutual friend Joe Reilly. In that time, despite the gossip I heard of his drinking, I never once witnessed him out of control but stories abounded in the neighbourhood of a man drinking himself into stupors. In between, he was trying to establish some kind of business for himself. He did approach me once, with an associate, to discuss how I could help him promote a project connected with open-cast mining in Lanarkshire. The grandiose nature of that did not seem to fit into his commercial naivety which had cost him heavily, like the failure of his pub business, where people took advantage of his good nature and prolific hospitality. So I knew that last business idea would come to nothing.

The day he went to his friend, now Lord Haughey and then Celtic director, to offer him his medals for sale, was a turning point in his life. Haughey knew that people were trying to use him to peddle fanciful commercial ideas that would never get off the ground. And given what Haughey had been told about his wild lifestyle, he read him the riot act. He warned Jimmy that he would catch up with him the next time he was drunk and make a video of him, and then when he had sobered up, he would show him the video to shame him. Haughey, who did buy his medals, for display at Celtic Park itself, believed that Jimmy left him that day shamefaced and determined to reform.

Another man was a huge influence in that regard, Ian Henderson, a loyal Rangers supporter, who went to AA meetings with him, striving to stay off the booze together, and befriended him for the remainder of his life. He encouraged him to keep fit. This Jimmy did with relish.

He would train in the public park near his home in Viewpark, day after day, remorselessly pounding the turf, dedicated not only to remain dry, but in the belief that physical fitness would be the route out of his past degradations. However, sometimes when he was driving his car he would feel pins and needles moving up and down his arms. Like most of us he would have easily dismissed that, except they persisted. These were the first signs of something strange happening within his body. One day Agnes, his wife, became concerned when he did not return in time for his evening meal, after he had gone to the park for his training session. As she had lived with a man who had led an unpredictable life that sometimes left her in a quandry, she wondered if he was lapsing into old habits. The past catching up with him? When she got to the park she was stunned. He was on his back on the turf. As he explained to her, he had fallen and discovered he could use neither his arms nor his legs to lever himself up. They were lifeless. And since there was no one around at the time he just had to lie there and wait for Agnes to turn up.

Despite that, he returned the next day to the same routine and continued with just a little more care about where he was stepping. But the incident that required Agnes to come to his aid had little to do with his feet. He returned one day and told her he had spat out his dentures to help with his breathing, but as he could not use his hands and fingers to retrieve them, they were still up there in the park somewhere. She had to scour through the grass to find them, in the hope that nobody would ask what she was looking for. Agnes returned triumphantly and as she handed them over almost ceremonially, like a queen gifting the freedom of the city to a subject, they dissolved in laughter, the tears running down their cheeks. What they were avoiding at that moment was the realisation that the simplest mundane tasks that we all take for granted were beginning to be literally outwith his grasp. And that became all the clearer when he stumbled on their patio one morning and was knocked unconscious when his head hit the French window's handle. It was a bitter home truth.

Of that I knew little at the time. All I heard from my friend Joe Reilly was that he was suffering from some form of rheumatism. He failed to turn up at an expected pub meeting with us, but I thought little of it at the time. What we certainly did not know was that he had been told at the Southern General Hospital that he had a terminal disease. Some time later I head the phrase, 'motor neurone' for the first time. But only when it was explained to me that it was the same as 'Lou Gehrig's Disease' which had taken away a famous American baseball player, as represented by Gary Cooper in the Hollywood film, did it really hit home with me.

What did Jimmy do when he heard of the fatal prognosis? He put his tracksuit on and pounded round the public park near his home. That was the theme of the rest of Jimmy's life – refusal to accept the inevitable. Had he been some docile patient simply awaiting the outcome he would not have elicited the amount of support that flooded into that household. Yes, he was a Celtic legend who would be voted by the club's global support in 2002, their Best Ever Player, and it is obvious there would be overwhelming sympathy and help. But they were providing this, not for some freeloader, but for a man whose words still talked about survival. Even when he was at the stage of having to be spoon fed or having his son wipe his backside for him in the toilet, in a reversal of roles that showed that this disease in its horribly bizarre progression, was restoring a man to childhood, there was never a whimper of complaint.

Equally he offered little resistance to those who queued up to tell him they could save him. Two women in particular came with a box one day which they said would emit rays that would penetrate his bones and deliver a cure. As they were proceeding with this, the Celtic doctor happened to visit and threw them out with a warning to Jimmy not to be taken in by 'charlatans'. But he had to try. The drug Tamoxifen had had some positive effects with breast cancer so they permitted him to try it out. But he took too many – swallowed them like Smarties and they turned his skin a bright orange. So orange he could have fitted in perfectly on the 12th of July.

Then money was raised by his friends to fly him to New York with his friend Ian Henderson, to attend the Beth Israel Medical Centre in 1st Avenue, where they had heard a project had been undertaken to counter the motor neurone affliction. But they had told him he would have to return at four-monthly intervals to continue treatment to properly assess progress. They could only finance one more trip, and even at that, his companion Henderson began to feel pessimistic about the whole procedure and felt the encouraging words the American professor was offering Jimmy were simply to boost his morale. It came to nothing. But at least they had tried.

His condition deteriorated. He was dying. He and Agnes agreed for him to try a snake venom that had been recommended by an acquaintance. They did not want to reject what friends were offering and with his voice weakening, his body now virtually inert, they saw no reason not to. She injected him with it three times a day over several months. To no effect, of course. John Reid, Baron Reid of Cardowan, recalled for me the emotional phone calls he received from his former constituent when he was Minister of State for Health in the Blair government between 2003/5. Being a lover of Celtic and an admirer of this former player, the calls were always put through to him personally.

'One day Jinky was quite agitated, "John," he said, "Do you know the Pope is against stem cell research. What are you going to do about it? You're in charge of health, could you not phone the Pope up and have a word with him about it. It could help me." I had to tell him I was really not in a position to do so but felt deeply sorry for him in that dilemma.'

However, their hope of stem cell treatment which they wished to embark on, against the strictures of his own church, were dashed by Dr Belinda Cupid of the Motor Neurone Disease Association, who told them that such treatment was useless and could do nothing to restore the chaotic jumble of nerves within the body. It would be like asking an infant to sort out the disordered lines in a telephone exchange box after someone had deliberately sabotaged it. It simply would not work. Neither would the drug Copaxone, about which there had been much discussion over its potential effect on the disease. So when the authorities at the Southern and General Hospital refused to administer it to him the media caused a storm. 'Jinky Drugs Ban Agony' screamed the *Sun*. The *Daily Record* echoed that with, 'Jinky Fury Over Drug Blow' which provoked much sympathy for the family and anger at the doctors in the hospital. However, the Celtic doctor, Roddy Macdonald backed the hospital's decision.

There was no way out. Jimmy lay helpless, his voice weakened, Agnes facing up to the physical challenge of lifting and laying him, and tending to him in general with remarkable courage. Visitors, including Rod Stewart, would come and go, some of whom would burst into tears as soon as they left the house. The emotions were understandable, since you could not go near him without the visual clash that took place between that motionless body and the memory of that figure on the field leading the pack a merry chase, as they tried to subdue the greatest jinker of them all. Mummifying that image seemed one of the most indecent acts of nature.

Ian Henderson was by his side on the evening of 12 March 2006. He held the phone for him as he was able to whisper a reply to Denis Law who had made regular calls to chat with him and talk about old times. Then he was phoned by his great friend Willie Henderson, the former Rangers winger who had teamed up with him through the years, touring venues around the country in a hilarious double act that both delighted and educated their audiences in how genuine the compatibility of Old Firm players could be. The former Rangers player told him he would visit him the following morning.

'Looking forward to seeing you, son.' Jimmy whispered.

Agnes decided to lie beside him later and fell asleep. When she wakened sometime during that night and looked at him, she knew he had passed away.

His death evoked multiple emotions. For the Celtic community it was the passing of a favourite son, whose brilliance and devotion to their colours eclipsed the more controversial incidents in his life. They turned up in their thousands to his funeral and to honour the passing of his cortege through the Glasgow streets. But there were others in attendance as well. For Jimmy had vaulted the sectarian barrier with an alacrity that matched his prowess on the field. Few, from the other tradition, had an unkind word to say about him. Those of us who had sat near him, as the cell walls closed in, astonished by how his quiet heroism continually rebuffed the certainty of death, began to appreciate the value of our own lives, but left us wondering whether we could summon up a similar strength to face our own oblivion. Jimmy Johnstone, superb footballer, wild partier, merry drunk, had now become our guiding light.

The Celtic connection matters here. Seated beside Jinky must be Sandra Whittaker who was helped by the club to run the race of her life.

CHAPTER 6

One-Hundredth Of A Second

TOWARDS THE END of the Scottish football season in May 1984 the crowd attending Celtic Park were treated to unusual half-time entertainment. You could say that filling in that 15-minute period in any football ground, to an impatient crowd waiting for a game to restart, is one of the major challenges for the Scottish performing arts. Brass-bands traditionally did their best, but became as dated as the hansom cab and in Scotland the skirl of pipes tried to fill the vacuum, although I always felt they were more appropriate at commemorations or celebrations, but not the no-man's land of half-time. They tried the American-style cheerleaders in some seasons, but even co-ordinated displays of flesh to largely lustful males strangely turned out to be as inspiring to them as a string quartet playing Mozart. Then clubs became quite open to more varied alternatives. In that spirit the Celtic manager Davy Hay accepted a suggestion that would switch minds away from the hazards of that 1984 season which saw them trailing Aberdeen in the League, to a different sport that would turn attention to a major event in another time and in a special place. He had been approached by an athletics coach, one Ian 'Rab' Roberston to allow two of his successful protégées to run a lap around the field as recognition of their competitive success and the fact that they were on the threshold of qualifying to compete in the Los Angeles Olympics in the coming months. He knew one of the girls well, as his own daughter trained with her in the athletic club. She was 21-year-old Sandra Whittaker, in intense preparation to fulfil her lifetime ambition of reaching an Olympic Games. She could hardly forget what she experienced that day.

'When we ran in events in Scotland it was usually to half-empty stadiums. So if we were going to compete in the Coliseum in LA in front of huge crowds, then our coach Ian Robertson, or Rab as we called him, approached Davy Hay and asked if we could do a lap round Celtic Park in front of a big crowd, just to get a feeling of what it might be like with so many surrounding you.'

At first glance this might have seemed to be taking preparations to ludicrous and quite unrewarding extremes, except Rab, the coach, was obviously a believer in Aggregated Multiple Gains or in the lingo of those in the know, AMG. In simple terms it means that at the highest level of sport, the difference between winning and losing could be down to a single-minded and meticulous focus on little things – minor details that when you put them all together, in preparation, could add up to lending you even the slightest advantage which could determine a positive outcome. A Celtic crowd could not be a Coliseum crowd, but it would create the sense of a multitude of eyes staring at you and might prepare you to insulate against a sense of overpowering crowd presence. The outcome certainly confirmed how effective a crowd could be in encouraging performance, as Sandra vividly recalls.

'I remember standing in the tunnel and becoming almost overawed by just the sound of the crowd outside. But, out I went on to the track, with my colleague Angela Bridgeman, adorned with our Celtic scarves that we had been given,' Sandra explained, 'We were told just to take it easy and slowly trot round to give the crowd plenty time to see us and to soak in the atmosphere and get to feel the presence of the huge crowd. We got a great reception after being introduced to the crowd. But then I thought I was beginning to hear some boos amongst the applause. So we got all the way round to the Jungle (*that now demolished enclosure at Celtic Park where, you could say, stood the heart and soul of the Celtic support*) and we certainly did hear the booing there. It increased a bit and I suddenly realised why. I said to Angela, "It's the Great Britain tracksuits. They're red, white and blue. They're linking us with Rangers!" One look at each other was all we needed. We decided that we weren't going to trot round any longer. We started to run as fast as we could.'

It has to be said that the relationship between them and the crowd was simply light-hearted, but it also suggested that athletics would still have to fight hard for wider public appreciation. Being a winner does help though, as Alan Wells in Moscow certainly did, to boost his sport by winning the 100 metres gold in those Olympics in 1980. Sandra had no illusions of how difficult it was going to be to come anywhere near Wells' achievement, if she were to make it to the Games. That was constantly on her mind, even as she was discovering the sensitivity of football colours to partisan crowds. But a few weeks later all doubts and anxieties were blown away when, even though she had been drawn in the outside lane, she won the Olympic Trials 200 metres final in Gateshead which confirmed her automatic place in the GB team for that event. Now every fibre of her being was concentrated on that moment when she would be called to her mark in the Coliseum Stadium in the steamy month of July ahead.

That was about the same time as it was confirmed that I would be part of the BBC team covering the Games. For both of us this would be our first Olympics. It should have been my second. The Kremlin's actions though put the Moscow Games of 1980 out of reach. For on Christmas Eve 1979 Soviet tanks and 30,000 troops rolled into Afghanistan in an invasion whose consequences are still with us to this day. With the Yuletide festivities in full swing, that Soviet action, at the time, seemed as relevant to me as the Dogger Bank weather forecast. After all it was occurring in a distant land about which I knew little, except through Kipling's 'Gunga Din' and reading the *Hotspur* comic as a boy in which anybody wearing a turban was a villain.

Wars happen. Life goes on. Except it took an unexpected turn for many of us broadcasters. The USA decided to boycott the Moscow Olympics because of the Soviet action. Maggie Thatcher could hardly ignore their decision and although she probably thought the American President Jimmy Carter was a closet Marxist, compared to his successor Ronald Reagan, she fell partly in step by strongly recommending UK sports organisations to boycott Moscow as well, although allowing them to make their decision independent of government. Equestrian sports, hockey and yachting obliged and stayed home. Other sports reduced their squads but decided they would compete. In that scenario the BBC decided they would not need as many reporters or commentators, so I ended up on the cutting-room floor, with my Russian phrasebook to this day unopened. In response, the Soviet bloc, which included 13 other communist nations, boycotted LA. The geo-political game of snakes and ladders was well underway as Sandra and I were heading for California, whose San Andreas fault would turn out to be more benign than the East–West political fault plates, grinding against each other and which essentially would devalue much of the standard of competition.

However, although we arrived in the USA in high spirits, in the first week before the Opening Ceremony we were becoming aware that this global sporting stand-off, sucking in the Olympics, was moving the emphasis away from the individual performance to the supreme importance of the medal tally and the ensuing League table. We knew this would obsess the media, as it would the politicians eager to twin any success with their ideology. Indeed, the LA Games were so commercial, in that free-enterprise way that fitted the zeitgeist of the Reagan era, the only nation failing to see the Olympic Torch arriving live in the Coliseum on television was the USA, because their channel was on a commercial at the time. All in all, I was beginning to think back to Orwell's dictum on sport, that it would forever be war, 'without the shooting' and that the much-trumpeted words of the Olympic creed, 'the essential thing is not to have won but to have fought well' was strictly for the birds, in an age of growing scepticism about the purity of the sport because of suspicions of illicit drug use. There was a girl there though, who was to help change my mind by her pristine honesty of effort.

Sandra had arrived. She was now one of the 6,829 competitors gearing up for the efforts of their lives. So here was a Lanarkshire girl, born in Bellshill – a cradle for great sports achievers, for which the Sir Matt Busby Sports Centre in the town stands testament – now about to face up to the special demands of an Olympiad. How would she cope with these unique pressures, on top of the frenetic rhythm of LA which to me resembled a scattering ant-heap, after having been kicked by a large foot? Might she be overwhelmed? Why should I have had any reservations about her temperament? Firstly, Sandra to me, at that stage, was simply a name, a statistic, a personality based merely on observing her fleetingly, over the distance of 200 metres. It would be a clever man to deduce anything from that

alone. Secondly, I suppose I clung to that dogged Scottish masculine mindset that women were basically frailer than us and that we
should start judging them from that perspective. Neanderthal views
did exist among the media and pronouncing on men in action on the
sports field, as I regularly did to the public, I had slipped into that
relaxed, self-comforting, but also self-delusional view that all wom-
en's sport deserved only one and a half cheers out of three. And at the
same time I desperately wanted her to succeed. When I had watched
her running on television previously I felt myself holding my breath
as she rounded the bend into the home straight, my legs tensing,
toes curling up, like I was her avatar trying to help her over the line.
Because she was a local girl. We shared the same sky, probably travelled the same daily routes. Running for GB? She was running for her
ain folk and perhaps particularly for those who had helped her along
the way, because of her own natural inclination.

'As a kid I just ran all the time. I would run between lampposts to
see how fast I could be. I would run shopping. Run to school. I just
loved running. So when I began to win things in school competitions
my coach Rab spotted me and asked my parents if I could travel into
Glasgow for special training several times a week.'

After she had won that Lanarkshire schools championship
200 metres in Coatbridge, she turned down the offer to join Shettleston Harriers, my old club, and went instead to Glasgow Athletic
who were top of the athletic clubs' league at the time and where
her father thought she would develop better. They could also drive
her wherever she needed training. It is clear when she spoke to me
about her early days that her parents handled her wisely and with
sensitivity. Their lifestyle was above the Lanarkshire social median.
Her father owned businesses and they could holiday in the south
of France regularly, as an example of a life that was decidedly a cut
above the average Lanarkshire family, you might say. And there is no
denying that if your life is not cluttered with anxieties about money,
equipment and you have freedom to pursue your obsessions, then
you benefit. Class actually can even determine which sport you take
up in the first place. Yes, she had certain advantages in life but never
that they would extend to her ever sitting on a polo pony. And so

began an entirely new lifestyle which was Spartan, in the sense that she clearly put preparation to succeed as a runner before much else.

'Up till then I had only been training once a week. Then it started to get really serious. In the summer we spent much of the time in sprint training but as my coach would say it was the winter when the hard work was done. This is when we would build up our strength and our stamina. So I would be involved four times a week in circuit training at Westbourne School and also at Bellahouston sports centre. We also had to add hill runs and running over longer distances which really extended sprinters. But on top of that I was going out for half-hour runs in the morning and when I worked in Glasgow I would run for half-an-hour during lunch time. In addition, I was training four nights a week in the summer and in the winter five nights. And some of the coached sessions would take up to four hours.'

It is a portrait of devotion to the sheer slog. But she was keeping company with others in her group who had been training since before their teens and so she was regarded as a late starter having only reached the serious competitive level when she was about 17. That clearly did not handicap her. For at the age of 19 she competed for Scotland in the Commonwealth Games in Brisbane in 1982. She was raw and admits that perhaps she was overwhelmed by the demanding unfamiliarity of such a level of competition which affected her. She failed to qualify for the 100 and 200 metres finals. But, running the first leg, she won a bronze medal in the 4x400 relay team. Her confidence and status were on the rise.

'Those Games were when I really took off. Having sampled everything around me during them I realised I wanted to go far. That was when I began to really commit myself to getting to the Olympic Games. I wasn't thinking of World or European Championships. It was the Games I had in mind. That was the turning point for me. I think when I came back from Brisbane I was a different athlete. My mental approach had changed. There was real hunger inside me to make it eventually to the Games. I really pushed myself to the limits. Sometimes I was on my knees hardly able to breathe but Rab would shout, "C'mon get on your feet. The lactic acid will build up, get yourselves round that track, you've got another three runs to go." And I did because I knew that if I didn't put in all that effort I wouldn't realise my dream.'

She was now in a city where dreams were manufactured daily in Hollywood, only a few javelin throws from the Coliseum. She was not a lone Scot though in the GB team in LA. She had the company of Alan Wells, there to defend his 100 metres title, Meg Ritchie (Discus), Geoff Parsons (High Jump), Lynne MacDougall (800m) and Brad McStavick (Decathalon). Before they had arrived in the city they had based themselves in San Diego, just south of LA, in a holding camp to help them acclimatise to heat and humidity. Given the peaks of performance that would be demanded of them, you could have likened it to the base-camp used before the final assault on Everest.

But, even on the brink of competition she never forgot the people who had aided her along the way. Perhaps in the canteen of the magnificent Games Village she might have thought back to the local butcher in East Kilbride who provided her with a weekly package of meat, in the liberal guilt-free pre-Vegan age. Her employer was also relaxed about the necessary time she had to train and be away from her base. Those acts in themselves, rather more than any nutrient, were perhaps more valuable in developing the warmth of community support, but at the same time increasing the degree of responsibility bearing down on her. More practically she received help from Celtic for one of the most chronic of athletic injuries.

'The main problem I had was with my hamstring,' she was to tell me. 'Eventually it was to end my career in 1987. But in the years leading up to the Games it recurred from time to time. I was fortunate because one of the athletic club members was the daughter of the Celtic manager Davy Hay. She passed on my condition to him and he put me on to their physio Brian Scott. So I would go to his house in Rutherglen where he treated me privately. He was magnificent. I owe him a great deal for the way he looked after me over a lengthy period of time and on terms that he worked out specially for me.'

But now, Sandra and I were set for a distant relationship, she sweating it out in the training areas and myself pursuing a wide variety of events to reflect the diverse nature of both LA and the

Games themselves. It was never going to be easy to meet up, even for an interview, given our contrasting commitments and the intense security that had enveloped the Olympics. International terrorism had increased four-fold since the Munich Olympics' terrorist attack on Israeli athletes in 1972 and protective helicopters now seemed to have taken on the habitat of starlings, there were so many of them – backed up by sniffer dogs, scores of human bomb disposal experts and a huge arsenal of specially assembled silencer-equipped machine guns. So, Sandra and all athletes were subject to the most intense security scrutiny they had ever faced. But that affected all of us. The BBC had put a camera crew at my disposal and I went after capturing different images that made me feel I was in the documentary business, exposing the fact that Orwell's dystopic picture of 1984 had not yet materialised, except for the hellish traffic that clogged the grotesquely misnamed freeways. The Games seemed to be swamped by LA's exotic normality. However, the media and the athletes clashed with their security psyche. Sandra had to adhere meticulously to the security conditions prevailing, which was a contrast to what you imagine a free-spirited Olympics ought to be. For us it could be almost farcical. It was in the LA Dodgers stadium when I went to illustrate to a British audience the Americans obsession for baseball – on show there as a demonstration sport. Our camera crew did not have the proper colour of badge to allow us to enter a specific area near the spectators to film, so this sour, officious woman security official called in the police to evict us. When they arrived a woman in the crowd got to her feet.

'What's going on here!' she shouted. 'I thought this was the land of the free not a police state. What did we fight the last war for? To watch some guys just doing their job getting slung out the Dodgers Stadium?'

As she said that I suddenly realised that she had struck a chord with the crowd. They started to get to their feet and applaud her. Inspired, she decided to give full vent.

'These guys are our guests! They're Brits! They fought alongside us during the war! Have you bums never heard of the London Blitz! These people suffered for our freedom and now they'll go back home thinking America's a dictatorship. You should be ashamed of your-selves, you bums!'

It seemed a multitude were now standing cheering her on and the security woman and the cop seemed to shrink under the cacophony. The transatlantic alliance renewed, we stayed and filmed. The man who appreciated that incident more than any, was the bulky athlet-ics commentator, the late Ron Pickering, who seemed to know as much about Sandra as she did about herself. He was a man of sharp intellect and towering passion. The lucidity of his arguments over such matters as sporting boycotts of South Africa or the cheating of drug-taking athletes (which we all knew was endemic), was sup-plemented by an almost evangelistic fervour, which won him both admirers and detractors. I saw him essentially as a man's man. He could down his booze with ease and was one of the best dispensers of the risqué joke in the business. In LA, during our rest periods we would sit round the hotel pool and he would hold court. He was to keep me in the picture of what was happening, both on and off the track, as I was concentrating on other events. He was frank with me about Sandra, but he did keep saying she had at least a good chance of reaching the final, if she were at her very best.

Having put the baseball international incident to bed and sent it off that night back to London for showing on *Grandstand*, I looked forward to watching Sandra in action the following day. I wondered about her mood. Would this almost suffocating mix of humidity and Olympic grandeur be too much for her? However, she certainly did have a personality trait which I have always felt was at the heart of any competitive motivation.

'I was a terrible loser,' she was to tell me. 'If I failed at anything I cried and cried. I remember a West District Championship when I lost the 100 metres, but won the 200. In the car afterwards my sis-ter, maybe winding me up, demanded to know why I hadn't won the 100. I recall punching and punching the back of the seat and crying. Terrible, I know, but that attitude was with me right through life.'

I referred her to some very bad losers I had known. Stein, Waddell, Ferguson, McLean. So as a type she was in good company. Impor-tantly the lady who was beneficial to Sandra at that crucial, tense time was the great Northern Ireland Olympic champion Mary Peters, who mothered the women athletes, escorting them to and from the designated areas around the track, but all the time soothing them with that charming brogue, which in these circumstances acted like a sedative.

THE COLISEUM

Mary accompanied Sandra as she made her way into the almost suffocating heat of the stadium where she had been advised by her coach Rab not to look up at the crowd. So… she looked up!

'I just couldn't help it. It was breathtaking. I couldn't believe the immensity of the crowd. But as I jogged around to the part of the track where I could practise some starts I suddenly heard my name being shouted by some folk waving the British and Scottish flags. "C'mon, Sandra!" They were strangers to me but they knew my name. It really was encouraging. However, I had to cut myself off from all of that and go into a mental state of mind where you say to yourself, "Right, here we go!"'

And then echoing what Pickering had said to me, she added, 'Every race I run would have to be like a final for me. I would have to reach further than I ever had before.'

That was evident in her first round when she qualified easily for the quarter-finals of the Womens 200 metres in 23.22, the fastest she had run that distance. She told her coach that she had run with ease. It buoyed her. Now she was a possible two races away from making the final.

'I felt so good. Fitter than I ever had before.'

But the world's best were around her. Like her nemesis Cathy Cook from Birmingham who was in another heat and whom Sandra had never beaten in any of the British competitions over 200 metres. And the competition was made even more daunting by the presence in the heat of such as Merlene Ottey-Page of Jamaica, Florence Griffith and Valerie Brisco-Hooks, both of the USA and all of whom would clearly be contenders for gold itself.

'Oh, the heat,' she recalled. 'It was as hot as I had ever felt. However, I was conscious of it but not worried. I knew all my muscles would be the better off for that. I just thought of what it had been like running on a bitterly cold day on a Scottish track. No, even with that kind of heat I began to feel a kind of privilege at being right in amongst all of this. And I tell you I felt the fittest I had ever been. In my first round I felt I could do better. I was just raring to go.'

The next few minutes would turn out to be historic for her.

She was drawn in lane 5. The first four to qualify. I would have preferred her to have been in one of the first three lanes, but then, what was I really to know about 200 metres strategy? But, observing all of this created a curious kind of intimacy with Sandra. I became so focussed on her that it was as if I was the only one watching in such a multitude. And since I hadn't the task of commentating I knew little of the other runners and little cared, other than about the presence of the favourite, the black American Valerie Brisco-Hooks, who as she warmed up, to the great acknowledgement of the hugely patriotic home crowd, looked struttingly, casually, magnificent. I must admit the Scottish word 'Pochle' came to mind when I heard the American had also been drawn in the inside-lane with its obvious advantages. A dastardly, unworthy thought – but where I come from cynicism is a natural attribute. Then they were called to their blocks.

'There was a little tingle in the pit of the stomach, when I heard the call, "Get to your marks", but I was far from nervous. I certainly did not want a false start. I knew that would set me back. That was on my mind when I bent down to my mark.'

When the pistol cracked I remember twitching like I had touched a bare, live wire. All I could see was a flow of runners making for the bend as if they were yet attached by the same invisible wire. Then they started to flatten out and I could see that Sandra was in a potentially healthy position.

'I felt I was flying. I really felt so light on my feet. I didn't feel any strain. I was just going for it and felt great.'

But she was being caught. I could see the Bahamian girl eating up the gap between them as Sandra herself was stretching to keep upside the Canadian runner. It was like watching iron filings being attracted to each other. Sandra herself, even years later, summons up those precious seconds.

'Sometimes in other events you would put about 85 per cent of your effort into it round the bend. And going down the straight you are aware of people around you but all you are thinking about is throwing yourself at the line. So I couldn't see her coming up on me. But not this time. I was flat out.'

The first two were clear enough, Rose-Aimee Bacoul of France first, Valerie Brisco-Hooks of the USA second but the other three behind threw themselves over the line in what looked an inseparable tangle. There was no telling in which order. But we all knew technology would. Above us was the giant screen, the teller of all tales.

Sandra breathed deeply, taking in gulps of air, as she looked up at it, like everyone else in the stadium where all would be made clear. She stood there awaiting the verdict. It came with that uncanny hush which can fall over thousands of people looking up at that screen, pausing, waiting. Up came the still-freeze on the finishing line, her body tilting forward, neck jutting. She was certainly behind the first two. But by how much? My eyes couldn't determine that. The bodies close around seemed to be merging, beyond separation by the naked eye. The clinical timing system then intervened and revealed all. She had been beaten into fifth place by one-hundredth of a second. One-hundredth faster than her time of 22.98. We are not used to such a finite measurement of time. At that moment it seemed almost indecent and beyond comprehension. I suddenly felt sad for her. I guessed what her mental state would be and I was hardly mistaken.

'I went back into the warm-up area and I collapsed in a heap. I couldn't believe I wasn't through. By one-hundredth of a second. Just think what that is like hearing that. So I sat in that area and watched the other heats and what pained me more than anything was I watched the other two British girls, Cathy Cook and Joan Baptiste qualifying in slower times than me. 23.02 and 23.11.'

In those days there were no places for fastest losers as is now the accepted practice. That weighed heavily on her.

'That's when the bad loser came into it. I felt it was a terrible injustice. How could they possibly get through when they were slower than me? It really hurt me. They had arranged transport for us to get back to the Olympic Village and I sat beside Lynn MacDougall, our Scottish 1500 runner. She was gutted for me. I just wept all the way back.'

Behind all of that, one-hundredth of a second separation between success and failure had been years of hard slog, of going through the pain barriers in essential training, of having had expert physio in time of need, of the parental care that nurtured her development in running from the earliest years, of the many in her community who offered her a variety of supports and now in her mind, as the Bard put it, 'in an instant all was dark'. But, in fact, that was not entirely the case.

There was a glimpse of something brighter that understandably might have been drowned in the emotion of abject disappointment. It was something Lynn MacDougall had to remind her of, something that Sandra had noted, but then laid aside in her mind, because of the indignation about a system which meant slower qualifiers had made it through and left her behind.

'Listen, Sandra,' Lynn said to her on that mini-bus. 'Remember, you've just broken the Scottish record.'

Now in the grand scheme of things and in the setting of an Olympiad where astonishing world records were being achieved – particularly by Valerie Brisco-Hooks, in the actual final of the 200 metres itself, in 21.81 – a domestic record might pale into insignificance: seen as a mere bauble by comparison, an afterthought, a sentimental consolation, something too parochial to bear consideration in such an august setting and especially about someone who had come fifth. All of these thoughts might have passed through the minds of those who don't appreciate the solo mission of athletes. Ron Pickering did. His words to me in our forum by the poolside after that event, pierced through the modern cynicism suffocating the Olympic creed. These words I do recall vividly.

'That girl achieved something special for herself. She bettered herself. That's what she came here for. That's really what the majority of them all come here for.'

The simplicity of that comment was augmented by the passing of time. Five years after her 22.98, the Berlin Wall was to come down – in 1991 there was the Gulf War and the Russian Empire began to crumble – Princess Diana died in a car crash in 1997 – on 11 September 2001 planes crashed into the twin towers in New York – in 2008 stock markets plunged – in 2010 David Cameron became Prime Minister of the UK – in 2011 the population of the world was recorded at 7 billion – in 2012 the Olympics came to London – 2016 saw the UK vote to leave the European Union. Meanwhile her record still stood. As we were preoccupied by these convulsive global issues, Scottish runners through the years were attempting to better those precious few seconds achieved on that glaringly hot LA afternoon, but kept failing. One after the other.

Then on the 2 June 2018, 23-year-old Beth Dobbin, the daughter of the Celtic footballer Jim Dobbin, ran in a UK Women's League Premier Division match at Eton, in a time of 22.84 to break that record. Sandra was first to offer her congratulations in words she might have been rehearsing for decades.

To this day that infinitesimal margin of defeat still nags at her. But that glorious sunny day in the Coliseum reminded me of how I grew up in an era accepting the norm that women ought not to wander too far from the kitchen. For me, that one-hundredth of a second did not represent defeat but was, instead, a vivid reminder of women's emancipation.

Beside Sandra sits a doctor. Olympic rower Dr Richard Budgett. His LA experience elevated him to become the scourge of athletic cheats against whom Sandra suspected she had had to compete.

CHAPTER 7

Stormy Waters

AS SANDRA WHITTAKER was mentally attuning herself in downtown LA, a fellow Scot was sitting in a boat on a lake in the hills outside the city about to take part in an event that was as foreign to me as falconry in Outer Mongolia and which I regarded simply as part of Olympic Games exotica. It bore, to my untutored eye, the clumsy title of the Men's Coxed Fours. But, there being a Scot involved who might just conceivably win a gold medal I was, as they say, agog. Everybody loves a gold. Even as an onlooker, if it identifies your nation it seems to lend you some personal cachet. The setting was Lake Casitas, on an early morning that belied the general aura of sunny California, by being wreathed in a mist that heightened the sense I was about to watch some clandestine event that was nowhere near the normal sporting diet that most Scots preferred to consume. But I was focussing like a laser on this Scot – Richard Budgett, who was about to take part in an Olympic event that had never been won before by Great Britain. However, Budgett admitted to me that a thought passed through his mind as he awaited the horn to start the race.

'You know as I tensed myself ready to let go I was utterly convinced that one way or the other, this final was going to change my life. Whatever the outcome, I just felt that so strongly. This will change my life.'

In his wildest dreams he could not have imagined exactly where the sounding of that horn would take him in life eventually.

I had come across his name by chance. It stemmed from a casual remark, made poolside in a hotel just off Sunset Boulevard in downtown LA. It was there we had daily pow-wows, involving Ron Pickering, Steve Cram and Stuart Storey, all broadcasters of great merit and steeped in the comings and goings within the Games, as well as gossipers *par excellence*. It was there they mentioned that a Scot could possibly win a gold, at a time when we felt that our cupboard was going to be very bare indeed, with Alan Wells not fancied to retain his 100 metres crown. Nobody at the time could remember his name, but they did assure me that he was Scottish. Perhaps they were in patronising mode given, as a lone Scottish broadcaster in the team, they thought I needed occasional sustenance. They were right. In the middle of the raucous complexities of the Games, clutching at a Scottish identity in this cosmopolitan alphabet soup of nations, seemed crucially important even under the GB umbrella. So once again, as with Whittaker, the Games had taken on a new complexion, even though my relationship with rowing at that time was almost confined to having spoken on air once about an incident that took place in 1974, off the shores of Largs, when a ginger-haired Scottish player took out to sea and lost his oars. But here was the real stuff – a Scot with hands on oars that could possibly elevate him to a great height in a sport of which I knew little.

Although, when much later I was able to talk to him, he said almost dolefully to me, 'Look, I was born in Bearsden. Is that really Glasgow?' This is a profound question that has engaged even the most learned of minds through the ages, with little conclusion, but I was loath to offer him my grannie's description of that neighbourhood, 'That's where the toffs live.' As far as I was concerned, as he sat slightly crouched in that slender boat, ready to fire away as a member of the Great British Coxed Foursomes crew, Sauchiehall Street was imprinted all over him. I had a problem though. My other activities were going to keep me in downtown LA and Lake Casitas lay miles away in the hills, had always acted as a reservoir for thirsty LA and was the source of the corruption theme of Roman Polanski's superb film *Chinatown*. It was also hosting all the rowing and canoeing events for the Games. So, in my determination to see this final I could only venture into the depths of the BBC recording area in the old Columbia Pictures studios.

The lake that morning was grey and misty, and with the air-conditioning in the editing suite seemingly in full blast, it enhanced the feeling that I was actually watching a regatta in Hogganfield Loch in Glasgow on a dank November's day. All I knew about rowing in general was that it was not for weaklings. That and the premise that if you were in the rowing scene you must have come from a privileged background, given the years I had watched the annual Oxford–Cambridge Boat Race, with my support for the Oxford boat based on their dark blue colours which I associated with the Scotland international football jersey. Budgett did admit to me that he clearly grew up in life with distinct advantages over many others.

'We left Scotland when I was only 18 months old and went to live in the south of England. I was able to be sent to public, or private school as you might call it, at Radley College. Of course, when you are there as a boarder and with the great facilities that are to hand and with a lake besides, you can spend a lot of time on your sport. That's when I really developed my passion for rowing.'

He was on a well-trodden academic route which he followed to Cambridge University to study medicine and where he could further indulge his passion for his sport.

'I rowed for my college which wasn't so all encompassing. That meant my medical studies could progress without much disturbance. And, of course I tried to get into the Cambridge "blue boat" so I could take part in the Boat Race, but although I reached the last 20 I was thrown out. Why didn't I make it? My style just didn't look the prettiest on the water. Remember in those days we didn't have rowing machines where they can test the power you generate. All they did was put you in an eights boat and if you looked good you were selected. I had an awkward style and they didn't think it suited. But when I went on to the University of London, to do my clinical studies, I rowed in a pair and it was then they could see how much I could power the boat in the water. My international career started there.'

To be informed that there was an aesthetic dimension to rowing came as a surprise to me, but at the same time indicated that we sometimes fail to appreciate the complexities involved in any sport, as my perception of technique was of the most basic kind – you grabbed an oar and you pulled. That was how I saw it as they prepared to pull away on Lake Casitas, with a Scot in a favourable position to win a gold medal, given that Budgett and his four other rowers with their cox had already stoked up a considerable reputation in their international outings. To add to the interest the BBC were discovering that rowing made for absorbing television. It was well covered by the cameras – there was no disorientation, in that you knew exactly where you were in the race given, in this case, the 500 metres markers all along the course and the steadiness of the mobile cameras. And, above all, it led to some vastly exciting finishes for a public which had been greatly misinformed about rowing through their annual peep at the traditional Thames Boat Race, where the contests could be finished half-way down the river.

I suspect the public had a false impression of the GB team in that they would simply be university types who sloped down to the river from time to time, as a bit of wheeze between studies, fitting the portrait of privileged part-timers who could parade in one of those fancy club blazers at the Henley regatta. No, the five men in the boat were ruthless in their commitment. No messing about on the river for them. And, of course, desperate to win gold for the first time in this event. They could have launched their boat and christened it 'Sacrifice' given what they all had given up to get there. Budgett, for instance, had a promising medical career in front of him yet he decided he would have to take a year out of studies to prepare for Lake Casitas.

'We spent hours on lakes or down on the Thames in gloomy conditions, just training and training. And, yes, I did sacrifice some of my medical career by doing that. So for the next three years I was part of the national squad and took part in the World Championships in 1982 and 1983. Nevertheless, despite all of that commitment to my sport, much to my surprise I passed my final medical exams.'

Quality coaching they regarded as essential to match their ambition, so they linked up with one of the best, Mike Spracklen, who did not endear himself to the crew at first when he demanded they train three times a day which previously had been unheard of. They were now into a kind of SAS mentality, under him. Thereby, Spracklen was to become one of the most successful coaches in the history of the sport. As they did so, they also moved forward to select who would be the final four to row in the Olympics. No sentiment whatsoever was attached to that.

'The decision was made that the coxed fours would be considered the most important of all the categories in the GB effort,' Budgett told me.

'There was a squad of eight oarsmen all competing to get into the final four. Now, in one of those fours we raced in an international regatta in Amsterdam, beating the bronze medallists from the World Championships from the year before, so that made us feel very good and that we were on the right tracks. However, funnily enough there was a young sculler (single oarsman) in that same regatta who had a look at what we were doing and fancied that he might be useful to us and wanted to be tried out for the team. Our coach knew him personally and recommended him. We put him in the boat, tried him out and decided to select him. So one poor guy was booted out to make way for this young man. He was Steve Redgrave.'

Budgett still talks about that dramatic change, like they had just added turbo-jet power to the boat. They had won their first race by a length without him. Then when the young Redgrave jumped into the boat for the next race, they won by four lengths. By that time, just about three months before LA, they began to think they had a real chance of gold. But uppermost in their minds, in terms of the opposition they would have to face, was the thought that because of the Soviet bloc's decision to boycott the Games, the Russians and their biggest threat, the East Germans, would not be competing. Even then the athletes from the DDR were surrounded by suspicions about their methodology, leading to universal puzzlement as to how a relatively small nation could have such regular success at international events. So, as a team, Budgett and his crew wanted to demonstrate that the absence of the East Germans would not devalue any possible victory in the Games.

'Off we went to Lucerne, the premier regatta before the Olympics. It's the big one on a beautiful lake. And our coach said to us, "If you beat the East Germans on the Saturday, I'll give you the Sunday off!" So we went on and beat them in a world record time! However, I admit that if the Germans had gone to the Games it would have been a very tough test for us.'

But, there were others to consider, like the current World Champions, New Zealand and the host nation USA, who would surely be inspired by the patriotic tidal wave sweeping through the Games. When the team of Budgett, Martin Cross, Andy Holmes and Steve

Redgrave, with their diminutive stroke Adrian Ellison, who looked as if he could have fitted into Redgrave's pocket, reached the States two weeks in advance of the event they trained in Santa Barbara where they were up at 4am every morning, as their event would eventually be at 8.00am – a time when Californian folk were into their breakfast pancakes and syrup, or perhaps their muesli and soya milk, given their New Age proclivities.

On 30 July the GB crew won their first heat in six minutes 18.79 defeating the USA and New Zealand into second and third place respectively. It was such a dynamic start that one of Budgett's GB colleagues, a member of the Eight's crew, said to him, on the night before the final on 5 August, 'You're so lucky. All you've got to do is to turn up and you're going to win!' They were the favourites but Budgett knew that the Olympic Games were unique and that upsets were part of its historic fabric. And, in far-off downtown LA, even in an editing suite with its constant bustle, I could feel the tension that comes when you are backing someone to win and, in this case, a fellow Scot only 2000 metres away from gold.

The GB boat lined up against the USA, New Zealand, Italy, Canada and West Germany. Budgett, unsurprisingly was on edge, tense, desperate for the start.

'I've always suffered nerves, whether in the Cambridge bump races, or the Henley Royal Regatta and certainly in the Olympics. But, of course, the key thing is, and you've got to do this as an athlete, use these nerves to optimise your arousal to get the best out of yourself. Yes, I felt extraordinarily nervous but after three strokes, that had gone.'

On that 6 August morning the news headlines were dominated by the announcement of the death of actor Richard Burton as a reminder that the Olympics could not shunt everything out of the front pages. Gold though gave you special entrée. And since a GB crew had never won this event before they were under close media scrutiny. At the sound of the horn, the USA immediately swept into the lead with a strong, confident surge, which to my untutored eye looked ominous. Knowing little about rowing tactics, I nevertheless came from that school of thought that in a sporting challenge it is always better to come from behind. Admittedly a crude concept of how to win any contest, but it fitted the more romantic notion of the fighting comeback.

'Our plan was to make sure we could overtake them at the 1,000 metre mark, but in fact they stayed ahead. We had raced in the semi so they knew what we were planning to do. So they surged. Even at the 1,500 metre mark they were still in front.'

But with only 500 metres left you could see the gap being eaten up, with the GB boat spearing forward and incrementally narrowing the gap. And there comes a moment in the final stretch of any race when overtaking comes with such momentum that you know before the final line that it is going to succeed. As Budgett vividly recalls.

'We came to the final 500 metres and they were still ahead. I'll never forget our bowman Martin Cross shout "Go!" Normally, he never said anything like that. And we just flew!'

They crossed the line, winners by half a length and slumped, exhausted, like galley slaves of the Spanish Main, except their rewards were going to be much greater. I felt one of those tiny inner glows at realising that in the massive array of names and statistics which would accumulate in the records of the Games, the Scot, born in Glasgow/Bearsden would have found a niche for himself among the golds but, sadly, without any other Scottish company in the end. He was to be the lone Scot with a gold in LA. His reminiscing of that day though is not based on self-aggrandisement but on stressing their essential strategy – the bonding within the crew – the demands of extreme training and the pragmatism applied to their selection process. He almost admits that the last factor probably tipped the scales.

'At 21 Steve Redgrave was the youngest in the crew. But everyone knew he was the top athlete amongst the four. Added to which he was extremely competitive. If you look at the footage you'll see he rowed himself into the ground in that final push for the last 500 metres. He's extraordinarily driven. It's all very well to have the right physiology but you also must also have the right mental attributes as well. However, not for a moment did I imagine he would go on and win another four Olympic golds. I was there in Sydney when he won his last, by a very narrow margin, and it was an intensely emotional moment. This is especially remarkable for a man who did it while developing diabetes and ulcerative colitis. Just astonishing!'

So too was the effect of his own gold medal which eventually charted a new course for him, thus confirming what his instinct had told him at Lake Casitas. Life, suddenly, took on a new course.

'I happened to be doing my GP training at Northwick Park hospital in London in 1986. The British Olympic Association decided to open an Olympic medical centre in that very hospital. That was for their athletes to go to if they were injured in any way. I heard about this, so I wandered down and I took my gold medal with me to show them and they said, "Oh! That's interesting!" So they agreed I could come down in my spare time and do some research into fatigue and under-performance. And from there everything followed.'

You have to take a deep breath to consider what did follow from that show of gold in a London hospital. He was to become Chief Medical Officer for the British team in both Winter and Summer Olympics from 1998 to 2008. Seven Games in all. Chief MO for London Olympics in 2012, becoming Medical and Scientific Director for the International Olympic Committee in that same year and in that role, oversaw the beleaguered Olympics in Tokyo, alongside his long-term association with WADA (the World Anti-Doping Association) where he is a member of the elite Prohibited List Expert Group.

His gold medal had taken him into a field that has become almost like a battlefield against agents of subterfuge who would go to extraordinary lengths to avoid detection in their use of performance-enhancing substances. All in order to win. There is no stronger motivation for a competitor or indeed for a nation state, to achieve gold, as became startlingly clear. But Budgett admits he was an innocent in LA in 1984.

'I hadn't the slightest knowledge of what was going on there. I really wasn't interested in anything like that. I just wanted to compete. Everything else was irrelevant.'

In fact, of the 1,502 athletes tested for drugs in the LA Games, 12 positives were reported including two medal winners, a Swedish weightlifter and a Finnish distance runner. But there were stories

and rumours circulating about serious misdemeanours going unde-
tected, like a news investigation carried out by the BBC that alleged
nine positive results had been covered up and the documentation per-
taining to them had been deliberately destroyed. All this was refuted
by the IOC, but it showed that there was a general mistrust among athletes themselves – believing that the reputation of the Games was being
shielded against shaming disclosures. Certainly the testing systems
had improved since the day in 1968 when Hans-Gunnar Liljenwall, a
Swedish modern pentathlete in the Mexico Olympics became the first
athlete ever to be disqualified in the Games, after having swilled back
two beers to calm his nerves before his shooting event. But the tests
then were not sophisticated enough to detect the increasingly complex
drugs being produced and the awareness of athletes, and particularly
some coaches, of how effective anabolic steroids were. In short, in the
conversations in our poolside forum in LA, there was little doubt in our
minds that there were cheats out there somewhere, amidst the glam-
our of the Games and getting away with it. The upright and moralistic
Budgett was the ideal personality to take this all on.

Through the years I had come to understand the dimension of
the problems Budgett would be facing. In Prague in 1977, I interviewed the great Finnish middle-distance runner Lasse Virén, after
he had won the famous Rude Pravo road race through the cobbled
streets of that city. This is what I wrote in the *Glasgow Herald* on 13
December 2012 looking back on the effect on me, of that meeting, as
part of an observation about Mo Farah's astonishing performances
in that year's London Olympics.

> The man I met that day was mere skin and bone – like a creature
> devised for a Tim Burton animation film. Around him had swirled
> allegations of blood-doping: that is, replacing blood to increase the
> oxygen-carrying red cells in the blood stream to the great benefits
> of middle-distance runners. Whether or not he had indulged in that,
> he seemed nevertheless, to personify the dehumanisation of running.

Whatever he was doing worked, winning Olympic gold medals for
the double of 5,000 and 10,000 metres in 1972 and 1976. He seemed

inhuman though. And despite the mounting accusations against him his denials worked as well. He was never charged for any breach of doping regulation. But he was an example of the extremes athletes might go to for success and how suspicions could circulate amongst competitors like a virus.

Then, just as Budgett was establishing himself in his medical career, I was to discover just how difficult it would be for any medical system to keep pace with the effrontery of athletes who would take astonishing risks to cheat. It was the next Olympics in South Korea in 1988, in that mix of ancient and modern city of Seoul. In one fell swoop a scandal polluted the Games. On Tuesday 27 September 1988, early in the morning, when the city was still awaiting the first rays of dawn, the telephone rang in my hotel room. It was the editor of *Grandstand*. I recall his calm voice, although what he was telling me deserved a screech or two.

'Ben Johnson has tested positive in a drug test. Would you go out to the village and see if you can get any pictures of him or any interviews with anybody?'

How could the winner of the Gold Riband event, the 100 metres sprint, even think he could get away with taking a drug? But when I did get to the Olympic Village the bird had flown. Johnson was already winging his way back to Canada and the hundreds of other journalists were drawing a blank as the Canadians were skulking away out of sight. The atmosphere in the entire Games after that was poisoned into continuous suspicion of virtually everybody. Who else was at it? It could have been anybody, really. And then the momentum of the scandal reached the very room next to mine in the hotel.

I had helped arrange a two-way interview with the London studio and the British sprinter Linford Christie who finished in bronze position in that now infamous race behind Carl Lewis from the USA. I stood beside him on a balcony overlooking the British team headquarters as he poured scorn on Johnson and accused him of betraying the culture of sprinting. It was an impressive defence of the purity of Olympic commitment. However, a couple of days later

I met Ron Pickering who in hushed tones said, 'You'd better come into my room for a drink. You'll need it. Say nothing about it at the moment but I hear a British athlete has been tested positive!' And I recall the long pause before he whispered, like the world had its ear to the keyhole, 'I think it's Linford.'

He produced his favourite malt whisky and we let it soften the blow. In many ways he was an admirer of Linford and he spent much of the time trying to reason this out as simply a mistake of some kind in the analysis process. Because, if it were true, it would be cheating, overlain with the hypocrisy of his criticism of Johnson. But, a few days later, when the truth came out, it was shown that they had found the banned stimulant pseudoephedrine in his blood. His claim that he had innocently taken ginseng tea, which does contain that element, was only accepted by the IOC disciplinary hearing by a margin of 11 to 10 and gave Christie the 'benefit of the doubt'. A magnificent athlete who won 24 medals in his career, including becoming the oldest man to win the Olympic 100 metres when, aged 32, he took the gold in 1992. Seven years later he was found to have the banned substance nandrolone in his system. In fact, he was found to have more than 100 times the normal level. All this culminated in a lifelong ban from the British Olympic Association.

Faced by such challenges Budgett, however, was not to enter into the fray of sports medicine like a Buffy the Vampire Slayer, constantly trying to peer into the dark side of life and catch cheats. His principal function was to oversee the general health of athletes and the effect of injuries. This, particularly during the London Olympics, was a massive and complex operation, over which he presided and within which the vigilance on performance-enhancing drugs was only a part. He was, for instance, the medical adviser to the British Bob-Sleigh team at two winter Olympics which did not entail much time looking at blood or urine. But, in that London Olympic role there was no escaping the public and media scrutiny of how the system could prevent cheating. Drugs were the stuff of the front pages. So, perforce, he landed in the thick of it and was publicly viewed as one of the guardians of integrity, as the world looked on in increasing scepticism about the validity of certain performances.

This is what Budgett told the Science and Technology Committee of the UK Parliament looking into performance-enhancing technologies, in preparation for the London Olympics in 2012, stressing how circular the talk of doping is among athletes.

'Some of the athletes to whom I have spoken and whom I then have known to have been found guilty of a doping offence, and it was not just an accident, justified it to themselves by saying, "Of course, lots of people are cheating, most of my competitors are cheating. So I'm just levelling the playing field." Their perception is that lots of athletes are cheating and that is as bad as really was the case.'

It is a kind of double whammy for the invigilators, knowing that athletes take it because they think others are, but who may in fact be drug-free. Or not, as the case may be. It is twisted and complex and Budgett's words indicate the vast scale of the problem he faced. And, of course, it implies that nothing is foolproof. This was certainly the case in the London Olympics which was regrettably tarred as the 'dirtiest Games' despite its great popular success with the British public. It was all about the kinds of tests which were available at the time, as Budgett continues to stress, having been the Chief Medical Officer at the Games.

'The retrospective tests did not come in until 2014. We did not have that ability until then. We retained the tests which meant we could deal with the cheats retrospectively, especially with those who had been taking the traditional anabolic steroids. They had been taking them for decades – in small doses, stopping them before events, knowing they could get away with it because it's washed out of their system. So now we could test them, not just over a week or two, but for months. So although a lot has been said about London being the "dirtiest" of the Games, the testing that was done not only caught up with people but led to other athletes deservedly being awarded medals that without these tests would have been denied them.'

The validity of that statement, and the consolidation of his own position, was seen in 2019, when, for example, Artur Taymazov, a wrestler from Uzbekistan became the eighth gold medallist to fail a retrospective test from the 2012 Games. In fact a total of 140 competitors in London were eventually disqualified, which was more than the two previous summer Games in Athens (41) and Beijing (86) put together. Budgett's explanation was to stress that the retrospective manner of indicting the cheats only proved the success of testing overall. It was a valid point.

But then Laurel Hubbard stepped into his life, when Budgett had attained the powerful position of Medical and Scientific Director of the IOC. The New Zealand transexual athlete was accredited to compete in the Tokyo Games in the 87kg-plus category – the first time someone of that nature had taken part. Hubbard failed and finished last in her group after three failed snatch lifts, but evoked great sympathy amongst some of her peers. Others were resolutely against her participation. It added to the heated debate in wider society about inclusivity, fairness, women's rights and human rights. Budgett had previous and firm views on this issue. In 2003 when he was with the British Olympic Association, in responding to a government inquiry, he wrote a letter stating, among other views:

> The BOA believes the effect of allowing transexual women to compete in their acquired sex would be to make competition unfair for women. The physique determined by two or more decades of life as a male would not be significantly changed (in the case of male to female transexuals) which would eradicate the concept of the level playing field.

Such a statement seemed clear enough to elicit sympathy from many, including myself. But contrast that with the discussions within the IOC surrounding the Tokyo Olympics almost 20 years later, which led to a new framework, drawn up in part by Budgett. It declared, 'until evidence determines otherwise' transexual athletes 'should not be deemed to have an unfair or disproportionate competitive advantage'. And then he later stated to the USA edition of the *Guardian* 'We're very aware that sex is not binary. It's a continuum. Transexual women are women.' That characterised the many re-interpretations of an issue that certainly would engage minds and encourage sometimes hostile debate well beyond the athletic track.

His scientific acumen helping in the fight against drugs was essentially about discovering and exposing cheats. This alternative issue was about evaluating human aspiration that would put him into an entirely new province. You can tell from his public utterances the tilt towards the sanctity of human rights, but in the IOC's overall and evasive decision to allow individual sports to pursue their own agenda in this matter, it created the potential for uncertainty, perhaps even chaos. I found his fellow Scot in LA, Sandra Whittaker, in sympathy with that post-Tokyo stance:

'I think there should be equal rights and opportunities for everybody. So I go along with what he has announced recently. However, they must get it right. They've got to come up with the rules that will lead to complete fairness for everybody.'

Budgett is now at the heart of one of the most contentious issues affecting society. Issues that can cause a noted author, JK Rowling, to be ostracised by even some of the actors who portrayed her creations on the screen and can have academics pilloried because of their views. In that context a firm resolution for the universal acceptance of transgender people competing fairly in sport seems far distant.

Dr Richard Budgett was the only Scot to win a gold medal in LA. Although he admitted at the outset that the race would change his life, little could he have imagined that it would sweep him into waters that now resemble the turbulence of the Corryvreckan of his native land, which ominously for him, has never shown signs of becoming a serene millpond. But there is nobody better equipped to steer world sport through these stormy waters than the Scot whose eminent sense of decency will shine through the murk of controversy.

Drugs? I have seated a very talkative man beside him to pour out his grievances about illicit substances. In a distant country Ally MacLeod heard of the stimulant Fencamfamin for the first time.

CHAPTER 8
Pipe Dreams

IT WAS A TRULY sickening experience to see a man being dragged to the gallows. Even though it was only on film and even though I wasn't old enough to have started shaving, the image sunk in deeply. I was watching James Cagney making his final walk in the film *Angels With Dirty Faces*. Ever since then, mention of the gallows has made the skin crawl. When I read about the hanging of Ruth Ellis in July 1955 and the public outrage that it caused, the Cagney walk would materialise in the mind as if it had been a real experience. Twenty-three years later, in the most unexpected setting, that same ripple of disgust passed through me that was to lead to that unique period of disenchantment which is simply identified as, Argentina 1978. It was, on 7 June, Argentina's autumn. The deep hues of the trees in the streets of the city of Cordoba did not fool us into thinking the country was in an idyllic state. For as we had approached the Estadio Chateau Carreras stadium for the World Cup game, we could see a line of men facing a wall just outside the entrance, their hands above their heads and guarded by two soldiers with rifles, reminding us that a World Cup was being held in a country run by a military junta which was constantly under threat from rebels named Montoneros. I never did discover who these men were or what became of them. But I certainly knew what became of Scotland in that stadium that day.

Inside it, at the end of 90 minutes, we were to hear the sound of other rebels who had travelled a long way and spent a lot of money, only to be deprived of what they assumed was almost a forgone conclusion – a victory. At the final whistle in Scotland's 1–1 draw with Iran – thanks to an own goal by one of their own side – I looked intently at the close-up picture on my monitor of Ally MacLeod, the Scotland manager, slumped on the bench. He looked grey and worn, his faced screwed up like a man suffering the passing of a kidney stone and the braying of disenchanted Scotland supporters in the background offered no anti-inflammatory for him. In fact it was the opposite. He rose from his bench and started to walk. He had ways to go to get back into the dressing room area and had to pass some fans bedecked in tartan. He looked bowed and dishevelled as he neared them. It was then the Cagney revulsion swelled up again. This man had the gallows look about him. Little wonder. For on my monitor I could see some of the Scots spitting at him, screaming abuse, like he had committed a capital crime. By the distorted look on their faces they would have mauled him had they been able to mount the perimeter wall, although by then they knew they were in a trigger-happy country and stayed put. MacLeod walked on, attempting a dignified forbearance in the face of this venom, although wise enough to know that getting off the hook with the media, after a disastrous afternoon, was as likely as him being invited back for a drink with the Argentine dictator General Vidal.

I had contrasting emotions. Like any full-blooded Scot I was suffering the frustration of just having watched my team play as if they had overdosed on Mogadon, against a nation appearing for the first time in World Cup finals and, on paper at least, ought not to have worried Brechin City's second-eleven. That is the judgement that the future Sky commentator Martin Tyler and I had come to, after watching them in training the day before the game, when they looked as if they had learned football only through a correspondence course. Rightly, they looked big and strong, but what chance would they have against a country like ours which invented the passing game and justifiably trumpeted our unique 'tanner ba' dexterity? The yokels, as we saw them, in fact helped us salvage a draw with an own goal, all of which added to the sense of humiliation that aroused the mob, literally spitting fury at MacLeod. I had witnessed really excruciating Scottish defeats in the past, but this draw was different. This was like every conceit we've ever had about ourselves as a footballing nation being shoved back down our throats and making us feel like vomiting. It was as if we had lost a marque of quality like, 'Clyde Built'.

But that initial feeling gave way to anger. The mob did that for me. These same people would have been among the throngs, that for the previous year had responded to MacLeod like he could part the Atlantic and march them all to South America, if he wanted. It was infectious. It was enjoyable. Who, in any case, in the early stages would have wanted to spoil the party by pointing to the cautionary tale of the Pied Piper? I was fortunate in that preceding year to get close to MacLeod, acting again as chairman for sponsored evenings around Scotland which drew hundreds to listen to his sermons. Some of those howling at him on that Cordoba day would have been in attendance at these events, when months before they had deified the man. We travelled many miles together around Scotland as he decanted his stories as one of the great raconteurs, in a sport full of them. I was swept along by his voice pounding on my eardrums with that rushing, breathless enthusiasm of his, that spurned intervention by anybody. But I did notice one factor that played constantly on his mind, which he used as a theme to those who came to listen to him. He was concerned that some figures in Scottish football saw him merely as an entertaining personality but without the necessary gravitas to control players. That undercurrent certainly existed. Indeed, Jock Stein summed up his appointment briefly to me with brutal economy, 'It's a joke,' he told me once. The ones who doubted him kept their silence. Outwardly brimming with confidence and optimism, as you talked to MacLeod intimately you became aware of a man desperately needing to prove himself to his peers.

You have to understand the context in which he had taken on the Scotland job in May 1977. He had replaced Willie Ormond, who had returned with an unbeaten team from the World Cup in 1974, but had failed to qualify for the second round of the tournament. So, there were decidedly mixed views on Ormond's tenure, most notably because of the conduct of some of his players on their travels. Before arriving in Germany, they had played pre-World Cup friendlies in Belgium and Norway, which one journalist described as the '*Tour de Farce*' and which led to the European-wide belief that Scottish footballers stacked booze in their team hampers as pick-me-ups during training. This ludicrously exaggerated belief was based on the publicity given to two players, team captain Billy Bremner and Celtic's Jimmy Johnstone who had a curfew-breaking night of raucous drinking in Norway and, perforce, everyone was tarred by the same brush. Ally was fully aware of that consequence. He understood the global media now had preconceptions of the Scottish professional footballer which were at the other end of the spectrum from the Cistercian Order and in a way he was auditioning himself as the man suited for the challenge. On one of our travels he told me a story and asked me if it would be suitable to bring it up to the audience ahead of us. After I had listened, I told him to go ahead with it, since it clearly was intended to show that he was fully aware of the wiles of the professional footballer and that nothing would slip under his radar, as it certainly had for Ormond. It was based on his experience in English football.

He had joined Blackburn Rovers in 1956 from St Mirren, for whom he only played one season. It was at Third Lanark, where he started his senior career in 1949, that he had caught the eye of the beholder, with a rampaging style down the left wing that always brought me in mind of a runaway combine harvester, arms and legs flailing. I watched him at Cathkin Park frequently in my youth, attracted to the Hi His, as they were called, not by the gawky looking winger but by the dapper, immaculate passer of a ball, Jimmy Mason, coming to the end of his career but still demonstrating the classic skills of the traditional Scottish inside forward. MacLeod was an entertaining but distinctly fringe attraction to that for me. At Blackburn he became almost an institution in the five years he spent there, playing 193 games and scoring 47 goals. It was his experiences among strong personalities down there which led him to believe he was streetwise enough not to be hoodwinked by the guiles and tastes of players which had so undermined Ormond. The story which he told was to show that his experiences had prepared him for even the shadiest conduct of professional players and that he was no innocent yokel. It was about one dark night in England, prior to an important FA Cup game.

In 1960 Blackburn Rovers were managed by a Scot called Dally Duncan, who hailed from Aberdeen, but had played all his professional football south of the border. He was capped 14 times for Scotland and became revered for scoring both goals in Scotland's

2–0 victory over England at Hampden in 1935, and then went into management with a reputation as a decent professional. He was generally respected by his Blackburn players, but at the same time had recruited, and been bequeathed, some men who burned the candle at both ends and could sniff out a night-club like a tracker-dog crystal meth. On the eve of that crucial game, Duncan took his players to a country-house hotel far from the madding crowd. He went to his bed just before midnight. Others did not. Led by Northern Ireland international Derek Dougan, future UKIP supporter, novelist and chairman of the PFA (Professional Footballers Association), they descended by a ladder they had found somewhere and absconded to a local hostelry in the team mini-bus, driven by the teetotal left winger from Scotland, where as fate would have it, a flock of nurses, benefitting from obviously flexible licensing hours, were indulging in a knees-up. Fraternisation quickly followed and the NHS workers were crammed into the bus and driven back, in the wee sma' hours, where they scaled the ladder together back into the rooms, and where, it has to be assumed, they were not about to play hands of bridge.

Sadly, when the party ended, as dawn was breaking, one of the nurses fell from the ladder and broke her leg. An ambulance had to be called. The night was fractured as well, by voices and the klaxon announcing help on the way. The players managed, at most, a couple of hours nap before breakfast reveille, where they sat down with Dally Duncan. Astonishingly he had heard nothing of the caterwauling, nor, even more bewilderingly, had any of his assistants. So, over their cornflakes and toast the players put on straight faces, as if they had done nothing more that previous night than browse through their Gideon bibles, before turning off the lights. As I listened to that story I was further astonished to hear that the revellers, despite having had virtually no sleep had gone on to trounce the opposition and had proceeded to the next round of the Cup. Ally was telling that story with the important emphasis on the fact that he was the outsider. As the non-drinker, he did the driving for the crew and could take a lofty position of silent disapproval which he hoped would demonstrate that if he had experience of the anarchical lifestyle of Derek Dougan and co. he could handle anything. And certainly miss nothing.

I was not wholly convinced, but at least he was conscious of how high the stakes were in maintaining good conduct in foreign lands to sustain morale. In any case he could easily charm an audience. And in these several weeks before Argentina, I could not possibly have spent so much time with MacLeod without being infected by his warm personality to such an extent I had to wonder how I could ever be hostile to him. That affection held constant throughout the experience of Argentina, whilst at the same time never really believing he was up to that daunting task. He certainly believed he was. For I do recall how he came on the scene as Scotland's manager with an unblinking self-belief that sounded like a redcoat at Butlin's shattering the dawn with a wake-up call. On the eve of his first encounter with the English on 4 June 1977 in front of the camera for me, pre-Wembley, he repeated what he had just said to a crowd of pressmen, including the vultures from Fleet Street, 'I don't dislike the English. I hate their guts.' Of course, he didn't. But, he wanted to strike a chord with the spellbound cohorts backing him. It was glorious, outrageous stuff that made you hold your breath, torn between astonishment and admiration for such bravado. I couldn't have asked for more, since it departed spectacularly from the orthodoxy of grunge that you normally got coming out of a manager at that juncture. But, in the pressroom, his statement only produced a muffled giggle from some of the Scottish journalists who understood Ally's script only too well and knew, that in his own backyard, he could get away with quips like that but also were aware that Fleet Street did not need any excuse to attack anything Scottish in football. They would not forget what he had said that day.

Ally was also pandering to a discernible change in the Scottish political mood. Nationalism was on the rise at that time. It had been shaped into a legitimate potent force by the SNP. Indeed, I was beginning to experience anti-English sentiment in my travels around the country, even outside of a footballing environment, with a degree of bitterness that exceeded anything I had ever experienced before. Football was becoming a perfect conduit for it. Ally seemed to be lapsing into that mood, even though some of the Fleet Street clique were already dismissing him as something of a clown. So on the back of Scotland's 2–1 victory in his first encounter with England and the ecstatic invasion of the Wembley pitch and the crossbars being mounted like they were ramparts of an evil empire, Ally could face a world beginning to accept that he was no bombastic fantasist. He was now so energised you could barely stop the flow of words coming from him.

That certainly impressed itself on me one evening in a hotel in the middle of Perthshire in the early spring of 1978, with the nation obsessed by the prospect of a World Cup on the other side of the world. Our travels together had taken us to a venue in a large banqueting hall packed with a crowd who rose to their feet in wild acclamation, chanting his name and then breaking into the song popularised by the comedian Andy Cameron, 'We're on the march with Ally's Army' with all the fervour of salvationists come to redeem us from sin. This was like being in on the birth of a cult, a movement that was charged with something more than a footballing obsession. It was like watching men and women experiencing a unique emotion that had lain in store for just this moment, like they had found a drug to make them forget the comparative bleakness of humdrum daily life.

But then came a mood change that night. My duty was to chair the discussions and channel them in some ways to reveal Ally's thoughts on the approaching World Cup finals to his adoring public. I decided to ask him a question that had entered my thinking, having followed the Scottish squad throughout his tenure, game by game, barely missing a kick. I can remember it to this day.

'Bruce Rioch and Don Masson are no spring chickens. Do you think that they might have peaked too soon for Argentina in June?'

I didn't regard it as a profoundly intellectual intrusion into the continuing lovefest that was going on. But it was at least a level up from the persistence of the semi-jocular, semi-serious questions like, 'Who would you like to play in the final, Ally?' I recall the sudden silence that descended on the faces in front of me, like I had accused Scotland's manager of some felony. Ally hesitated. Then from within the audience I heard a grumble of discontent, followed quickly by some guffaws, which morphed into sneers. They were turning on me. Ally seized his moment.

'That's the media for you,' I recall him saying.

I was no longer 'Archie' who had accompanied him around the country, where the only risk was ducking the rose-petals being thrown at him – a kind of Sancho Panza to a Don Quixote, now that I come to think of it. But I had now broken cover. I was now the embodiment of MEDIA – representative of that vulturous pack which would feed on the carrion of any manager when it suited. For I think he long suspected, even then, at the height of his popularity, that skulking in the background were those who would stick the knife into him when the time came. Of course, he was to be proved right.

And, indeed, although I was slightly irked, I shoved that evening aside, since much more important tasks related to Argentina were on hand. But then you never knew what might emerge from him, something I had realised from the first moment I interviewed him on his appointment as manager of Aberdeen in 1975. At the tunnel mouth of Pittodrie he was confident enough to predict that he would win the club something. Well, they all do, don't they on their first day in that kind of job? At least, as far as I can recollect he did not hold an Aberdeen scarf above his head for our camera. But there was something about his presence at Pittodrie which I could barely reconcile with my preconception of Aberdeen as an institution, led then by one of the wisest counsels in Scottish football, chairman Dick Donald.

Donald always conveyed canniness, sobriety to me, even though he was a successful entertainments entrepreneur in the city. He seemed to typify the douce image of the granite city to us outsiders, where we imagined a strong puritanical thread ran through daily life. That this was probably a huge misconception did not alter the fact that the loud, demonstrative MacLeod did not seem to fit the nature of the club and that Donald was taking a huge risk. However, Ally found hard-won acceptance in defeating Celtic 2–1 in the final of the Scottish League Cup on 6 November 1976, Aberdeen's first trophy in six years. With the sudden departure of Ormond from the SFA to Hearts in May 1977 Ally accepted the post of Scotland team manager and thus began an era that bit into the Scottish psyche in a manner that echoed that other disastrous transatlantic Scottish venture, the Darien Scheme of the 17th century, where investors in new plantations in Panama lost fortunes in their failure. Nobody lost fortunes in Argentina in 1978. It only felt as if we had.

Ally had already been given a double dose of reality to pack into his suitcase for the long journey from Scotland. Firstly, England had beaten Scotland 1–0 at Hampden on 20 May, but his players received the loudest ovation I have heard for a defeated Scottish side, since it had been an absurd result, given our superiority through-out. Then eight days later the squad bade farewell to a crowd of 25,000 who had turned up at the stadium, just to wave them off into to the unknown – a feat of astonishing salesmanship by the SFA that might have encouraged them to start selling bottled air in Glasgow's George Square.

As soon as he put foot on Argentine soil I felt as if Ally had put his foot down on the brakes. From the outset he was on the defen-sive. SFA secretary Ernie Walker, casually and innocently spoke some words at the Press Club in Cordoba City, about a few players mount-ing a fence to escape from their rundown hotel, heading for a casino but alerting security guards, who apprehended them. Not to worry, Walker told the international press there, all of whom were like cus-tomers outside Harrods waiting for the doors to open for the Boxing Day sales, eager for a Scottish 'incident' and rushed in after the sec-retary said it was of no great consequence and a minor event. Even news editors back in Scotland, no doubt fed up with the usual clichés bombarding them from the other side of the world, grabbed this item like the Scotland squad had just mounted an assault on the junta. It was splashed around their pages. The same reaction followed in places as far apart as Reykjavik and Timbuctoo, because isn't this the sort of thing Scottish players do? Déjà vu couldn't possibly cover it, for those of us who had trawled after Scotland in Germany four years before.

This distraction took the edge off Ally, as far as I could deter-mine, when he faced us all. But we were quite unprepared for what was to follow. So was he. If you were able to focus on this one man throughout the footballing journey which began in Cordoba on 2 June and ended on 11 June in Mendoza, and peered through the footlights of World Cup football you could see, at the back of the stage, an eminently decent man slowly disintegrating, uttering despairing soliloquies that only heightened the sense of loneliness and helplessness that he was eventually to endure. The first of these was on the morning of 3 June. Peru had beaten Scotland 3–1. To a man the Scottish media present were numbed by that, so you could easily imagine what it was like in the Scottish camp in that mansion of gloom in the small town of Alta Gracia, which might have been built for such an aftermath. Ally came from within it to face us the following morning with a colossal sense of anti-climax hanging over us all like a toxic cloud. We were as intense and anxious as he clearly was, because most of our own predictions had been wafted away like confetti in a breeze. We were all implicit in the hype that he had engendered, so there was an unease among the Scottish media who, although professionally prepped to stick the boot in, had to do so with the cautionary recollection of what had appeared, optimistically, on their pages on the morning of the game. The Fleet Street mob were freer of that condition and with England back at home eliminated, adopted the 'I told you so' superior tone in their questioning.

So I found myself, in that interview with him that morning, wanting to help him, not crucify him. We talked about his team selection, about losing the initiative after the Joe Jordan goal had put us in the lead after only 15 minutes, the crucial loss of a goal just before half-time and the missed Don Masson penalty at 1–1. When I got to that passage where the Peruvians scored two goals in six minutes including the climactic, brilliant free-kick by Cubillas to put them 3–1 in the lead, I could see Ally was suffering. His handling of it was to praise the astonishing goalkeeping of the eccentric Peruvian goalkeeper, Quiroga who, in truth, had made a sequence of saves that justified his performance as one of the legitimate reasons for losing the opening game.

Ally was paining, but shocked though he was, we watched him gather strength as the interviews proceeded, until by the end he seemed to have convinced himself, if not his entire audience, that we could put that defeat behind us, as it would have little effect on the other two fast approaching games against Iran and Holland. Then it was revealed that Willie Johnston had taken Reactivan, apparently to help with hayfever. Except it contained the illicit stimulant Fencamfamin and duly was sent home by the SFA, principally for lying to the medics. The attendant publicity unhinged Ally. I watched him having to be restrained or else he would have assaulted the mild-mannered ITV interviewer Trevor McDonald, who had asked him a simple question about the facts. There and then I was not the only one to wonder if his warm personality was on the verge of imploding because of the use of a banned substance, by a careless footballer. Ally, thereafter, looked as if he was nursing some terrible secret from his past life, the geniality largely evaporated when in the presence of the media. He was not aided by what his men had to face up to next.

Now in the panoramic memories I treasure of the 16 World Cup games I witnessed between 1974 and 1998 I have created a kind of Bayeux tapestry in the mind, with scenes and images that are woven together to remind me of the wild swings in emotion we all experienced. Samples are: Billy Bremner's strangulated attempt to meet a cross in front of an open goal in Frankfurt in 1974, a simple touch of which would have led to a deserved victory over Brazil; Archie Gemmill's masterpiece in Mendoza in 1978; the tragicomical efforts of Willie Miller and Alan Hansen to go for the same ball that led to the Russian goal in Malaga in 1982; the bitter face of SFA secretary Ernie Walker calling the Uruguayans 'animals' in Mexico city in 1986; Mo Johnston's astonishingly cool penalty against Sweden in Italy in 1990 that prevented a collapse in Scottish morale; the look of mortification on Tom Boyd's face after his 'own goal' in Paris in the opening match against Brazil in the 1998 World Cup.

But there also exists an empty space on the tapestry – as if, mentally, I hate to return to that very depressing day that was to scar Ally permanently. We go back to where I started this chapter – 7 June 1978. If we are looking at depths of inadequacy in the history of international football, as far as I was concerned, that day was the Marianas' Trench of how low we could sink. I had been angered by the Scottish crowd, but that was nothing to the incandescent rage

1971. Tommy Docherty. The newly appointed Scotland manager was a restless soul already staring ahead to a future well outside his native land.
© The Daily Record

1943. Jackie Paterson, on the right, had a punch which I always imagined to be his Excalibur. His winning a World Title in only 61 seconds, after employing it, justified my romantic notion. © The Daily Record

1960. Jim Baxter signing his original contract. He signed with his right hand and went on to terrorise with his left foot. © The Daily Record

1971. Eric Brown (the Bomber) on the eve of his captaincy of the GB Ryder Cup team, illustrating, to newcomer Harry Bannerman, the aggression which characterised his leadership against the Americans. © The Daily Record

2001. The mercurial Jimmy Johnstone shortly after being diagnosed with motor neurone disease. That slight look of incomprehension on his face was simply a prelude to how courageously he faced up to the inevitable. © The Daily Record

1984. Sandra Whittaker. A record-breaking run in
the LA Olympics nevertheless did not qualify her for a
medal. © The Daily Record

In 1984 Richard Budgett was the only Scot to
win a gold medal in the LA Olympic Games.
He had predicted before his event that the
day would change his life. Little did he realise
it would elevate him eventually to one of the
most powerful positions in world sport.

1978. Argentina. Ally MacLeod, faceless in the eye of a storm. Nevertheless in his time as Scotland manager he did evoke a unique national emotion.
© The Daily Record

1985. Jock Stein and Alex Ferguson. The Sorcerer and his Apprentice.
© The Daily Record

2003. Bill McLaren, while being the paragon of commentating, treasured his domesticity and the closeness to his wife Bette, particularly as they shared a passion for golf.
© The Daily Record

1983. Jim McLean. Beneath his customary Grim Reaper image pulsed a unique footballing brain. © The Daily Record

1986. Graeme Souness launched a football revolution that attracted some unusual camp followers. © The Daily Record

I felt after watching what my BBC London colleagues were to do to him the following day. They certainly had remembered Ally's pseudo-jocular comments about the English way back.

Firstly, they had been all over MacLeod from the moment Scotland had qualified for the finals. But they had never been comfortable with the fact that England had been left behind licking their wounds. Having to concentrate on Scotland, as the only UK team there, was an act of sufferance for too many of them. So, given Scotland's failure to put this rudimentary Iranian team to the sword and playing as if in temporary paralysis, BBC London targeted the Scotland manager. They skilfully edited a segment of pictures from that day – set against those from the months before – thus contrasting the joyful, optimistic pre-World Cup Ally with the miserable wretch sitting on that foreign bench. But it was also a calculated mockery of us Scots who had trooped along willingly behind this man. It was BBC London's less than subtle portrayal of nationalistic hubris. It was also payback time, for the Scottish antics at Wembley the year before. Thus, they unleashed this montage of pictures in a tone of poisonous ridicule.

Ally looked crushed the following day at the press conference, on a hillock in the grounds of the hotel, where a stray dog muzzled him and he stroked it back with the comment, 'Well, at least I have one friend here today.' He was broken. It was hard for me to take. Yes, I had never thought he was fit for the purpose of this special task, but nevertheless I had come to know him as a decent man who deserved more than mindless rage at this juncture. He looked as if he was wishing that one of those carpets he had commercially endorsed in the months before the finals would turn up and magically fly him out of this mess. Indeed, one SFA official said to me years later, in a fit of metaphor, 'After the drugs fiasco and the Iran result, Ally hid under the bed. He locked himself in his room. He just disappeared when the going got rough.'

I was not to see him again until just before the last game in Mendoza against a highly fancied Holland side. He was subdued, almost casual in his interview and seemed as if he was in the same suitcase-packing mood as the rest of us, and glad to be putting this pestilence of a tournament behind us. The script did not quite go according to plan. Scotland were to win 3–2 with Archie Gemmill's goal a tiny fragment of Scottish creativity that we thought had completely deserted us. The fact that we had failed to qualify for the second stage only through inferior goal difference, added its own aggravation. The following day, almost as if the Andes weather was determined to create an appropriate background to a dismal retreat, Mendoza airport was shrouded in fog and we were all cooped up for several hours waiting for our flights and holding inquests in small huddles, conjecturing how long Ally could last. The victory, twinned with the exit from the World Cup tournament was summed up by author Alan Sharp, who had come down from Hollywood for the occasion, when he muttered to me from under his broad fedora hat, 'We've just discovered a new way of losing.' However, watching Ally in those almost interminable hours waiting for the fog to lift, I could tell he knew that a temporary reprieve was not going to save his neck. He was fully entitled to reach out for some credit for a victory against an accomplished side and at one stage declared to the press that we had shown our real Scottish quality by beating the Dutch. To which Frank McGhee of the *Daily Mirror* wrote the following day, 'This is like losing the world war and then inventing the atom bomb.'

It had come too late for Ally and all of us. Nobody was really buying into his attempt to salvage something of his reputation out of this one exalted victory. In fact, he was about to face an uninhibited backlash that stretched back across the Atlantic, to a nation largely soured by the month's events and epitomised for me by the view of a Dundee shopkeeper who offered clients a free hammer to break Andy Cameron's record of *Ally's Tartan Army* – on sale at a penny each. So, in view of the exuberant optimism continually expressed by the manager himself, he was to be hauled down from the pedestal we had placed him on, like toppling the statue of a figure associated with the slave trade.

But it was those twisted Scottish faces of hate in the Cordoba stadium that still turns the stomach after all those decades. It was remarkable to watch choirboys turning into a baying mob in the space of two weeks. But, at the same time, it had set me wondering as to how much the media, including my own contributions, inflated the Ally phenomenon. Did we really call out the dangers of the hysteria in any sense? There was one test I did fail. The BBC had invited Ally, at our expense, to come with me to Peru to watch his future opponents play the host nation Argentina in Lima and make a film of that fact. He declined. He was too busy fulfilling various commercial endorsements at home to bother. That it was a professional duty for him to watch Peru in the flesh, in any case, was glaringly obvious. He never did achieve that. I wrote or said nothing about that lapse of judgement but should have. I was not alone in being tethered to the idea that nobody in that World Cup year should rock the boat.

The paradox in all of this was that I never met anyone who disliked Ally. He was the kind of person you would have wanted to thrive in this sport, populated as it largely was, by men who faced the world each morning as if they had spent the night sleeping on a bed of nails. He was a tonic in a world that could make you queasy so often. Indeed, his induction to the SFA's Scottish Hall of Fame, came posthumously, in 2015, 30 years after that victory over the Dutch in Mendoza, as a reflection of how reluctant succeeding generations were to acknowledge the breathless excitement he had generated in our game. His passing away cruelly through Alzheimer's disease on 1 February 2004 had certainly been a factor in softening the views of those in authority who had blatantly disowned him. And there were three days, in particular, that one can never forget and in truth have never really been equalled and why I could not fail to recognise him in this narrative.

Consider the 2–1 Wembley victory of 1977 that was overshadowed by the pitch invasion by Scots who proceeded to tear up the pitch and break the crossbars. This was one aspect that certainly got out of control, but indicated that Ally's exhortations were introducing us to something that Scottish football had been denied for so long against the English – triumphalism. That view was discreetly accepted by even the top brass of Scottish football. Of course, the rampaging went much too far but you could feel that Ally had aroused the feeling for so many, that the future for the national side was limitless. Then weeks later, in the precipitous Boca Juniors stadium in Buenos Aires, Scotland played against the host nation Argentina and in achieving a

1–1 draw in a game, even the local and usually very partisan media thought the visitors should have won. Nobody that I know in the stadium that night, or on our further travels, tried to put the brakes on the wild expectations that arose from that single game, as Ally, by his very nature, milked it for all its worth, as he had every right to. 'We are potential finalists,' he told local TV later. As we had survived the lion's den atmosphere in the heart of a football-obsessed country, nobody was inclined to ridicule that assessment. Those of us there were beginning to feel that slightly relaxed tipsy feeling that was a very rare phenomenon and unforgettable.

Then, above all, it was capped at Anfield, Liverpool, in the September of that same year, with the defeat of Wales in front of a majority Scottish crowd, which produced the fiercest cacophony of sound I had ever heard. It was Ally sound. It was a combination of heart and lung. It was total belief. It was unique. That emotional pinnacle has never been reached by any of the crowds following the national side since then. I link all that to his first day in office facing the press. In a self-deprecating touch, which he was fond of lapsing into, but which only augmented his supreme self-belief, he touched his large and prominent sloping nose and declared in his first statement to the media, 'Concorde has landed!' And, indeed, despite all, he did generate some sonic booms which still ring in many ears.

Sir Alex Ferguson could sit anywhere he wants I suppose, but I place him beside Ally as former national managers and because the granite city played such a major part in both of their careers.

CHAPTER 9

The Aberdeen Rose Bowl

IN THE MIDDLE of the night of 7 May 1970 a violent electrical storm broke over the city of Milan. It persisted stubbornly through the morning until the streets were mimicking the look of Venice. At Malpensa airport, just outside the city centre, all flights had been cancelled. The terminal itself was eventually to look like an internment camp for refugees as hundreds of people from all parts of Europe stared at departure boards, which for hour after interminable hour were monotonously announcing 'Ritardo'. Translation was unnecessary. Aggravations inevitably sparked off some friction between people vying for space and refreshment, for we were all discovering this particular terminal would not even have catered for the needs of the abstemious Independent Order of Rechabites, and we noticed the Carabinieri were circulating among the crowd, as furtively as pickpockets, on the assumption that someone somewhere in the throng would snap under these claustrophobic conditions and Etna would seem to erupt.

For there were two opposing phalanxes of people under the same roof and in different frames of mind. The balance was simple. There were winners and losers. There was triumphalism off-set by dejection. All cheek by jowl. It is a credit to everyone that, apart from a few expletives that rang around the concourse, there was mutual respect among the opposing throngs who, the night previously, had been seated in the San Siro stadium voicing support for their teams. It was hangover time, in different ways, for Celtic and Feyenoord supporters, as the European Cup was heading for Rotterdam. That was the harsh fact which separated the respective supporters by more than their colours. You could tell by the body language who had won. In general terms the Celtic support were quieter, morose, having been shocked by how well their opponents had played to win the Cup in extra-time and thus denting the reputation of their great manager Jock Stein, in whom they had placed so much of their trust.

That is why one single face caught my attention amidst the frustrated, suffering green and white throng. The oddity of it actually startled me. For there, surrounded by grieving Celtic supporters was a face that seemed glaringly out of place. A bit like that face in Alfred Hitchcock's film *Strangers On A Train* – the scene at Wimbledon when all heads keep turning, side to side, following the ball, except one which is static and staring. The face in the terminal, surrounded by green and white, looked straight ahead, with an occasional amused twitch, in response to some of the banter directed towards it. The man wearing that barely flinching expression knew full well that he had been spotted by the fans around. Here, in their midst, was a 'blue-nose'.

Alex Ferguson, calm, composed, looking for all the world like a man waiting patiently for a bus and although a Falkirk player at that moment in time, could not conceal the fact he was from the other tribe. For all that he had been a successful player for other clubs, including having been the joint-leading goalscorer in the Scottish League with Joe McBride of Celtic, in the 1965–66 season when he was with Dunfermline, his two seasons at Ibrox and his honest admission to having been a diehard Rangers fan since childhood had stamped him with a brand which is never erased. Was this some dare he had taken on to be amongst those who had taunted him for his part in Rangers heavy defeat by their club in the Scottish Cup final only a year previously? What was he doing here? Given his background and the fact that he was now playing for a provincial club it was difficult to take in what attracted him to these circumstances. He could have watched the game on television without risking the ribaldry of those who were into mocking him. It was not until decades later when I saw him with the European trophy in his hands in Barcelona in 1999 that I thought back to that lonely face in that crowded patch and it suddenly struck me that all these years before, I was witnessing a typical Ferguson act of audacity, into which nobody at the time thought there was any significance. Here was a Rangers reject flying all the way to watch their great rivals and, at the time, in the brief and jocular conversation I had with him, pointing out how well he was accepting the cheery but critical banter of the Celtic supporters around him, it merited not even a second thought.

But, in the light of what then proceeded in his life, all of us who saw him there could claim we were in at the start of his burning ambition to push on with life and that conventional boundaries meant nothing to him. Here was somebody attracted to the big-time, like a moth to a flame, just as we assumed that as he was entering the provincial waters of Scottish football, he was also heading for professional oblivion, given his expulsion from Ibrox for what the club thought was an act of negligence in the Scottish Cup final of 1969. I recall that very day, that very minute, as it was my first Scottish Cup final commentary. For Fergie it was a moment that would change his life. A corner on the left was awarded to Celtic after only two minutes. The usual choreography followed. For Billy McNeill had trotted down from his defensive position to take his customary stance just inside the penalty area, a ploy so blatantly obvious that it was as if the Hampden Park PA system had just announced his arrival in the box, so that nobody would miss him in the crowd of 132,870, the biggest attendance ever for an Old Firm match. In watching the ball land on his head and then take flight in a looping curve, ending up just inside the far-post, it was almost as if he could hardly believe himself that he had been granted so much freedom to put Celtic ahead so soon. The *Glasgow Herald's* Glyn Edwards described the Rangers defenders as, 'marking no one but their own teammates'. Gair Henderson in the *Evening Times* was more pointed,

> Where, oh where, was the cover in the second minute, when Billy McNeill was given the freedom of the field to head the opening goal and hammer the first nail in Rangers' coffin?

In a way these words could have formed the epitaph for the career of one individual, because in the next few days information leaked out of Ibrox that the blame for that crucial lapse was being heaped on the shoulders of one Alex Ferguson, who had been assigned to cover the Celtic captain. Now had Rangers fought back from that mishap and made a game of it, then perhaps that incident would have been forgotten. In fact, they were eventually trounced 4–0, and to pour acid into the wound, it was the first Scottish Cup final Rangers had lost in 40 years. History had intensified his culpability. So, charged with being AWOL, court martial for the Govan-born boy followed. Training with the youths instead of the main squad thereafter at Ibrox, was the equivalent of boot-camp for him and public humiliation made his continual tenure there impossible.

Until that day in Milan, the man who was to become Sir Alex, but referred by all and sundry in the media and other parts as Fergie, had dropped off my radar, as he went on to play for Falkirk and eventually Ayr United. In those early days of the 1970s it was the continuing Stein juggernaut that was preoccupying most of us in the media and even impending wars would have seemed peripheral given our intense involvement in what was turning out to be a unique phenomenon in Scottish football. So I paid little attention to the news of his progression into management, firstly with East Stirling, then in 1974, on to a club which he clearly saw had more potential – St Mirren. It took his success to alert me to how he was progressing in the world. Reports were flowing in of his youthful St Mirren side mopping up the opposition in the Scottish First Division, accompanied by exuberant interviews to the media by a young manager relishing every second of his push towards the limelight with what the press now called, 'Fergie's Furies'. However, this was 1977, in the middle of the Ally MacLeod era and the prospect of the World Cup was monopolising much of our thinking in the media. Nevertheless, I found myself taking off to interview Fergie at Love Street, as his fresh young side, whose captain Tony Fitzgerald was only 20, eventually captured the First Division title.

From that day in the spring of 1977, right through to the 18 October 1986, when on a windy day in Leith, Aberdeen arrived in Edinburgh to play Hibernian in a league game, I enjoyed perhaps the most exhilarating managerial relationship I ever had. It came to an end that October day, abruptly, dramatically, but could never obliterate the feeling that over those nine years, with Fergie steering, we had shot the rapids together, especially after he had been appointed manager of Aberdeen in May 1978. It was a time of convulsion in Scottish football – the disappointments of Argentina – Billy McNeill replacing Jock Stein at Celtic – John Greig taking over from Jock Wallace at Ibrox. So it was refreshing to come across such buoyant optimism inside Pittodrie and certainly from someone who had taken his previous club St Mirren to an industrial tribunal for wrongful dismissal, but which, going against him, cast doubts on his competence and trustworthiness. It had concluded, 'It shows him as one possessing, neither by experience nor talent, any managerial ability at all.' Think of an ancient scribe noting of the teenage Alexander the Great that he, 'will never be able to mount the saddle', and it might give you an idea of the scale of misjudgement that report contained.

THE GRANITE ERA

When you walked into Pittodrie in these early days and had not the slightest inkling of where this was all going to end up, for him or the club, it was like taking a spacewalk; feeling free from the gravitational pull of the Old Firm and engaging with a personality who kept you safely tethered to his rampant self-belief. Of course, like many others I was slightly taken aback by his appointment there, given the wide publicity of the tribunal's findings against him, as well as measuring it against the personality of the Aberdeen chairman Dick Donald who was the very epitome of canny reflection. However, Donald had been influenced by a man sitting in Glasgow. Like many officials or owners in the game at that time, they would lift the phone to Jock Stein, almost as a matter of course, to seek his judgement on people, given that he was now considered the oracle of the age. Donald asked him his view on Bertie Auld, one of his favoured Lisbon Lions, as a potential manager. According to what the Celtic manager ultimately told me, he strongly dissuaded Donald from that option. He suggested Fergie instead. Stein admitted that Auld, whom he considered vital to the great efforts of 1967, never really forgave him for that, when all was eventually revealed. It was another instance of the lack of sentimentality and the sometimes breathtaking candour of Stein, whose intervention helped changed a club's history.

Thus, the man on whom Fergie seemed to model his methods on inspiring players, had helped lever him into a job which was to lead him eventually to stratospheric success. At the outset, whether consciously or not, the new Aberdeen manager adopted a stratagem that Stein had used effectively when he took over at Parkhead in 1965. He became political like Stein. The Celtic manager had known that his great rivals Rangers commanded greater respect and exerted more influence on the media then because of their current supremacy in the game. Stein linked that also to the historical sectarian-based bias that many had against his club, linked with the general impression that the media were historically pre-disposed to Rangers. It was a powerful motivation for young men to fight against perceived prejudice by a media who wished to devalue their true worth. The 'blue-nose' world was against them. It worked a dream.

Fergie's political motivation was geographical. The West of Scotland press was the object of much of his scorn, which he transmitted to his players by megaphone, to convince them to go the extra-mile to achieve the recognition they rightfully deserved. Of course, Fergie, who went on to more sophisticated mind games in the future, had the personal fortitude to take on the powerful beasts from Glasgow. To me it was the mirror image of what happened in 1965 at rudderless Celtic FC. So, in my first visits to Pittodrie I could also see a lot of Stein in him, in his energy, his love of the post and the challenge he had been given. In 2007 when he was manager at Old Trafford and just before a match in Lisbon against Sporting Lisbon in the Champions League, he actually asked the club's television channel to film him walking around the Estadio Nacional, where Celtic had lifted the European Cup, in overt homage to Stein. That poignant scene was never released publicly.

At first these Fergie interviews were formal, but later a more intimate relationship developed. I was recognising quickly enough that here was a voice that people would ignore at their peril. Nor that he would take defeat lying down, particularly at the hands of the Old Firm.

This was particularly so when I interviewed him about the Scottish League Cup final against Rangers on 31 March 1979. It is a game that aroused him to the heights of his belief that in finals like these the officiating would be as evenly balanced as that tower in Pisa. With the score 1–1, and Rangers having equalised late in the game, Doug Rougvie the Aberdeen centre half was sent off for what we assumed was an elbow on Derek Johnston's back. The Rangers striker fell, poleaxed, and was treated eventually for a full five minutes. Fergie, like myself and many others, even in the press box, did not see the incident and as it was off-camera as well, there can be no real verification of the referee's decision to expel the player. Rangers went on to win 2–1 in extra-time. Now it did not matter that Jim Reynolds of the *Glasgow Herald* was to write, 'Rangers played Aberdeen off the park', or that Hugh Taylor of the *Evening Times* criticised Aberdeen who, 'for so much of the game they appeared to lack confidence with too many moving around as if they were fated to lose a final again', thus suggesting that not much had changed around Pittodrie. What mattered was the decision of a referee to send off one of his players and of course Fergie was not far off the mark to suggest that it had lost them the final. For without Rougvie in defence, Colin Jackson was there to head in Rangers' winner in extra-time.

But the controversy had obscured one more salient factor. Aberdeen had taken stage fright again. Although a deflected equalising goal by Rangers must have been difficult to stomach, they had been inferior to Rangers for most of the 90 minutes. It reminded me of the day his predecessor Billy McNeill had brought his Aberdeen side to play Rangers in the Scottish Cup final of 1978. With the sun beating down on us, I stood chatting with the Aberdeen manager at the tunnel mouth just before he went in to deliver his team-talk. It was hardly innocent chit-chat. For he rooted me to the spot with an almost heartbreaking comment that sprung from his experience of big-time challenges with Celtic in the Old Firm cauldron.

'Some of our players just don't get this,' he said in astonishing frankness. 'Even Bobby Clark is in that dressing room at the moment shitting himself because he's coming out to face that.'

The 'that' he was nodding towards was the massive Rangers support. He was conceding that Aberdeen's players had an inbuilt inferiority complex in this setting and was conceding the disadvantage he, as a manager, was having to face – he, who as a player had never experienced thoughts of inferiority in a green and white jersey. So on the basis of that League Cup final defeat it appeared that nothing much had changed in the Aberdeen psyche since Fergie had arrived. But it had. Fergie never would forget any seeming injustice.

For, many weeks later at the beginning of the new season, in my first sit-down with him inside Pittodrie, off-camera, he could still vent cold fury when you mentioned the final and directed it mostly at Derek Johnstone who he felt had conned the referee Ian Foote into sending Rougvie off. There was nothing unusual in a manager griping about a refereeing decision. But the fact that something had lain dormant in Fergie's mind for so long, but emerged with venom like it had only just occurred, ought to have been a salutary lesson, that he was a man with a vivid memory and could store grudges like they were in a nuclear missile site ready for use in perpetuity. That was utterly lost on me at that time.

In season 1979/80, Fergie's second, Aberdeen beat both Celtic and Rangers, home and away in the Scottish League Cup, and there was every justification for respecting and even fearing a man who had stepped into a club that was always promising more than it could deliver and had shaken it to its foundations. I was genuinely excited about this and because of that I went to Hampden Park on 8 December 1979 for the Scottish League Cup final against Dundee United, believing that if Aberdeen were to mount a serious challenge to the Old Firm and exorcise their ghostly recent appearances at Hampden from their system, then they had to prove their worth and lift this one. In that sense, I suppose I admit that I did want them to win it for that reason alone. This was not to discredit Dundee United under the crafty guidance of Jim McLean, who was a master strategist and for whom Fergie had the greatest respect. For at that stage, however well United could play, in the longer term, if there was one club with the resources and talent available to win a league title it would be Aberdeen before anybody else. And if it failed, then there was a possibility that Scottish football would continue on its orthodox way with historical imbalance, even though the Pittodrie–Tannadice success had been recognised by the media as the 'New Firm'. I believed that much of the reconfiguration of Scottish football was at stake in this final.

However, above all, I recollect the weather and the attempts by both sides to master the 'glaur', for on a miserably wet day with parts of Hampden in danger of becoming like the fields of Passchendaele, skill was aplenty, but of goals there were none. Aberdeen ought to have won on the number of chances and Fergie, post-match, expressed his ultimate anger to me at the referee for not awarding a penalty when Steve Murray, the former Celtic player, seemed to pull Drew Jarvie down in the box in injury time. The goalless affair then moved to the replay at Dens Park on the following Wednesday, where I recall Aberdeen supporters smashing bottles against the underside of our commentary position, as they watched their team, outthought by Jim McLean, go under by 3–0. This time a relatively complacent Fergie made his position clear to the world, as summed up to Hugh Taylor of the *Glasgow Evening Times*, 'No excuses – we were never in it. We had our chances and didn't take them. Truth is, I have never seen United play better.'

THE TURNING POINT

He told me afterwards that he did feel as low as he had ever been after that final replay, but on the other hand I did sense he also judged this to be a temporary aberration – that United would be no real obstacle to them advancing in the League. That was his primary target. The evidence of that seemed to mount after that Cup failure. They started to win significant league games. About this time, as the New Firm were making an impact on Scottish football, the BBC were being criticised for concentrating inordinately on the Old Firm. But 'facts are chiels that winna ding' and the reality was that audiences were intrigued by the new challenge and under some of my prompting we steered a newer course. About the end of March of that season, after a period of some bad weather that cancelled many fixtures, including those of Aberdeen, I found myself travelling to the north-east more regularly in those few months than I had in my entire previous career.

For Aberdeen were on a run. In recent times they looked as if they had been lacking in self-belief, any time they went south of Dunblane. But, as decided proof of how Fergie had built communal backbone to both team and support, they were to travel to Celtic Park, their nearest challengers, and beat them 3–1 late in the season, to authenticate their status as potential champions. This was on a sequence that would see them undefeated in 15 league games. So my visits to the granite city became almost habitual. I would always travel on a Friday to avoid possible travel disturbance on the day of the game itself. But there was an ulterior motive. I would be able to talk to Fergie after training inside Pittodrie. And he was definitely up for it. I had something initially in my favour. I was not seen as part of the West of Scotland press and in truth, it was not my remit to be snooping after stories. He knew that. So his tongue was as loose and as relaxed as any manager I have ever had to converse with. All this took place mainly in Pittodrie's boot-room. As I write that I can almost smell the leathery, earthy air that hung around us and still see Teddy Scott, former player, coach, trainer and general factotum, without whom you feel the place would fall apart, fussing around us and occasionally throwing in a quip to stir the pot. It was like being in a footballing sanctuary that stimulated the imagination, and the repartee and stories and gossip flowed between us like cronies in a favourite howff. It's a tableau I fall back on with a fortifying degree of nostalgia, when even now I try to comprehend how the roof eventually fell in for me.

I certainly was benefitting from Aberdeen's burgeoning success, since I did appreciate that he and perhaps all those around him felt they were on the cusp of unprecedented success and – although he could express some anger about an individual from time to time – Fergie was generally at ease with the world. This was a passport to some frank revelations about many of the personalities in the game that came from his lips, knowing full well that nothing he said would escape to the outer world. So, like Stein, he liked gossip and pushed for as much information about other people in the business that I was prepared to offer him. It helped that we had a lot in common. He was a strong Labour supporter and trade union enthusiast like myself, thus the conversations could segue easily from football to other social issues. I almost felt privileged that he seemed to be accepting me as a confidant, if not wholly intimate friend, fraught as that clearly was with the danger of being accused of becoming a cheerleader, not a dispassionate observer. However, I was genuinely excited by this boom that paralleled what was happening at that time underneath the North Sea.

In that sense I admit I was unabashed about expressing my enthusiasm for this new Aberdeen phenomenon. As Billy McNeill once said to me during Aberdeen's ascendancy in the domestic game, 'I think you've become a Fergie man.' That in itself indicated progress, for hardly ever would an Old Firm manager have given a second thought to who was managing at Pittodrie. On 3 May 1980, nature provided the perfect background for them winning the championship. It was at Easter Road, Edinburgh. From my high vantage point you could see Arthur's Seat poised and respectful in the glorious sunshine, almost as if on the final whistle it would give a nod of recognition to an Aberdeen side trampling over the newly relegated Hibernian side 5–0, as Celtic were eking out a scoreless draw against St Mirren, in a game they needed to win to take the title. It was then I witnessed the most ecstatic response I had ever seen a manager make. When the word broke to him that the title was theirs, Fergie took off. He started to sprint. It was like a man chased by a swarm of wasps, frantic and at first sight aimlessly, until you realised he was heading for the sizeable Aberdeen support at that end, and where I was to witness the original blast-off for an ascension that would lift him almost to the status of demi-God by the time he left football management forever, 33 years later.

For all that he sounded, at first, like he was in an advanced state of delirium, his more rational state surfaced when I interviewed him and he was able to remind me that it had been 15 years since a provincial club outside the Old Firm had won the title. Pride oozed out of him. I wondered if he could ever exceed that moment of nirvana in his career, little realising he was only warming up.

In the next six years, from the day of that Easter Road celebration, those boot-room dalliances were supplemented domestically when Fergie and his wife Cathy would meet with us occasionally and when he was in our vicinity would sit in my house until the wee sma' hours talking about life in general. I had the audacity to believe that whatever else befell us in future, our working-class roots and the sense of having climbed different ladders, but with a kindred sense of purpose, would underpin any relationship. The winning of the Scottish Cup in 1982, 4–1 in extra-time against Rangers, which put them into the European Cup Winners Cup tournament meant the conversations we had during that campaign took on a new electrifying tone. I missed the earlier rounds but covered the two remarkable games against Bayern Munich, who they beat 3–2 on the night and on aggregate. The following morning I can still see his face saying to me, 'I think we're nearly there.' They were certainly in the semi-final, but I gleaned from that first conversation, after perhaps the most tumultuous night Pittodrie had ever experienced, that he was actually turning his mind to a final in Gothenburg, without being explicit about it.

I watched their hammering of semi-finalists Waterschei in Belgium, 5–1 and the anti-climactic 1–0 defeat at home which aroused his ire, but the reality was that reaching a European final trumped everything. When Real Madrid qualified to meet them in that final I did get the feeling that most of the media privately believed that Aberdeen had come thus far, but would proceed no further, against such distinguished opposition. Now, unfortunately the BBC did not have the contract to cover the European Cup Winners final, but thankfully, working in London for Breakfast Television at that time, they sent me to Gothenburg on 11 May 1983 to send back reports on the game, although the game was beamed live on television throughout Europe.

That night was miserably wet in the Swedish city, in stark contrast to the other Scottish European finals involvements I had experienced in Lisbon and Barcelona. It gave this final the look of a wintry Scottish local derby in January, although slightly warmer. The romantic white shirts of Real lent it credibility, reminding us all that we were clearly within sight of the pinnacle of European football. I had a flexible position in the ground, for as a reporter I could leave my seat and go on to pitch level. Which is what I did when, in palpitating circumstances, Aberdeen were 2–1 up with only five minutes remaining in the extra-time period the game had entered. I could see Fergie in that agonising posture of a man thinking he is betwixt heaven and hell. It affected me as I kept looking down at my watch and following the Italian referee Gianfranco Menegali who looked insufferably indifferent to our anxieties, with time seeming to be deliberately standing still to allow this great Spanish side to redeem its reputation.

Then the final whistle went. Aberdeen had won. Fergie, after being engulfed by his colleagues on the sidelines, rushed on to the pitch, slipping slightly as he went and started to hug Willie Miller in particular. I bided my time. When he turned and came back towards pitch edge he saw me and we hugged. In fact I lifted him off his feet when he threw his arms round me. We were compressed in a moment of mutual relief and celebration, his body almost quivering with joy. In the interview with me about an hour later, he was actually constrained by comparison, as he expressed his thanks to so many who had helped along the way. Ten days later I interviewed him again on a pitch, this time at Hampden at the end of a Scottish Cup final against Rangers, which his side won 1–0 after extra-time. He was to give me one of the most memorable interviews in the history of the of a Cup final, because of its shock effect on me and the vast viewing audience.

'That was a disgraceful performance,' he blasted.

There was a pause as I thought he was about to launch an attack on what he thought was the over-physical tactics of his opponents Rangers. Then he went on.

'If the Aberdeen players think I'm going to accept that standard then I will be looking for new players next season. The only excuse I can make is that they looked knackered and as if they needed a holiday. But I'm still not prepared to accept it.'

He was attacking his own players who had just lifted two trophies in the blink of an eye, as it were. I nearly dropped the microphone after it sunk in what had possessed him. If he hadn't been staring intently at me I might have thought he was jesting. But, no. This was a man obsessed, a perfectionist for whom the lowering of standards was approaching sacrilege. I should have learned a personal lesson from that but instead let it pass by me, with the general acceptance of the rest of the media who thought, 'Ah, well! That's Fergie for you.' The day after, he did make a public apology to his players blaming the stress he had been under in previous weeks for his eruption and by the time I saw him at an end-of-season football awards ceremony shortly after that he was joshing with me in a hearty manner like a victor at his peak, as he certainly was. I vividly recall the day we sat in the boot-room towards the end of his reign when he could look back on massive achievements having won the European Cup Winners Cup, the European Super Cup, three league championships, four Scottish Cups, one Scottish League Cup and a Drybrough Cup and sitting beside him you were fully aware that this man had turned his opposition into Lilliputians. That was the day he opened up to me to verify many of the rumours swirling around him. He told me in a manner that carried both regret and slight contempt when he admitted the Rangers chairman John Paton had once approached him to lure him to Ibrox.

'How could I go back and not sign Catholics? What would I tell my friends who are Catholics? "You lot aren't good enough for us!" I just couldn't do that,' he told me.

He had always felt that marrying a Catholic had led to a lack of affection for him from within the Ibrox boardroom and may have expedited his exit from the club after his Cup final misjudgement. I felt privileged to have been offered a verification of the rumours, and of course was a strong supporter of the SFA's ultimate decision to appoint him temporary Scotland manager after the tragic pitchside death of Jock Stein on 10 September 1985. The World Cup in Mexico beckoned for him the following year.

My first interview with him there was placid. You could tell he was feeling his way carefully and he deliberately skirted around the growing controversy about Kenny Dalglish's decision not to be included in the squad, because of injury as he stated and the non-inclusion of his Liverpool team-mate Alan Hansen. It was tempting to link those absences as a deliberate snub, but Fergie resolutely rejected the point I put to him that some English commentators were claiming that he was favouring his own club players, Willie Miller and Alex McLeish. It was the start of a tempestuous time. Defeat to Denmark in the opening game led to the usual recriminations, amplified by the press to such an extent that as a reprisal for some of their comments about the team's accommodation, all of the media were banned from the camp. I managed to get word through to Fergie by shouting to one of the security men that we wanted an interview with the Scottish manager. He responded in such a way that I could only conclude that he gave not a jot what the secretary of the SFA Ernie Walker had commanded and came out to the gates and stood, in full flow, in front of our camera in straight defiance of the people who were paying his wages, prefacing everything with the comment, 'That bloody man won't stop me from talking.'

It was a personal gesture on his part that helped salve some of the disappointments that were to follow – defeat by West Germany 2–1 and that infamous no-scoring draw against Uruguay in the final match after which he ranted about the Uruguayans and said, 'That was a debacle out there. I know we are out of the World Cup but honestly I am glad to be going home because this is no way to play football.' But it also sounded to me like a farewell speech to international football management altogether, having now experienced how so many issues could be beyond the rigid control he could attain in club football. He had other aims in life.

In the early part of season 1986 there was a feeling of post-World Cup depression pervading Scottish football and my visits to Pittodrie were conditioned by the general feeling that Aberdeen would never be the ultimate home for this breathlessly ambitious man. He talked to me about rumours about moves but I gleaned nothing much from the chat.

THE RUPTURE

Then came 18 October 1986. It was such a momentous day for me that I felt like asking people eventually, 'Where were you on that day?' like you would ask those reflecting on the destruction of the World Trade Centre in New York on 11 September 2001, or President

Kennedy's assassination on 22 November 1963. It had that kind of impact – a seemingly average day usurped by the unexpected. When I walked into the old reception area of the old Easter Road that day to verify team selection for the Hibernian–Aberdeen League game before commentary, I was expecting nothing more than the pre-match rituals of asking for team selections and a few words from both managers about their prospects for the day. My defences were down for what actually occurred. In the gloom of that vestibule leading to the tunnel entrance to the pitch, there was a group of figures standing discussing some matter. I paid little attention until one of the figures broke away and came towards me. It was Fergie. He was bawling. His first sentence I have now personally immortalised.

'What the fuck do you know about football?'

It was hardly a rare question directed towards me throughout the decades. But this was uniquely venomous. At first I thought he was addressing someone behind me. But as he came nearer I could see a face contorted not just with rage, but in an almost rictus of pure hatred. And I was unmistakably the target. At first I baulked. I simply had no idea what he was talking about. There had been no storm cones raised between us – ever. Whatever he felt about me privately it never manifested itself other than through a decent relationship and some intimate conversations through the years. But, as he thundered on, I gleaned that he was accusing me of criticising his goalkeeper Jim Leighton, who in midweek had been in goal for Scotland and in my view had been responsible for at least one of the Belgian goals in their 3–2 victory. Over the years I have long mulled over how I felt at the time in facing this verbal blitzkrieg from a man with whom I had shared a genial intimacy many times. The nearest I could think of was as if your own father had slammed the door in your face and told you never to darken the doorstep again. I experienced a 'Who me?' incredulity. My reaction was not just one of shock at hearing this coming from a man I had long admired, but raw anger at being so confronted. Fergie had for long, and justifiably, referred back to his hard working-class upbringing that informed and aided him in his tumultuous career. He was not alone in that respect. I had many a fight round the backcourts off Shettleston Road where I learned the hard way that you had to stand up for yourself. This I certainly had

148

to do then and there. In this case I knew that there was no way back. This was terminal. Nose to nose our saliva and obscenities crossed paths like tracer bullets. It was road-rage brought indoors, although he probably saw it as his Rolls against my Mini. The onlookers including his assistant Archie Knox and the Assistant Chief Constable of the Lothians looked on in stunned amazement – at least at first – at the vemom of the verbal battle.

For it was brought to an abrupt end by the intervention of that high-powered policeman, who sternly warned us that he would take action if we did not desist. Desist we did, he to Aberdeen's dressing room, me to a commentary position feeling a curious triumph that I had stood my ground. However, not for one moment did I believe that that anger stemmed from one incident. His annoyance must have been festering for some time before that and, despite all appearances to the opposite, despite the warmth I was experiencing when previously we had met, he had in fact, been 'nursing his wrath to keep it warm'. And then let blast.

Of course I was never ignorant of the perils of off-field associations with anyone in football if you were to remain of independent mind and express views that might cause offence. Even starting off in the media and wet behind the ears, I wasn't slow to grasp the fact that football managers in general do not react to criticism, of themselves, or players with the tolerance of John the Baptist. And, at that period in history, when Jock Stein commanded at Celtic and Willie Waddell towered over Ibrox, you had to have the kind of courage that Hemingway once described as 'grace under fire'. There was plenty of hellish fire then, to be sure. That is why Fergie ensconced in Pittodrie was a real tonic. He had responded to my appreciation and certainly made me feel at home in the heart of Pittodrie. At which point any student of human behaviour might accuse me of naivete – that in the sensitive nature of competition you could never nurse a real friendship in the football cauldron. On the other hand, you take what you are offered from anyone in life in a relationship and we cannot all be skilled enough to know when we could be drinking from a poisoned chalice.

When Fergie eventually was to be known deservedly as Sir Alex Chapman Ferguson CBE and universally recognised as one of the greatest managers of all time, principally because of his feats while at Old Trafford, I looked with a certain wistfulness at a rose-bowl on an engraved wooden plinth sitting in my living room. It was presented to me by the Aberdeen Supporter's Association in 1983 for having voiced continual encouragement for the team in their triumphant European season. It was Fergie who had prompted them to do so. It is tangible evidence that our chats in the boot-room, sharing gossip, inquests, analyses and a healthy cynicism about the structure of Scottish football, had been with a bonding that went beyond anything else I had ever experienced in the game. The gift still stands there as confirmation of a genuine relationship that could never be dismissed as delusional and a reminder that, at the very least, I had enjoyed the privilege of frequently rubbing shoulders with a man who had seemed, so often, more than a mere mortal.

Sir Alex was always attracted to high class quality. So at my fantasy table he would enjoy the company of Bill McLaren whose distinctive voice set a new tone for commentating and helped me raise my game.

CHAPTER 10

The Hawick Troubadour

IN THE AUTUMN and winter months of 1969/70, Nelson Mandela, imprisoned at that time on Robben Island, noticed his white jailers were becoming more and more agitated in the confines of the prison. They spewed out a greater degree of anger against the inmates, as if some intensification of imprisonment had been decreed from on high. Despite a news blackout there, the jailers, in fact, were responding to the information they were receiving, that not only were the Springboks being beaten on rugby fields all over the UK and Ireland, but that many people there were militantly objecting to their very presence. The detestation of the apartheid regime was being broadcast throughout the world, to their great discomfort. Demonstrations had been held against their presence by anti-apartheid campaigners at Twickenham, Leicester and Newport but erupted into serious violence at Swansea on 15 November 1969. There had been a wholescale pitch invasion and a battle ensued, not just between the police and protesters but by vigilantes, hired for the occasion, whose idea of rough justice led to serious injuries among the protesters.

So when they arrived to play Scotland at Murrayfield three weeks later in the first of their international encounters, the police, realising that the young student rector of Edinburgh University, one Gordon Brown, was organising a hefty protest in the city, they were on high alert. As the *Glasgow Herald* reported, 'Bus loads of reinforcements were brought in from Fife, Lanarkshire and the Lothians, to back up the city force.' Seven-hundred of them were present, in and around the stadium, which was disfigured by the empty terraces behind both goalposts, emptied for security reasons. The commentator for that game was a man who took it all in his stride and for whom, as a fellow broadcaster I had great admiration, Bill McLaren. However, that controversial day was fated to bring us together in unusual circumstances, almost a year later. It was not to be a happy union of minds.

We were both part of a sports panel in front of a live audience for a BBC broadcast, in the baronial splendour of Drumlanrig Castle just north of Dumfries. As I reflect on the arguments that emerged that night, even after all that time, I still interpret it as a clash of cultures and not just a divergence of views on the presence of the Springboks in our country. It really stemmed from our respective origins.

I had first encountered the Hawick man inside the old BBC building in Queen Margaret Drive. There, in a corridor of that former art gallery, which could induce an immediate hush and careful footfall when you entered, like you were trying to avoid standing on eggshells, he stopped me in the passing and asked me, surprisingly, who I thought was going to win the Scottish First Division that season. This was in 1963. He was full of bonhomie, the voice resplendent and although I was not aware of it at that time, an inspiring example of survival against TB which had attempted to destroy his left lung as a younger man. I was slightly in awe of him. He was, even by the early 1960s, an internationally recognised commentator whose voice, once heard, could never be forgotten. Indeed, I have to say that he is one of the few people I encountered in broadcasting whose voice seemed to fit my preconceived image of the man. So many others failed to match. To me, he simply looked as he sounded. In his day the painter Naismith would have portrayed him as a sturdy Scot with a kindly but resolute profile, mirroring the avuncular baritone tones of his commentaries. A dominie with a kind heart, as he actually was.

But, from that first meeting all the way through the next 40 years, Bill McLaren was a presence that always hovered around me whenever I put a mic to the lips. His name was used constantly in the corridors of the BBC and indeed out in the streets, as if it represented the gold standard of commentating. As a fellow commentator it was like having a stalker after you, with a query constantly in the ear, 'Well, you've managed the Munros, but could you take on Everest?' Clearly it was believed Bill had achieved that and you were left feeling you were still striving in the lower foothills. On a very personal basis though our relationship, although mostly distant, was based purely on genuine mutual respect, even though we promoted different sports and were entirely different personalities.

In the early 1960s it was not as if we had much time to sit down together and discuss profound matters in Scottish sport, for at that stage Bill, firmly established though he was in the public firmament, seemed a furtive figure to me. All the BBC correspondents would rush in with their reports, for whatever sports they covered on a Saturday afternoon and if they did not retire to the BBC club for a drink and a chat afterwards, they would rush back out again. Bill was a 'rusher', no drinker. As he travelled from Hawick to all parts of the central-belt of the country to cover significant games, he would often return to the BBC in Glasgow to report on radio and television and then rush back to Hawick, 'like the deil was on my tail', as he once said to me. Nevertheless, we would bump into each other occasionally in the corridors, or in a more luxurious moment in the BBC canteen, as he took a quick coffee or tea, before his young Lochinvar journey back to his adored Borders.

Bill was always encouraging to this newcomer whenever we met, however briefly. Nor was he ignorant of the world of football and could quiz me avidly about the background to some of the controversies in my sport that he was fully aware of. So much so, that at one stage the sports editor of BBC Scotland Peter Thomson, once aired the view, very loudly to all and sundry around, that Bill would make a perfectly fine football commentator and wondered if he could persuade him to cover both codes. I have no knowledge of words ever being exchanged in that matter, nor did I ask Bill at any time if he had any conversation on that. Such a conversion would have been as stunning as hearing he had uprooted himself and moved to live in Gala.

Before then his landscape had been as far distant from me as Middle-earth in *The Lord of the Rings*. I knew that they spoke a different language down there, especially when they talked about that 15-a-side game which was woven into their culture, as if from some heavenly loom and as distinctive as the cloth that was harvested in their mills. It seemed by common consent they had the best rugby players on the planet, particularly if they came from Gala or Hawick. To hear a report on Scottish rugby, on radio in my youth, without a prominent mention of these two towns, was like hearing an Atlantic shipping forecast without mention of Rockall or Fastnet. I reckoned they must be the Old Firm of the rugby world. I recall mentioning that analogy once to Bill, a Hawick fundamentalist, whose gentle reprimand was a reminder that I resided within the stockade of Glasgow insularity. No, he made clear that his 'ain midden' drew no comparisons with any other place in the planet. That 'toon' rivalry was like no other. What came over to me, perhaps simplistically, was a game down there that was more egalitarian, more in touch with the daily rhythm of life, the game of the commoner as opposed to that of the privileged. What is more, Bill did not resemble the 'rugby type' to which I had become accustomed in the West of Scotland.

For I admit I was heavily laden with a resilient bias. I disliked the penumbra of class distinction that seemed to surround the rugby culture. Raised in the east end of Glasgow, rugby was as alien to me as the Eton Wall Game and carried the same cachet of privilege that was consolidated by those posh private schools I heard about in distant parts of my city. These institutions normally provided the educational background of the Tory candidates who would face the largely fruitless task of standing for election among the grey tenements of my neighbourhood, thus underlining for me the social chasm that existed between the round and oval ball. Of course, some state schools did have rugby teams but they were few and far between and I imagined, only set up for those boys ungainly enough not to be able to trap a round ball with either foot, and only made possible by having at least one teacher in the staff brave enough to take on the task. I particularly resented those schools which excluded football from their sports agenda, as if they wished to demonstrate they were banishing an inferior ethic. I equated it with any censorship of books imposed on a school library. Of course, the mandarins of private education were not slow to point out what they perceived to be the crudities of the football culture. And the Old Firm, in particular, were not slow in providing them with plenty material to convince the fee-paying parents that kicking a ball about was the road to perdition.

THE DEBATE

All of which provided a background to that night at Drumlanrig Castle where the issue of sporting protests against the Springboks was raised by the audience to the panel. I relished the opportunity. As a former anti-apartheid campaigner in my student days I made my case against the acceptance of playing against a team which represented an immoral political system. Bill pounced on me. I could see that he was particularly disturbed by the support I voiced for the Black Power salute by Tommie Smith and John Carlos at the Mexico Olympics in 1968, a precursor, perhaps, of 'Taking the Knee'. Bill, in almost school-masterly tones, rebuked me for my opinions. There was no place for politics in sport, no matter the great sympathy there might be for the downtrodden black people of South Africa. Sport was sacrosanct. Players deserved to get on with their games without interference. I could tell he was quite shocked by my views. But his lucid and persuasive argument carried the night. Indeed the applause of this predominantly middle-class audience in support of what he was saying, began to make me feel like a Trotskyist who had blundered his way into a meeting of the Women's Rural Institute. Frankly, I think his voice alone would have carried the day as I sensed it carried the sound of familiarity that rang with affection in their ears. On my own part I was surprised at the level of hostility he displayed which echoed some of the thoughts of the hardliners within the South African rugby community. A sudden and chilling distance had been created between us. I recall driving back north actually regretting that we had been sucked into this in the first place and that we could well have done without it and that in a way it seemed irreparable. I need not have worried. For it narrowed considerably though, a few years later, to such an extent that it might even have been called a bonding. It came through a blend of two factors – the professionalism of broadcasting itself and a sincere love of country. This took place in, of all places, Twickenham. It all sprang from the consequences of a game at Murrayfield which provoked new thinking within our department, entrenched as it was in feeding a regular diet of football to the public through *Sportscene*. It was the Scotland–Wales encounter of 1 March of 1975 which turned minds away, if only temporarily, from our slavish devotion to the people's game. That contest, the setting, the outcome, the consequences, were all remarkable on that grey Edinburgh afternoon. It was tumultuous. From the top camera shot the crowd looked so immensely packed inside Murrayfield, you had to wonder how anybody could breathe down there, let alone give vent to any emotion. Occasionally those sitting outside the perimeter wall looked as if they might invade the pitch, for their own safety and not just from rejoicing at the sight of Scotland's Dougie Morgan and Ian McGeechan using their feet to score three penalties and a drop goal respectively to amass 12 points. These supporters exercised massive self-restraint that might not have been in the instinct of a football crowd. Only for a time though. Nor could we have anticipated a climax that might been written for the pages of the *Hotspur*. It went like this.

Wales score a brilliant try four minutes into injury time. There are only seconds left to take the conversion which will end the game in a frustrating draw. The Welshman Alan Martin has to attempt it from close to the right touchline. There is some derisive whistling by the Scottish supporters, purportedly to detract the kicker – a tendency which, alongside booing, would eventually be denounced by the purist Bill, with the severity of Moses denouncing the worship of the fatted calf. Martin seems unconcerned. But his kick sweeps past the outside of the post and bedlam ensues, with the almost overdue pitch invasion taking place, like a stay snapping in a too-tight corset, in the realisation that in their 12–10 victory only Scotland can now win the Triple Crown. And it would be at Twickenham on 15 March 1975.

I had suspected, in the months leading up to Wales visiting Murrayfield in March, that the Scottish public in general, including perhaps those extremists from my code, who would rather trawl through Marks and Spencers with the wife than watch the Calcutta Cup, were beginning to be aroused by the performances of the Scottish side. When the attendance on that Saturday was announced officially as 104,000, it not only was recognised immediately as a world record for a rugby match which would last until the year 2000, when 109,874 watched the All Blacks beat Australia in the Stadium Australia in Sydney, but shocked many in the football world who had long boasted of its massive crowds in Glasgow. It's also logical to think that Murrayfield might just have been lucky since this was only four years after 66 people had been crushed to death on Staircase 13 at Ibrox at an Old Firm match. But, something intriguing was happening to the Scottish sporting psyche which was influenced by the fact that Scotland had just ended an 11 year winless run against Wales. It prompted Ian Archer, reporting on the match, but a football man to his toenails, to write in the *Glasgow Herald* on the Monday morning,

> This was not a regular rugby crowd. To its usual numbers were added many who on other days might never have considered giving Ibrox, Parkhead, Tynecastle or Easter Road a miss – but who are now anxious to sample the Murrayfield atmosphere. The whole spectrum of sporting Scotland was there, sardine-like on the terraces.

But still one game short of the Triple Crown.

Part of the reason for the growing acceptance of rugby in the living rooms around the land was Bill McLaren himself. Rugby could be an impenetrable game to those who were not aficionados. Many viewers would watch a maul developing, like the tangling of two large octopuses, all arms and legs, and without any sense of coherence, until Bill's authoritative but unfussy voice unpicked the complexity, like an Egyptologist translating hieroglyphics for us. That was one of the major ingredients of his appeal to the British public, in conjunction with his impeccable impartiality when the inner Scottish voice must have been screaming 'Hallelujah', from time to time, at a Scottish success or, on the other hand and perhaps more often, cleverly disguising his misery.

I thought the mood was therefore ripe for us to relegate football to a subsidiary role in our programme and give rugby the prominence that it duly deserved for such an event. The way to do that was to take all our resources to London for the occasion and broadcast our evening programme from Twickenham in recognition of the historic occasion and hopefully capture the celebrations. A gamble certainly, but the idea was accepted by the hierarchy, since Bill, above all, gave it his blessing. So, to set the scene for what promised to be an epic game, we decided to travel to Hawick, the week before, to record on camera his thoughts about the forthcoming fixture. And, in any case, I needed my visa of public acceptance at Twickenham stamped by the Voice of Rugby.

THE HAWICK INTERVIEW

Bill had just come from playing at his local golf course with his wife Bette. He eased himself into a chair in the lounge and given my switch from a crowded and clamorous Glasgow, into this idyllic part of the world, I could not resist the image of him as a laird just having returned from pacing his estate. It was a wholly revealing day. For Bill was so different from my conception of what the rugby animal was like, that after this meeting I almost felt queasy about holding my rigid views on his sport. The archangel Gabriel could not have done a better job than he of convincing me that, in essence, I had been too readily blinded to the similarities in our differing codes. His couthy conversation about team spirit, conviction, inspiration, leadership were easily translatable into football chat and had nothing to do with social structure, but more about how, when it came to it, we tilled the same soil, for the same sense of accomplishment in a team game, regardless of the shape of the ball. After all he was from Borders Rugby – with huge capital letters – and so different from that uppity rugby world of Former Pupils that was so alien to me.

For the first time I was learning that he was as besotted as much by golf, as he was by rugby. I could hardly get him stopped talking about his favourite courses. He recited a list of them he and his wife played regularly, and was at pains to extol the challenges and beauty of Gullane, as if he and Bette kept renewing their vows on those special links. It was good that he was warming to my presence although I was there to talk about his first love and a very special day. He switched with ease eventually and flowed into his rugby mode, where it became clear he was a proud traditionalist, calmly revealing his devotion to the traditions of rugby. It was like being back in bible class as he expounded the virtues of the amateur game and the purity of playing just for the love of it, in a tone and line of argument that was difficult to rebut, playing on the fact that deep down we are all lovers of the amateur in any sport. His argument was that the game that he was devoted to was a blend of interests of equal merit – the selectors, the coaches, the captains, the players – all of them contributing to self-beneficial togetherness. A manager of the ilk of Stein, Waddell, Ferguson was quite unnecessary.

And, at that moment in Hawick in 1975, the world that Bill was describing seemed intact and imperishable. It was denoted in his assured tones that distanced his culture from the surging tide of commercialisation impinging on all sports. It simply couldn't happen to rugby, he seemed to be saying. But in 1971, four years before my visit to the Borders, the IOC had decided to eliminate the term 'amateur' from the Olympic Charter. It was not simply about semantics though. For at the same time they also legitimised the sponsorship of athletes by NOCS, sports organisations and private businesses. It was in fact the veritable opening of the Pandora's Box that was to spread the contagion – as Bill would certainly have seen it – remorselessly throughout the sporting world. So I believe it was delving into the rugby world of his youth that indicated why radical change in his sport was something anathema to his nature.

For midway through the interview his face seemed to become burnished by a sheen of vivid recollection, his eyes seemingly looking beyond me, as if he was being hailed by a distant voice. He was telling me of how he had been affected by a famous victory and the elation he must have felt at the time was revealed in only three words from within his narrative, 'I was there!' He was talking about the last time Scotland had won the Triple Crown, on Saturday 9 March 1938, in that very same stadium in south-west London. I was reliving that day with him. In print, on a page, I can do no justice to his rhythmic retelling of an unforgettable day in his life, but it is certainly worth the attempt. Just entering his teens he had taken that long, arduous train journey with family to watch the game. Although he did speak about it on camera, it was sincere but brief, since we had prospects for the coming fixture to consider above all. But, off-camera at the end, in his own inimitable way he conjured up a scene of a young Hawick boy, in his early teens, bewildered by the vastness of this city,

the size of the crowd, the spectacular sight of Twickenham, the pum-
melling of his nerves and his description of a try – a famous try – by
a man, whose name clearly could never have left his consciousness
through his entire lifetime, Wilson Shaw.

It was his description of Shaw's try I will always recall, in that
Hawick lounge 37 years on from that London day. The Scottish
captain had won the game for his side with an electrifying dash,
with only two minutes remaining. He painted a picture of a swift,
jinking, pacey player of genius, side-stepping and body-swerving
opponents to touch down near the corner flag and win the game
for his country, in debatably the most dramatic try ever scored by
a Scot. The Calcutta Cup and the Triple Crown had been secured,
21–16. There was also a wistful note of regret though when he
reminded me that it was the last time Scotland would play there
until after the Second World War, which was only a year away.
It was a reminder of how life would change dramatically for him,
for in that very month of March in 1938 the Germans enacted
the infamous *Anschluss* with the invasion of Austria and its eventual annexation. A process whose ultimate chain of events would
propel the young Hawick lad into the armed forces four years
later, and put him, as a lieutenant, into the front line of one of
the most savage battles of the European campaign, the assault on
Monte Cassino.

TWICKERS

But he could not hide a concern about the forthcoming Calcutta
Cup. For from the time shortly before the First World War when
Twickenham became the home of English rugby, Scotland had only
won there on three occasions, 1926, 1938 and 1971. The longest
winless run of any country at a rival's home ground in the 134 year
history of the championship. None of the existing squad had been
born the last time Scotland had won at Twickenham. It was the kind
of persistent failure that can turn into a self-generated belief, for any
team in these circumstances, that a jinx hovers over them. I recall
him mentioning that very word. So, for Scotland to win again in

the year 1975, after such a long time would be like transporting the BBC commentator back to his boyhood, and deep down throughout that game, it seemed clear to me he would be wishing for another Wilson Shaw to emerge, without a hint of that inclination ever being revealed to his audience of millions.

And, indeed, there were millions. This Triple Crown challenge had caught the imagination of the British public in a major way. A mood reflected by the interest of the BBC who were to televise a rugby game live for the first time, one week before their first ever live coverage of a football match. In Scotland the mood was particularly intense, for hadn't England lost their three previous championship matches? Were they not ripe for picking then? That notion was gathering steam. But as a regular attender at that other London venue, Wembley, I was as confident of making predictions in games against the Auld Enemy as I would be attempting to cross Niagara on a tightrope. Nevertheless, around Twickenham that afternoon there was no disguising the optimism of the many Scots attending. They had not 'taken over' the stadium, as was the natural equation of Wembley where the 'invaders' normally outnumbered the natives, but they were plentiful.

That nervous knot in the stomach was there with all its gnawing familiarity as I waited for kick-off, not just because I was about to see Scottish colours take on a historic task, but also because I badly needed a win personally, for having convinced everyone we just had to be here for the event, away from our conventional *Sportscene* setting. I had clamped the headphones to my ears so I could listen to every word Bill spoke to the multitudes. Whatever was to happen on the field it would lead me to the line of interviews after the game. But, unknown to Bill and myself, something unique had happened in the Scottish dressing room prior to their entrance onto the field, which was a harbinger of the changes to come in the game and contradictory to the man from Hawick's conception of tradition. To get the full story of that I traced one of Scotland's outstanding forwards Ian McLauchlan, 'Mighty Mouse', to the island of Islay where he is in retirement from a successful business career and with whom I had many lively broadcasting interviews in the past. He told me of a dressing room achievement of which he was naturally proud.

'I captained Scotland for the first time in that Murrayfield game against Wales when we had that record crowd. I was determined to stamp my own authority on the side but there was a problem I had to overcome. At that time the team was picked by the committee. In essence they were in charge. Twickenham for them was their week-end away in London. Now Hector Monro was the President of the RFU at that time. And a very good one at that. So when I captained that first game I approached him and said that I would want the committee to leave the dressing room before I gave my team-talk. He said to me, "Are you sure about that because they won't like it?" I said that's what I wanted. So that day at Murrayfield Hector came down to the dressing room and sat down on a bench and wished the lads good luck and then turned to the committee and told them to leave. I don't think he had forewarned them, for they were aston-ished. But after a moment or two they realised it was the President talking to them and they headed for the door. But the last man going out turned and said aloud about me. "You know of course, that if we lose today, he'll never play for Scotland again!" We won, of course.'

So Mighty Mouse's team-talk in the absence of the selection committee, minutes before the Triple Crown challenge, contained a realisation of the physical menace that was in store for his side as the England coach John Burgess, in the spirit of the Duke of Cumber-land, the butcher of Culloden, had stated in advance, 'I've seen this Scottish pack rucking. If it's blood on their boots they want, that's what they'll get.' In the days before, I had interviewed one of Scot-land's great maulers, Nairn MacEwan, who had made a name for himself for travelling weekly between his home in Inverness and his club Gala, before he established the local side Highland as a force in rugby. He knew what was coming, he told me. And came it did, in exactly two minutes. In a maul I saw MacEwan go down holding his face. His jaw had been broken. Bill McMurtrie could not deliberately cast aspersions in his Monday morning article in the *Glasgow Her-ald* but, in his clinical description, left the reader to draw their own conclusions, when he wrote:

> Scotland lost MacEwan in a fearsome opening by England. He had to go to hospital and two other Scots had to have prolonged attention on the field, McHarg and Steele. The lock was dazed, the winger later had to have stitches in a cut ear.

I felt a plummeting depression when I saw MacEwan leave the field. As Ian McLauchlan admitted to me, 'His going off so soon really upset our plans.' You did not need to be deeply into rugby to feel that this was a seminal moment. It carried with it a sense of dislocation. This wasn't supposed to be in the script. Bill, high up on his commentary platform, sounded non-plussed to me, taking it all in his stride, although deep down I have to suppose he must have been paining like me. The crowd around seemed cheery, which probably was not such a good sign. There were ruffles of displeasure when Scotland scored with two penalties by Dougie Morgan, to an English penalty by Bennett and to lead 6–3 just into the second half. But, in that half, expectations nose-dived. Almost literally so, when Andy Irvine, Scotland's full-back and the English winger Alan Morley raced for the ball which a punt forward placed it over the Scottish touchline. It was a controversial moment, which Ian McLauchlan has barely recovered from in all that time.

'To this day Andy swears blind that he touched the ball before Morley. The referee was so far away from that incident but awarded the try to England.'

Bill did not question a decision that even VAR might not have clarified. If that was not enough, from where I was sitting and listening to Bill, as the game neared its end, Dougie Morgan stepped up to take another penalty which would have won the game. It was astonishing that he was able to commentate without emitting a sob as the ball sailed past the outside of the posts. So the mythical Triple Crown seemed even more mythical, to any Scot, as the referee pulled down the shutters on the game at 7–6 to the Auld Enemy. Having originated the idea of broadcasting from Twickenham, in the first place, I felt the defeat as badly as anything I had ever suffered at Wembley. What made matters worse were when some inebriated English Hooray Henrys, who had infiltrated our broadcasting area, began to hurl cushions at us to disturb the recording of the programme for later that night. Cushions, no less! It was so Twickenham!

Meeting Bill afterwards was like sharing unspoken grief, as we were too adult to whimper, but inwardly feeling like that, even though deporting ourselves with dignity as befits a wake. Scotland had lost and it hurt us both. There had been no 'Wilson Shaw try' or anything like it but the British public would not have detected even a trace of disappointment in Bill's voice as he had mastered the situation with customary aplomb. As for my own position, I was now having to introduce a programme from a site that I had encouraged BBC Scotland to accept, but whose value was now almost negated by crushing anti-climax. I felt that offering it to the Scottish public would be like offering a burnt sirloin to epicures. Metaphorically we did it through clenched teeth.

Although I did not meet Bill again for years, I felt that the memory of clashing at Drumlanrig Castle had been supplanted by the Twickenham experience. We had so much more in common. His life though, brushed against mine in distant but curiously tangible ways. Firstly, his BBC producer for his international commentaries was Bill Taylor, my closest friend at school in Coatbridge. He kept me apace of working with the man, in glowing terms, almost like he was talking of his own father. Then, while I was working at national events in radio I sometimes broadcast alongside Bill's son-in-law Derek Thompson. He was an excellent broadcaster, with a sumptuous voice, but his lifestyle, to say the least, did not seem to chime with the Presbyterian rectitude of Hawick from whence his wife Janie had emerged. I never met her but I was not surprised to hear eventually that the marriage collapsed, to the great distress of Bill, particularly as he knew, as others did, his daughter had been faultless in her marital relationship. Then in 2002 I was attending the Open Championship at Muirfield and came across Peter Brown, the former Scottish rugby captain with three Calcutta Cup victories to his credit in that role, a Muirfield member and acting as a steward at the event. He told me that Janie had died of cancer and that Bill and his wife Bette were so deeply stricken they were finding it difficult to cope with life. Brown, a devout Christian himself, then said to me, in unforgettably grave tones, 'Bill says he's lost his faith.' The former Scottish captain sounded as if he felt an anchor in his life had come loose, because

Bill, virtually in all respects, exemplified steadfastness to those who knew him well and also to his audience, who were attracted to his cool and unemotional analysis set against the turmoil of a rugby field. I have no knowledge of how Bill worked through that spiritual dilemma but simply record that incident to show how traumatic his daughter's death had been to him.

We were never to meet again, although we were supposed to. We should have come together on the stage of a hotel in Glasgow in 2005 to receive lifetime awards from the Scottish branch of BAFTA. But his Alzheimer's condition was so advanced by then that he had ceased to comprehend much of life around him and couldn't attend. He was to die five years later. By that time his beloved game had been 'open' for 15 years, prompting Rob Andrew, England's professional rugby director to reflect to the *Guardian* in August 2015 that, 'It was like the Wild West when the game went professional. No one had a clue what we were worth.'

If Bill had been able to broadcast in that cowboy-like world he would surely have filled the role of the kindly preacher man. And I have little doubt he would have commented with enthusiasm on 9 June 2018 when Siya Kolisi led out the Springboks as their first ever black captain. I am equally sure it would have contained that signature acclamation of his, 'They'll be dancing in the streets of Soweto tonight!'

So why not put Bill next to the man who made many in the city of Dundee dance in the streets for him? Jim McLean, anyway, thought many of his opponents should have been playing in Bill's sport.

CHAPTER 11

The Wise Man From The East

IT WAS ON Braid's Brawest, that idyllic fairway on the King's Course at Gleneagles that I was made to feel like a fugitive. It was in the early 1970s. As I ventured to take a 5-wood to the green, I was being accused, by one of the foursome, of being part of the media whose tunnel vision of Scottish football failed to look beyond the city boundaries of Glasgow. Purely by chance – as I thought – I had been placed in this foursome, in a golf outing sponsored by a brewery, which had assembled some worthies of the media to mix with golf-inclined football managers and players. It was a genuine attempt at fraternisation which, nevertheless, carried the risk that Shakespeare took, in bringing together the Montagues and the Capulets on the same stage. I suppose the brewer imagined that golf could neutralise any hard feelings, quite ignoring the competitive instinct which some managers take into their very sleep and who have decidedly long memories on matters which irk them. For myself, I thought the only confrontation would be in settling how many I took to get out of the rough at any time. I was wrong. Thinking back to that outing, I am reminded of the writer Hilaire Belloc's recollection of something that blotted out all other pictures in his mind, when he wrote, 'I can't remember the name of the restaurant. I can't remember the name of the girl. But the wine was Gevrey-Chambertin.' Of that day, I can't remember the name of the brewer. I can't remember the names of the other two in the group. But the fourth man was Jim McLean, the manager of Dundee United.

I could hardly ever forget his intense presence and his desire to get things off his chest, as golf became only a sub-text to the main drift of the chat which was about Scottish football. And it was there on the 13th hole, moving down to where my ball lay hidden and never to be found again, that he was lambasting the media's obsession with the Old Firm and that we were in cahoots with the administrators to ensure that nothing much would ever change in the structure of the game. Incisive, biting words to that effect. I pleaded innocence of course and made my case, but I could see he was as impressed by that as he was by my frequent hooking.

I have to pinpoint here what Jim's status was at that juncture in his career. He had recently taken over as manager of Dundee United from Jerry Kerr, whose management style had stabilised United and greatly boosted their credibility. Although, it has to be said, did not necessarily endear them to the power brokers in football, who felt they contributed practically nothing to the dynamic of Scottish football, even though they could proudly boast of home and away victories over the holders of the Inter-Cities Fairs Cup, Barcelona, in 1966 in the first round of that competition.

So, what on earth was this former inside forward of average attainment as a player and recent first team coach for that other club down the street from Tannadice Park, going to achieve with an unfashionable club, of modest attendances and flimsy finances? Not much, I thought, in common with most observers in the business. Indeed, on reaching the 19th watching Jim sip his non-alcoholic beverage, in between regaling us with his views, I was trying to be politely, attentively deaf to it all. My attitude resided in the question, who was this wee man from a provincial club up there in the east to tell me anything about our business? He would probably be out on his ear in a couple of seasons anyway, if not before.

My assessment of Jim McLean during that golf outing, was as prescient as the Hollywood talent scout who utterly dismissed Fred Astaire with the withering assessment, 'Can't act. Slightly bald. Also dances.'

I had only met Jim once before then. It had been abrupt and curiously painful, like when you accidentally bump your funny bone. It was at Ibrox in 1972 just after Rangers had brought home the European Cup Winners Trophy from Barcelona. I knocked on the United dressing room door, as I normally did, to elicit the team selection for the game which was normally handed to me as the match commentator which, of course, all added to my sense of importance. It was answered by a wee man in shirtsleeves with a quizzical look on his face who told me that I was not getting his selection because I would probably go and blurt it out to Jock Wallace, the Rangers manager and furthermore I had been talking crap about his team in my last programme, and then shut the door in my face.

This had never happened before, even with Jock Stein. So how dare he? Who was this little-known upstart having the temerity to send the BBC packing? What I could not have realised at the time was that this was not gratuitous obduracy, but a man who had planned out that day meticulously and part of which was keeping Rangers in the dark about how he would set out his stall. Then a year later came that day at Gleneagles, that evokes memories of all that followed – of the many games, many adventures, many challenges and of that significant afternoon I would force him to put alcohol to his lips, for the first time, in celebration of a historic triumph.

Out of politeness, what I did not tell him that day was of how much the odds were stacked against him. In 1973 I interviewed Tom Hart, the chairman and owner of Hibs who could be crudely belligerent in his role as a power broker. He was a central figure in the moves to form a new elitist ten club Premier Division. His lip almost curled with disdain when he mentioned Dundee United. He spoke about them like they were from the Romany community deemed not worthy of pitching their caravans on his patch. After all, they had voted against the move to reconstruct the league. He must have had some personal dislike for some of the people on their board because you were left feeling that United was run by a firm of undertakers. Indeed, some of United's critics at the time would facetiously describe the board as the 'Tannadice Glee Club'. Sadly, for Jim, at that stage Hart was not alone in his view. The facts spoke brutally.

Seven days before United went off to play the 1974 Scottish Cup final against Celtic, an achievement in itself as the club's first final since 1940, beaten by Rangers in the Scottish War Emergency Cup, they attracted only 3,800 at home. In the previous game against Partick Thistle, it had been 2,700. Jim, in later years, when he spoke to me about those times admitted that he was in deep despair about the lack of response. Dundee's *Sporting Post* had warned as early as 1973 after Andy Gray, the club's rampaging and courageous striker, had scored four goals in a 6–0 win over Dumbarton, watched by only 3,500, that, 'It would be a tragedy if such attendances would force them to sell Andy Gray.' After all in that final 1974/75 season of the old league, Gray was equal top goalscorer with Willie Pettigrew of Motherwell with 20 goals and inevitably in October of 1975 he was sold to Aston Villa, but only after he had been largely instrumental in securing United's place in the new condensed ten club Scottish Premier Division – to the disapproval of some of its founding members. United's membership though came close to being a one season wonder.

There are two images that stay with me which encapsulate the breadth of United's achievements. One was of the first season's final day at Ibrox on 4 May 1976, with United requiring to avoid defeat to stay in the elitist league. The other, a missed chance in a foreign city years later that might have cost them a European trophy. Watching Hamish McAlpine, the United goalkeeper, with five minutes remaining, hitting the post with a penalty against Rangers and then rushing back to his goalmouth like a stag pursued by the hunt, succeeding to secure a goalless draw, merges in my mind with the scene, eight years later, in Rome. It was there I saw a United player balloon the ball over the bar from a favourable position that might have taken United into the European Cup final. These indelible pictures illustrate the tale of a modern odyssey of a football club that awakened Europe to the city of the Broons and Desperate Dan.

In 2003, after he had severed all ties with United, he agreed to talk to me in his home about his time with the club, for a television documentary that regrettably did not eventually come to fruition. His tone was remorseful. Regrets came forth like he was emptying them from a packed suitcase after an eternity on the hoof. At times I almost felt embarrassed at his eagerness to bare his soul, especially as I had become accustomed to dealing with a man constantly wary of people resisting any attempt at familiarity. I told him I used the Scottish Cup final of 4 May 1974 as a baseline from which I could measure how extraordinary the next 22 years would be for himself and United. It was not because they recruited new admirers that day. Celtic, who had just completed their ninth successive league championship, defeated them 3–0, apparently without breaking sweat. Ian Archer was in total agreement with me when he summed up the contest in the *Glasgow Herald*: 'This was not a great final on the field. Celtic were drab by their own high standards and United diffident to the point of invisibility.'

According to what I could see they would never be any more than a provincial side who would fill the role of sacrificial lambs for the more powerful. They seemed ripe for bullying in any crunch. That would be their lot in life. But, of course, I knew little then of the resolve and the technical ability that resided in the grey matter of the lad born amongst a culture of self-reliance and gritty resilience to the quirks of life, in industrial Lanarkshire, almost 40 years before.

When I talked to him after that 1974 final, on the pitch, he gave me a brisk technical analysis of what went wrong with his side, the first of many frank interviews with him, which would have been more effective with the public had he not sounded so often like he felt like jumping into the Tay and ending it all. I would come away from his interviews perplexed that a man, who was attempting to tell home truths that were eminently worth listening to, could not find the panache of his good friend, but keen rival, Alex Ferguson, who, whatever he faced up to never sounded like a phone call to the Samaritans would be the next step. For instance, a couple of years after that scare at Ibrox, I met with Jim at Tannadice to talk about a forthcoming game. Somewhere in the middle of the chat he suddenly launched an attack on the new league structure, like his very life depended on it.

'Ten clubs are in the league. But two of them will never be relegated. Celtic and Rangers. The other eight are just fighting to avoid relegation. So what happens? It becomes negative. Fear of the drop dominates everything. And if you're thinking like that it becomes a fight. I want a league of up to 16 or even 18. Do you get attractive football in this one? Look at Graham Payne. He's a skilled wee player, but he's getting kicked off the park, every week. Play the ball through the middle? I'm going to go long, definitely long. No way am I going to get my players to keep passing through the middle. That's what this league has brought me to.'

In actual fact it didn't. We were then at the birth of a United who would go on to play an exciting passing game at pace. He simply wanted to be heard as a voice of sanity in an over-commercialised world, where the purity of the game was being tarnished by an incestuous elite who disregarded the general health of the game, and he knew I was providing him with the best platform to sound off to a weekly audience of millions on a Saturday night on BBC. The trouble is, he sounded too often like the character who appeared on the Scotch and Wry comedy show after *Sportscene*, the *Reverend I.M. Jolly*, although lacking Rikki Fulton's caricaturing ability to generate laughs. Nevertheless, I would travel all the way back to Glasgow utterly convinced, that in his long talks with me, I was privy to one of the most radical thinkers in the game who was a source of enlightenment, superior to anything I was hearing within Parkhead or Ibrox, whose regular domination simply encouraged complacent orthodox thinking – at least in the mid-1970s.

ON THE WAY UP

But from the early part of the next season when they topped the league for the opening 12 weeks, I began to see more of him in the number of times I followed United in Scotland and later around Europe, as they began to make more headlines and fill our screens more regularly. Here I have to stress I learned much about him through my friendship with Dundee journalists who would have to deal with him daily or weekly and over whom he held sway like the potentate of small feudal community. The phrase, 'Wee Jim', would spill from their lips almost with apprehension, as if anything they said would get back to his ears. In that respect you could liken that to the effect Stein had on the media in his first years at Celtic Park. So I had to balance my own views of his dealings with me, against those of the local journalists, who were not slow to add to my knowledge of the man.

I had to listen to a litany of criticisms about his erratic behaviour, his rages, his harsh treatment of some journalists and the stories they heard from the dressing room from players who would admit that his blatant tyranny in there did not preclude them from playing out of their skins for him. Maurice Malpas, that outstanding defender, summarised for me the oddest of relationships:

'We linked up against him in a way. We wanted to protect each other and the way we could be shielded from his anger was to go out and play for each other and win. He might have known that that was a good psychological ploy for him. It certainly worked.'

It was an astonishing mix. I had heard nothing like it before. I actually felt that some journalists believed I was being duped – that I didn't know the real Jim McLean they had to deal with. In the times I wined and dined in their company they were building up the picture for me, of a highly talented ogre. Consequently, I would always approach Jim with the caution of a bomb squad approaching a suspect package. One misstep and I was for it, so they were suggesting. I tried though to feed him some cues to break away from the rigours of football in the hope of reaching some sort of rapport. He wasn't really having it. For instance, in 1978, United comprehensively beat Rangers 3–0 at Tannadice – the first victory over them there in nine years and the first time they had scored against them at home in seven attempts since the inception of the new league. You could not easily forget the jubilation in the home crowd that followed.

So when I talked to him afterwards it was the first time I had heard genuine enthusiasm in his voice as he was in full spate rightly praising his players. Then, as he was about to walk away, I asked him if he would go out on the town that night to celebrate the noted event. The shutters suddenly came down. 'No,' he replied, like I had just made an indecent proposal.

'Doris and I will be too busy. We have to go over the books tonight.'

Now, to this day, I have no idea what he meant by 'going over the books'. But I had this almost immediate Dickensian picture of he and his wife hunched over ledgers, penning in details about the comings and goings of players, whilst supporters and players were out painting the town red. It almost sounded like he had been reprimanding me for suggesting he would engage in such libertine behaviour as partying on a Saturday night. When I expressed my surprise and jokingly attempted to be shocked by that, he defended himself. 'Doris and I go out every Friday night for a steak. That's what we do.'

So there. Social life was timetabled with the exactitude he brought to his tactics on the field of play. I left Dundee that day with a portrait in my mind of a mercilessly driven man who was unique amongst his peers. Our professional relationship, although far from intimate, grew as United rose from the trench of mediocrity and charged over the top.

As first there was a misstep, but no retreat. United and Aberdeen had played out a goalless draw after extra-time, in front of a meagre crowd of 27,173 at Hampden in the Scottish League Cup final on 8 December 1979, on a treacherous, damp surface that seemed to disjoint too many players at crucial times. It was a day when I was confronted again by the abrupt candour of the United manager when he stared at the camera and announced, 'I don't think we deserved a draw.' Said with a sense of relief, but also left me with the feeling that he knew Aberdeen had blown it. They had. At Dens Park in the replay on the following Wednesday, United outthought and outplayed their opponents in a manner that suggested his team was maturing towards potent self-belief. Willie Pettigrew with two goals and Paul Sturrock with the third, meant that United had won their first trophy in 70 years. In defence of their trophy, after reaching the final again in the following season to be played against their neighbours Dundee, from the lower First Division, Jim reluctantly allowed us for the first time to film part of training, only because his rivals down the street had agreed also. Eventually we had to edit the tape with great care because, quite oblivious to the camera he launched into an impassioned session during which I thought he might burst a blood vessel. And this was simply about his players sprinting between traffic bollards.

I had watched training sessions before in other places but never with such a fanatical involvement of a manager. I recall mentioning that to Andy Gray, years later, who admitted he had seen the best and worst of his former boss.

'I had two years with Jim,' he said, 'and I could not have had a better coach. I used to think he was bullying me. He used to bring me back for training in the afternoon, on my own. "Why me? The swine!" I used to think. But it's only afterwards you realise he was making you a better player.'

As Jim once said, 'I only crossed bad balls to Andy. It was the bad balls that helped him. With the good balls he would score too easily.'

There was only going to be one winner in that particular final, of course, and United duly won the second trophy in their history, on 6 December 1980 by the same score, 3–0, on a pitch that was like an Arctic waste. Now they were being discussed by the media as often as the Old Firm. All you need to do is peruse the names, like Gray, which would emerge from around the years leading up to United winning the League title in 1983, to appreciate how, from anonymity, he scouted and produced players who would become household names throughout the land – Richard Gough, Dave Narey, Maurice Malpas (all of them internationals) evoking memories of a disciplined athletic barrier. And of others like Davie Dodds, Derek Stark, Billy Kirkwood and John Holt, who always made you think that they were pure McLean inventions and probably would not have made it elsewhere, but crucial to the structure of his side. And then, up front, the searing pace of Paul Sturrock, Eamonn Bannon and Ralph Milne, which made United renowned for their counter-attacking. That was in Jim's mind when he talked about the game that put United on the brink of winning the League title that season. He said of their 3–2 victory on 20 April 1983, over Celtic in Glasgow, after having lost their first game to the same club in that month, 'I think Billy McNeill definitely made a mistake that day in being so attack minded and left them exposed to the pace we had with Milne, Bannon and Sturrock. It was right up our street.'

On the day history was made, with the title eventually coming up their street, I deliberately concocted a television tableau that Jim himself would cast up with me, from time to time, although with the courtesy of a meagre smile. United, playing their neighbours Dundee again and needing a win to take the title for the first time, were decided favourites. They played like that. With United two up through a neat chip over the keeper by Ralph Milne and an Eamonn Bannon rebound goal, after his penalty had come off the keeper, Jim only began to dance up and down the touchline ranting, when Ian Ferguson for Dundee pulled it back to 2–1, the final score. The title was theirs for the first time. As I walked over the pitch towards the jubilant players I thought back to the rebuff I had suffered when I had asked Jim about how he would celebrate that special victory over Rangers in 1978. Surely a historical achievement would reach parts of him that other occasions could not. I had something in mind, but had to be cautious given his reputation and the fact that I had driven him to desperation the year before. We had been preparing to return from a European tie against Radnicki Nis, Yugoslavia, where the local team with the palpably obvious assistance of a referee, who came from only 25 miles away in Bulgaria, had beaten United 3–0. At the airport in Belgrade I was detained, understandably, by the uniformed authorities of this still authoritarian state, because I had left my passport in our hotel and we had to wait until they received verification of such back in Nis. The United plane was held back at the end of the runway, engines tuning up and a manager's blood boiling. I am told one of his quotes was, 'Leave the bugger where he is. Get us aff!' But they did wait and I was transported out by car eventually to enter the aircraft to loud boos and an incandescent wee man generating enough heat to power the aircraft.

So, at Dens Park that day, I took a deep breath before I joined the jubilation. I went through the normal rigmarole of question and answer about the game and then came the confrontation I'd had in mind for this most abstemious of men. I put it to him that tradition demanded a drink be taken from the cup, which was still glistening with champagne. Now was the time. I handed him the silver trophy filled with golden bubbles. There was a shifty look at first and I had in mind that other fundamentalist teetotaller Jock Stein who had lifted the European Cup to his lips in Lisbon in 1967, but at the last moment desisted. But, suddenly Jim took the trophy, lowered his head, looked over the edge of the edge of it and to a live audience of millions on *Grandstand*, muttered, 'Close your eyes, mother' and sipped. The ogre of repute had become a sentimental human being.

In that sense, he would claim it was emotion, not rational thinking, that kept him at Tannadice when the offer came from Ibrox to become Rangers manager in 1983. Apart from any other factor, having been born deep within a Rangers culture in Lanarkshire, it is something he could scarcely dismiss lightly. I went back to my notes

I took at the time, when talking to Jock Stein about that day. He told me very precisely about their conversation, so what follows is really Stein's account. I noted firstly that they did not meet in the car park at Hampden, as even I had thought at one stage, but parked at the Ostler's Halt, a roadhouse on the outskirts of Glasgow, opposite where Calderpark Zoo used to be. They sat for some time in Stein's car and talked. The former Celtic manager could not have been more adamant that when Jim left him that day McLean had decided to accept the offer. He told me what had been said, which was verified for me by Jim himself, when he spoke to me years later.

'Jock said to me, "Who won the League last season?" I replied, "We did." "Will you win it next year?" he asked. "I don't think we'll win the League," I said, "but I think we've a good chance of winning a Cup." "Then you're a failure," he said.'

Stein was convinced that his argument had settled the matter. When he returned home he told his wife that Jim McLean was to be the next Rangers manager. Stein went on to say that when he turned on the evening television news that night and heard that Jim had turned down the offer, he nearly fell off the couch he was lying on.

The issue of Rangers blatant sectarian policy of excluding Catholics from their playing staff had been at the forefront of Jim's mind. I talked afterwards to Jimmy Robinson, a Rangers director and whom you might have described as a thorough traditionalist.

'He was told he could sign any player from any category, no restriction,' he clarified for me and that stance was ultimately verified by Jim himself.

But he had turned away from it despite that assurance. His explanations that evening played heavily on his association with United and personal respect for the people who had been loyal to him through various controversies. He could not bring himself to cut the umbilical cord. Stein's interpretation though, as a man whom I found could assess people like he had a doctorate in social psychology, was more brutal.

'He took cold feet, that was it!'

That might have been verified by McLean in that long sit-down with me in 2003 when he clearly told me directly, 'I deeply regret

I did not accept that at the time.' And would continue to harp on it when he told Hugh Keevins of the *Daily Record* on 19 March 2010 of that eventful meeting with Jock Stein.

'My only regret, and one that has lived with me for nearly 30 years, is that I once turned down the best piece of advice he ever gave me.'

Perhaps part of the reason for the regret may be that he returned to United to become involved in part ownership of the club and in the long run, facing an internecine dispute within the shareholding group that would require Tolstoyan length and insight to understand.

THE WAY OUT

His admiration for Stein, of course, had intensified when the Scotland manager appointed him as his assistant for the World Cup finals in Spain of 1962. This was an oddity for us observers for the simple reason it was remarkable to see him in a subsidiary role. There would we watch him, hands behind his back, strolling after Stein in the training ground, like he was the sorcerer's apprentice and looking almost unhealthily tame, given we all knew he could spiral quickly into a tornado. How and when to intervene in the decision-making process clearly bothered him throughout that tenure, because he was admittedly in awe of Stein.

'He was God to me,' he told me bluntly.

But did he take it too far? After the debacle of the Willie Miller/ Alan Hansen partnership in the last World Cup game in Malaga, against Russia, and the tragi-comical blunder between them which effectively cost us a goal and qualification for the final stages of the competition, Jim opened up to me about his acceptance of that final selection.

'I'm still ashamed to this day of the way I did that job and I'm ashamed I may have let Jock Stein down after he had shown a great deal of faith in me as a coach. Quite honestly I was a disgrace as an assistant manager.'

However, in disregarding Stein's advice on Ibrox, the beneficiaries were the United flock and the media, for that rejection meant that because of his passionate pursuit of success at a level which had never seemed likely for this club, the city of Dundee had become a moveable feast. We were travelling to all parts of the continent with a club that many in these foreign parts knew little about. That was the beauty of it. This was a new and attractive Scottish identity, informing all of Europe to look at the map of our country again and learn that it was not simply a big blob called Glasgow. They scattered Scottish football to the winds. Prague, Monaco, Monchengladbach, Eindhoven, Vienna, were just some of the places we visited, by kind courtesy of the man who had turned his back on Ibrox and with a tactical verve that his excellent striker Paul Sturrock never failed to identify, even when managing in English football.

'Most people talk in the Premiership about playing 4-5-1. Well, McLean was using that system with us all that time. I was the fulcrum at the top of it and we had so many late runners coming from midfield that many teams couldn't handle us.'

They continued to shock. The two cities that told me most about the mentality of this complex man were Rome and Barcelona. On 25 April 1984 they played AS Roma in the second leg of the European Cup semi-final, leading 2–0 from the first leg. On the day before the game I was privy to one of the most astonishing press-conferences I had ever attended. He took centre stage in front of a wide selection of European journalists and, perhaps aware of that fact, indulged in part history lesson, part confessional. His theme was roughly, that if you thought about this logically then United shouldn't really have been in Rome, but still ought to have been playing for the Forfarshire Cup, not the European one. You could understand he was trying to emphasise the almost miraculous transformation of the club. Yet, because of his flat monotone, I recall an Italian journalist from the pink *Gazetta Dello Sport*, saying to me afterwards, 'Was he getting his excuses in first?' For allied to that historical background was his admission of mistakes he had made in the past that he would not want to make again. It was disarmingly frank, but downbeat, almost defeatist and it slightly disheartened me as I wondered if that mood was being transmitted unconsciously to his players. Of course, he knew he was in for a torrid time within the stadium as the Italians, including the paper I mentioned above, had played up fabricated reports and in his case, jesting remarks, about his players being virtual junkies. The rowdy stadium crowd sounded like invasion was imminent, even from the outset. And yet, the image of Ralph Milne ballooning the ball over the bar from a Bannon cut back, early on, that had he scored, meant Roma would have had to score four to reach the final, still overlays everything else. In fact, the Italians scored two in the first half and a penalty in the second, to win 3–0. From on high, I looked down as Jim walked round the track, at the end, towards the dressing room area, surrounded by his Praetorian guard of coaching colleagues fending off hysterical Italian players who clearly wanted to scrag him. There was an impassive dignity to his demeanour, deliberately unresponsive and clearly unaware of the almost impossible feat he had achieved in returning Rome to the days of the nutty Emperor Nero and thumbs down for the Christians.

Years later it emerged that an attempt had been made to bribe the referee Michel Vautrot of France. This would not have surprised those who had to compete inside the Italian sports culture at the time – summed up to me by Scottish World Champion boxer Walter McGowan after fighting Salvatore Burruni for the World Flyweight crown in that very same stadium and losing controversially on points, when he said to me, 'To get a draw in Italy you've got to knock your opponent out.' The Frenchman denied all culpability. But what still shines through the murkiness of doubt and suspicion which some of the United players were to chorus, about dubious refereeing decisions during the game, was the purity with which Jim assessed any football match, even this incendiary one. His clinical analysis of a game had not deserted him even in the face of such violent confrontation.

He told me simply, 'We just weren't good enough that day' and then went on to say, 'If Ralph had scored, and I hoped he would, then I doubt if I would have got out of that stadium alive.'

We all did though. Three years later, as a much wiser man through bitter experience, United arrived in Barcelona leading the host side by 1–0 from the first leg in the quarter-final of the UEFA Cup. Pre-match, this wasn't exactly sunny Jim, but he did not indulge in any remorseful monologues as I recall. Fleet Street were well represented because of their interest in Terry Venables the Barcelona manager and they were to discover that United existed on a plane completely different from others. What followed was simply one of the finest triumphs I ever had to commentate on. One goal behind in the match, United scored two in three minutes in the last four minutes to reach the semi-final of the UEFA Cup. The thundering John Clark header before Ian Ferguson scored the second, drew me off my seat, mic in hand. I was transported by the sheer audacity of that second win and the clear evidence of a tactical genius at play. What seemed strange to the English was the reaction within the club. Everybody around me was on a high coming down from our lofty commentary position in that canyon-like stadium. But half-way down I came across the United board members with Jim, all standing expressionless on a landing, silent, verily like they had been at a wake. On the way back from the stadium the English journalists, invited to join us back to the hotel on the team bus, were amazed at how quiet everybody was after such a climactic triumph. No carousing. A slight murmur of conversation was the peak of emotion on display. They simply did not understand the McLean ethos. Hootenannies were not in the psyche of their Spartan-like commitment that he had nurtured. But as Jim would admit to me in 2003, 'I just wish I had let my hair down and enjoyed some of these victories with the players.'

The last time I spoke to him though, on a football pitch, he need not have blamed himself for his solemn mood. It was 16 May 1987, at the end of the Scottish Cup final against St Mirren which they had just lost 1–0, after extra-time. This had come only ten days after they had lost the first leg of the UEFA Cup final in Gothenburg 1–0 and only four days before the second leg at Tannadice. He was beginning to think that fate and the inflexible, crowded football calendar, were conspiring against him.

'We were awful,' he told me. 'Even Eamonn Bannon, in the 69th game of the season was absolutely knackered.'

For a man obsessed with football he also knew that the body can only take so much. His very success had paradoxically turned toxic. Mid-season they might have swept Gothenburg away. But, four days later, they learned to their cost that the marathon had hollowed them out and they could only draw 1–1. The trophy which had lain in wait inside Tannadice for safe keeping was never touched by McLean during its stay.

'I now wish I had my photograph taken with it, because it's the nearest I ever got to it,' he told me, although with a relaxing laugh, during that long baring of the soul in 2003.

What he would not discuss with me that day or else, very clearly, I would have been shown the door, was his inexcusable assault on the BBC journalist John Barnes on 14 October 2000. His *mea culpa* on some of his actions was never going to include that. Although the charge of assault that the police delivered to him was never pursued by the procurator fiscal in Dundee. It was abundantly clear it had scarred him, ruined his always shaky reputation at SFA level and finished him in football, after he severed all practical ties with the club before that very day of the assault was out. Two years later he would give up his shares in the club.

It had been a shameful episode which made some people in my trade, who really never stopped loathing him, feel like celebrating, as if all had been revealed, at long last, as to what they had tolerated through the years. According to their lurid accounts wee Jim had been hovering on the edge of delinquency ever since he stepped into the post. Then, in the next breath as if they were speaking of a different man, they could rhyme off his record, almost with pride – raising the First Division League flag above Tannadice for the first and only time; winning two League Cups; six appearances at Hampden in finals; 18 continuous years in European football, including reaching a semi-final and final, in separate competitions; and never falling below fifth in the League since 1976, until he left. All from a man, who according to my own eyes and with the considerable evidence of so many others, had no interest in courting affection with a world he believed was conspiring against him and leaving him with no option other than to adopt what might be called the siege mentality.

'I certainly couldn't have done it any other way,' he told me. 'I had to give my whole being to getting success. Do you know that if we lost on a Saturday, Doris, my wife wouldn't be able to talk to me until the Monday? Even sometimes when we won she still couldn't talk to me. Of course, I regret many things. I regret having missed the upbringing of my kids, especially the older boy.'

It was uncomfortable listening to him baring his soul. In many ways I wish he hadn't, almost as if it was going to be difficult in the final analysis to square his great triumphs with the fact that his family had, on his own admission, become collateral damage along the way. But his death from Alzheimer's disease at the age of 83 not only generated great sympathy for him and his family. It also increased the acute awareness that without him, the pages of Dundee United's history would hardly be worth reading.

McLean's regret at not moving to Rangers might make interesting conversation with the man I place next to him. For Graeme Souness did go to Ibrox. And Scottish football was never the same again.

CHAPTER 12

The Odd Couple

IT WAS A press conference that was scheduled to be ordinary and bland. Instead it turned out to be unique. It lasted 5.60 seconds. Thereabouts. It was so startling it compelled you to force tiny estimates like that into the mind. As far as I know there is no category in the Guinness Book of Records for durations of press-conferences, although one candidate for merit would be Volodymyr Zelenskyy, the courageous President of Ukraine who claimed a world record for holding one which lasted 12 hours and left journalists having to fight against the onset of *rigor mortis*. Then, at the other extreme, would be that blink of an eye afternoon in the heart of Ibrox Stadium. The figure who was supposed to address us all, simply mumbled a couple of barely discernible harrumphs, then took off, the door slammed behind. That was our lot. The sheer audacity of such a manoeuvre reverberated longer than the actual shivering of the timbers within the room. There were many experienced journalists packed into the small room, just off the marbled foyer, who were only ever struck dumb when their expenses claims were rejected, but now seemed to have been turned instantly into pillars of salt, like Lot's wife, after having waited patiently for some words of wisdom. That eerie silence was followed by a babble of voices, the gasping of breaths, expletives and a growling consensus that they had just been treated like unwanted guisers at Halloween who hadn't even been wearing fancy dress for the occasion. The late Alan Davidson, close friend and astute writer for the *Glasgow Evening Times* simply muttered, almost in awe, into my ear, 'Jesus Christ, what a man!' He was referring to the vanishing act of the Rangers manager, Graeme Souness.

The initial feeling of just being handed pariah status, by a man who certainly held many of the press in contempt, was quickly replaced by an understanding of what Souness's slick manoeuvre really did signify. It was an act of defiance. The sound of the slamming of the door in our faces was intended to be heard in that 19th century townhouse in Park Gardens, many miles away on the other side of the River Clyde, which housed the man who appeared to be Souness's nemesis, Ernie Walker, the general secretary of the Scottish Football Association. The building was not unknown to Souness who had appeared there – somewhat reluctantly, it has to be said – from time to time, to be censured one way or another by an organisation dominated by Walker, whose relationship with Souness lent the public the impression it was rather like that the Governor of Texas had with the outlaw Billy the Kid – overlording a system which seemingly had one man in particular in its sights. This perception was gathering public acceptance even outwith the Ibrox legions. Souness's peculiar reaction to us that day was targeted particularly at the Scottish Premier League, who had insisted on him adhering to contractual agreements to appear in front of the press, but in effect, he was thumbing his nose at the entire spectrum of officialdom, of which Ernie Walker, as we all knew, was the chief manipulator. Souness, even though supported by a rich industrialist and packing the crowds in at Ibrox whilst winning trophies, clearly could not prevent himself from sounding as if he was in the grip of a persecution complex. He was also keenly aware that Walker set the authoritative tone throughout the whole of Scottish football.

Although this situation was always couched, by himself and his admirers, as the classic struggle of one man against a mindless, nit-picking bureaucracy – whipped into a frenzy by a hostile press and supported by thinly veiled contempt from the other side of the city – you could almost interpret it as a duel between two men representing clashing values. In those glorious two decades, between Lisbon of 1967; through Barcelona in 1972; Gothenburg in 1986; ending in St Etienne 1998, the sixth World Cup finals in seven attempts; Scottish football had gained universal credibility and respect, despite our own occasional tormented relapses, as anti-climax followed anti-climax in international football. But midstream in that era, during that short period between 1986 and 1991, Scottish football was to change in ways which would affect us to the present day. Nothing would ever be the same again. Circumstances clamped these two men together in an odd way. There was the very public relationship and then the private one which told a different tale. However, when all was said and done, in considering the competing forces they represent I judge only one of them to have been the winner.

Ibrox had set the atmosphere for revolution in our game without us knowing where it was taking us. However, Walker, even when he watched Souness being interviewed by me in Santa Fe, New Mexico as the new Rangers player-manager – all of us heading for the World Cup in Mexico – had more than a fair idea of where the game he presided over would end up.

The SFA general secretary, who by then had been dubbed the 'Ayatollah' by Celtic's irrepressible wit, Bertie Auld, did not like the line of direction Ibrox was taking under the new manager. That, you could say, was the ideological bit. But it was Souness's troubles that paired them in the public eye, as the new Rangers player-manager strayed off the straight and narrow, with almost metronomic recurrence. Walker did not blink in the ensuing public glare. Pistols at dawn seemed afoot. Although any time I spent with Walker and we talked about the former Scottish captain privately, he would actually talk in almost affectionate terms about Souness. This was the mature Walker, so different from the man I had first come across. Appointed to his position in 1978, his transformation was astonishing to many. In his previous role as assistant to his predecessor, Willie Allan, he had always seemed a geekish and anonymous figure in his long coat and soft hat, as he trailed after the stooped and usually crumpled figure of his boss. So when it came his time to step into the limelight and appeared in front of television cameras, sometimes under press bombardment, he belied the intensity of his feelings by being calm, and coolly articulate, like someone had done an Eliza Doolittle job on him. But that was only because too many of us had paid scant attention to him and wrongly assumed he was simply another apparatchik come to bore us all into submission again. Closer to him you saw an entirely different personality.

Walker had immediately set about prising the SFA away from the almost Dickensian culture that existed before he took office. Bill Wilson, who was eventually to become commercial director for the

SFA, had to deal with the previous secretary, Willie Allan, on behalf of his PR agency, on one of the first major commercial deals that was on offer in the UK. He wryly recalls the attitude of suspicion and reluctance in telling me:

'Scotland used to make a profit when we played against England at Hampden and make a loss when we went to Wembley. There were no other real sources of income. Now I was working for an agency and was proud of the fact that after several months of discussion, I had persuaded Umbro to pay the SFA £10,000 for wearing the strips which they would distribute free to the players. That was a fortune in those days. Prior to that, players like Baxter, Law and Crerand had to pay for their strips, that came from a sports shop in Paisley, would you believe. So I put this unprecedented offer to Willie Allan. I remember his response. "Oh, dear, dear, Mr Wilson! Strips free! And giving us money at the same time? I think you had better run along now and just make sure you know what you are saying!"'

That disbelief in the potential of the commercial world was one of the first shibboleths attacked by Walker in that staid, plodding organisation and in giving full backing to the aggressive hunter-gatherer that Wilson turned out to be, as commercial director, the SFA would attract £6 million a year, in different deals, by the time he had left his post. Walker was to describe Wilson as the 'best signing I ever made'.

So by the time Souness had arrived at Ibrox in 1986, Walker had created a fiefdom at Park Gardens that suggested benevolent dictatorship. Each of the seven men who chaired the seven committees within the organisation had been handpicked by Walker and were his personal friends. They wined and dined together in their travels around the world as members of the international committee. Thus, conviviality and genuine comradeship being at the heart of their relationships, it is little wonder that no rebellious hearts beat anywhere near him. The consensus SFA voice was Walker's. He didn't write their scripts. He didn't need to.

Although, on one occasion, I did come across a rebellion of a sort when at a dinner table with Walker, Jock Stein and my producer Nevin McGhie in Madrid, just after the draw for the 1982 Spanish World Cup finals, I almost spilled the Rioja down my best bib and tucker when I heard the SFA president, Tommy Younger, launch an attack on the erstwhile unimpeachable Scotland manager Stein. He suddenly and loudly criticised his match record as the national manager and said any other man would probably have got the sack by then and that it wasn't acceptable. Knowing the ferocious 'Celtic' Stein well enough, I thought Younger was about to have the *paella pollo* dumped on his head. But instead Walker promptly intervened and firmly put his chairman in his place in no uncertain manner, as Stein drummed his fingers on the table, as if itching to really let fly. With searing, cutting words he forced Younger into a surrender with the classic exit line, 'No hard feelings, Jock.'

Souness would have been aware of the authority which Walker now commanded like that, having been a player and captain of the national side, and neither man would ever be hesitant in recalling the night when fate brought them together in tragic circumstances and which revealed a bonding that was a mix of shredded nerves and an intense love of Scottish football. It was the evening of 10 September 1985. Scotland had travelled to Ninian Park, Cardiff, requiring to avoid defeat to qualify for the play-offs for the World Cup in Mexico the following year. The score was at 1–1 after Davie Cooper had equalised controversially from the penalty spot, as a result of the ball striking the arm of Welsh defender David Phillips. There were only ten minutes remaining. Walker admitted to me he could not bear watching till the end. With so much at stake he left his seat and sought sanctuary inside the stand. He was then to tell me that, to his astonishment he met Graeme Souness, who was suspended for this game. He had flown over from Italy to lend his support to the squad and now was admitting he could not bear to watch either. Walker asked him if he wanted a drink to calm the nerves, but the lady behind the bar in the boardroom refused to serve them, having been given instructions not to open up until the final whistle. Walker knew of another small VIP room where they could help themselves. Seconds later he tried to serve Souness with a vodka and tonic, but his hands were shaking so much the drink was spilling all over his suit. He was also able to recall that he poured lemonade rather than tonic, just about the time when they both became aware of a curious silence descending from above and heard the commentator from a nearby television set announcing that Jock Stein, the Scotland manager, had collapsed and was being carried from the pitch.

That scene exposed the frailties of men who could do nothing to influence the outcome of a football match that meant so much to them and was almost instantly compounded by their despair at being witness to Stein's last breath in the medical room. Both men took some time to recover from that night, although in the longer term the antidote to lapsing into chronic grief, was Scotland eventually qualifying for Mexico after play-offs with Australia. It just so happened that just before both men took off on a flight to Santa Fe for their final World Cup preparations at altitude, Souness had become Rangers new player-manager. He was attracted to Ibrox by new chief executive David Holmes, a decent, soft-spoken, Labour-supporting man who too many now seem to have forgotten. Now his new appointee sat comfortably in the sun in Santa Fe, very close to where they exploded the first atom bomb at Los Alamos, although some of Graeme Souness's early statements to me, in interview by poolside (where else?) had plenty of plutonium-charged material in them when he said, 'There will be no holding me back from signing a Catholic at any time!' Followed by, 'And I don't care if Celtic beat us four times in the League so long as we win the championship!' Hardened as I was to the abrasions of that special rivalry his words seemed almost charmingly delusional and indeed he was to find out that asking the Rangers support to accept four defeats by Celtic, in a season, would be like asking the survivors of the Titanic to recommend lifeboat travel.

AT ALTITUDE

Souness and Walker suffered in Mexico. Walker, through one startling, injudicious statement to the media and Souness in coming to realise that he was 33 and had to play at an altitude of 2,240 metres. His muscles rebelled. It was not so noticeable in the first 1–0 loss against Denmark, but in Querétaro against West Germany the realisation sunk in to himself, as it did to Charlie Nicholas, who having been badly injured against the Danes and unable to play, was my co-commentator.

Nicholas has always maintained this to me.

'He was the fittest player I have ever come across. A great physical athlete. Strength everywhere. And a mental toughness.'

However, that day, against West Germany he played like he was treading on a field of treacle. Watching him from on high with the sweat lashing off us, it was like he had suffered the fate of Samuel when he foolishly let Delilah loose on his hair. The imposing strength had vanished. He was ponderous. Play swept past him like he was a pedestrian trying to cross a busy thoroughfare. It was painful to watch and Charlie and I were of the view that we had just seen him playing his last game for Scotland, which sadly was associated with the 2–1 defeat.

Alex Ferguson decided not to play him in the final game against Uruguay, a selection which can still arouse debate among those long enough in the tooth and provoked by remarks such as Richard Gough at the time when he said to me, 'Here was our captain, our leader, and he wasn't going to be there. I felt uncomfortable about that.' Walker backed the manager, in a subtle way, as Craig Brown recollected to me.

'On the morning of the game, all the coaches and the manager were sitting down at breakfast when suddenly Ernie Walker walked in and asked to see Fergie privately. We all thought that he was probably in for a rocket because we had lost our opening two games and were hanging by a thread and he was away for a good ten minutes. But when he returned he expressed his surprise at what had happened. "That was curious" he told us. "He's just told me that no matter what happens today, win, lose or draw, the SFA are behind me and will support me."'

So Walker took his seat among the dignitaries in the Neza stadium, and probably experienced a surge of optimism when Uruguay created a World Cup record by having José Batista sent off in only 60 seconds, for what could only be described as an assault on Gordon Strachan. There then followed a turgid, brutish, goalless game, only noted for a glaringly missed chance in front of goal by Stevie Nichol of Liverpool, which Scotland supporters in general felt any of their grannies could have scored. That fact, along with the elbowing, spitting and wild tackles by the uncouth ten Uruguayans, under the complacent eye of the referee, led the incensed Walker to rise from his privileged seat at full time, with one aim in mind, to head for the media. He gave the Scottish press the headlines they badly needed. He arrived in front of the press in his usual unflurried manner, as if he was about to announce travel arrangements for the retreat back home. There was a Latin hubbub all around and the air-conditioning didn't seem to be working. On the back of our exit from the tournament it all seemed hellish. Affected by that mood, he let fly. No roar. Soft bitterness in fact.

'There was no game of football here today. We found ourselves on the field with cheats and cowards and we were associated with the scum of the earth.'

It was almost eerily effective in its low-key bitterness that silenced the babble of Latin voices around us. In an instant, though his words conveyed a change of personality, from lofty office-holder to that of 'Disillusioned Duntocher', uttering words he knew would be circulating among the angry tartan legions, but which we suspected might be causing FIFA a corporate cardiac arrest. It surprised me that he was playing so blatantly to his home gallery, because even at the time I thought he was well over the top. What later began to sink in for him and the more discerning of the supporters, was that Scotland had played 89 minutes against ten men and couldn't score, and although some of the Uruguayan players looked like they could have eviscerated an All Blacks pack, they had the outstanding player afield in Enzo Francescoli who justified his title, 'El Principe'. How would Souness really have deported himself against the thuggish South Americans? As you ponder that, jump forward to Saturday 9 August 1986, at about 3.30pm.

THE OPENING SALVO

The World Cup was in the past. Souness and Walker were no longer under the same SFA roof and that separation was dramatically emphasised when on the stroke of that half-hour Souness, in his new role as Rangers player-manager at Easter Road, left a gouge on the shin of George McCluskey of Hibernian – as un-Uruguayan as you could find anywhere in Leith – in the opening match of that season, literally stamping his imprimatur on the Scottish game and was sent from the field. That might lend a clue as to how long he would have lasted against the 'scum'. It was the first of his three expulsions as a Rangers player and the start of a rumbustious playing career in Scotland that left you wondering if he really cared where boundaries lay in any game. But whatever you thought of him, for us in the media he had introduced one of the most stimulating, provocative chapters in the sport since Stein had arrived on the scene with Celtic in 1965 and wakened the huge Rangers following from the slumbers of a mediocre age. You felt that there was some kind of reckoning for him, after that first game though – something that would make or break him.

It came on 26 October 1986 when the Old Firm met in the Scottish League Cup final that, for me, as the commentator on the day, was an unexpected but glorious feast of controversy. Now you can attach many epithets to these clashes but this one definitely qualified for the rubric, 'Fire and Brimstone'. In the background lurked the notion that Celtic were the only club in the country who could stop the developing Ibrox momentum turning into a runaway juggernaut. Celtic wanted to burst a bubble rather more than winning a Cup. That club, not noted for their lavish spending, desperately wanted to show that success could be achieved by traditional and more modest means. At the score of 1–1 Rangers were awarded a penalty with only six minutes remaining. Ian Durrant had put Rangers in the lead in the first-half only for an equaliser by Celtic's Brian McClair with 20 minutes remaining. For what it is worth, Jim McLean, the successful Dundee United manager was my co-commentator and valued for his almost puritanical utterances about anything in football, declared, 'Definitely a penalty', as Roy Aitken and Terry Butcher tumbled together in the box. But in that kind of setting nothing is cut and dried. What then followed was a complete breakdown on the field of some of the Celtic players venting their fury, losing their discipline and Mo Johnston being sent off with a deliberate genuflection, that was less to do with spiritual comforting and more to do with solidarity with his own supporters, whom he would spurn in later years when he arrived ultimately at Ibrox. Another, Tony

Shepherd was sent off by mistake and then reinstated, provoking Davy Hay, normally a rational and moderate man, to declare that he would encourage Celtic to apply for membership of the English League to free themselves from the unjust treatment he believed was meted out to his club.

Souness did not play in that match and given the volcanic nature of the game was probably best out of it, because his whole character was being judged on his on-field behaviour and the marked lapses of judgement that peppered his career. This is how the public saw him and assessed him. His tackles seemed to come from a raging desire to be in control of events. You can find a collection of his challenges on several websites on the internet, one of which is actually portrayed as an instructional film for physiotherapists on how to cope with serious injuries. An Icelandic hospital was the recipient of one incident when the 18-year-old Siggi Jónsson from Sheffield Wednesday was taken into A&E there on 28 May 1985 after a wild lunge by Souness in the World Cup qualifying game against Iceland, which Scotland won 1–0 only in the last four minutes. Jónsson was never to be the same player again. That incident even affected his manager Jock Stein who told Ian Archer of the *Glasgow Evening Times*, 'It was a foul which upset us more than Iceland. Souness wasn't the same man after it.' And led to his suspension for the last game in Cardiff and those nervy last minutes with Walker that evening.

However, that recklessness was largely tolerated by a man like Stein and many others, on the pragmatic basis that they would rather have him play for you, than against you. He was simply a greatly influential presence ever since he made such a difference against Holland in his debut in international football in Argentina in 1978. Stein admired his measured approach to life in general, with elements of style that loudly proclaimed his identity. The Scotland manager used the word 'Class' to me about Souness before a game in Spain once, adding, 'You need somebody like him around that the others can look up to', and even some of his severe critics had a sneaking admiration for him because of his self-appointed gladiator role in the macho culture that dominated his sport. But he also had a poise and self-confidence about him that swayed the likes of Charlie Nicholas, who was even impressed by the colour co-ordinated wardrobe Souness took with him to Mexico that really chimed with his own image of 'Champagne Charlie'.

But by January 1988 Walker was reading the runes about a future based on Souness's impact. He expounded that to me in an unusual setting. Not in his office, where he often held forth to myself and others – like the notable day I met him with two other journalists, Ken Gallacher of the *Sun* and Alan Davidson of the *Glasgow Evening Times*, in the autumn of 1986, to chat about the repercussions following the Mexico disappointments and to reflect on the public debate that had arisen about the surprising appointment of Andy Roxburgh as Scotland's new manager. The question we were after was eventually put simply: 'Who really appointed Andy?' After a contemplative pause and a tiny puff on his cigar, he simply replied, 'I did.' Two words confirming both his enduring command of events and of the ultimate control of his institution. But the reason his first comments to me about the Rangers 'revolution' made such an impact, was because of the unusual setting. It was at a Burns Supper. Walker loved Burns, golf and a dram, in equal measure. Knowing of my similar fascination with the Bard he invited me to the Hagg's Castle Golf Club, where he was a member, to celebrate the birth of Robert Burns. After he had lustily sung the climatic and maudlin 'Star of Rabbie Burns' with the rest of us, he settled down to another dram and amidst the usual debris of these occasions, he uttered the phrase which was to be echoed more and more throughout the land.

'Look what's happening at Ibrox!'

He was not referring to their on-field success where, at that stage, they had won the League title for the first time in nine years and the Scottish League Cup, but to their increasing number of foreign imports, which had been facilitated by the ban on English football in Europe at that time. In the League Cup final against Celtic in that first Souness season in 1986, Rangers had three non-Scots in the winning side, including the English captain Terry Butcher and first choice England goalkeeper Chris Woods, plus Northern Ireland's Jimmy Nicholl. Four years later, as Walker was in the process of demitting office, Rangers lifted another League Cup in a victory against Celtic and fielded seven non-Scots, with another on the bench. The drift of

Walker's observations on Ibrox that night, which seemed about three times longer than 'Tam o' Shanter', was his worry that Rangers would merely be starting a trend that others might follow, particularly Celtic. A developing alien culture was definitely not to the liking of the man who defied government advice eventually to replace 'God Save The Queen' with 'Scotland the Brave' as the national team's anthem.

The other trend was one which I know deeply disappointed Walker, Souness's apparent indifference to the diktats from his office. Clearly, on the surface, the SFA secretary issued stern disapproval of the indiscipline of the former Scottish captain, but up close and personal with Walker, you could tell he was saddened by his appearances in front of the disciplinary committee, as if he was reluctant to dispense with his liking for the man. He did not have the same view of Rangers' new owner.

For Rangers Football Club, from November 1988, was now in the hands of David Murray. Holmes had disappeared, vanquished by this entrepreneurial coup. This initiated a spending spree on transfers that were to have both immediate and historic consequences. He had come at the behest of his friend Souness who, in keeping with the entrepreneurship of their relationship, would become a major shareholder in the club. Such ambition seemed to make him more sensitive to any unflattering press response to games. After one game against foreign opposition he was particularly irked by a report written by Jim Traynor of the *Glasgow Herald* (in later years to become PR adviser at Ibrox) who criticised his tactics in that defeat. Souness was livid and responded at the press conference some days later. As Traynor recalls, 'He bounded down the marble staircase at Ibrox, made a beeline towards me and almost fell on top of me in his eagerness to let it all come out. Everybody was diving for cover.'

The exchange went like this:

Souness: (raging) *My daughter knows more about football than you do.*

Traynor: (*sotto voce*) *Well, if your daughter knows more about football than me maybe you should get her to come along and help with your tactics.*

Souness: (exploding) *You're nothing but a... a... wee socialist shite.*

Traynor: (proudly) *Well, thank you very much.*

A week later Traynor was astonished at the difference.

'He could not have been more charming with me, as if nothing had happened between us. We were on great terms again.'

That somersaulting behaviour from aggression to cordiality, became a feature of many of his relationships in Glasgow.

However that 'socialist' reference, as the worst possible impromptu insult Souness could think of, fed into the growing perception amongst his critics that Ibrox had become a Thatcherite enclave in a country which was about to face the detested Poll Tax, legislation of which was introduced into Scotland in 1989, the year Rangers took off on their nine-in-a-row League title run. So, adding to the distaste many people still expressed about sectarianism within the institution, was the perception that he was a Tory crony, at a time when there was an appalling male unemployment rate of 42 per cent in the district of Govan (where Ibrox is sited) and an overall rate of 25 per cent in the West of Scotland. However, I knew many members of the Labour party and trade-unionists who flew up joyfully to Ibrox on the wings of recurring triumph, feeling that being *in absentia* from politics for 90 minutes was worth accepting, if league titles and cups were coming their way. On the other hand, he did provoke among his traditional opponents a degree of hatred that was intense as anything I had ever experienced with any other Rangers player.

So, if ever a man was in need of a distraction, it was Souness, approaching season 1989/90. It came in the signing of the Catholic-born, Maurice Johnston, on 10 July 1989. Given the historic significance of this it is hardly credible that it all happened within a few steps of Souness walking down the marbled steps inside Ibrox one day. He spotted Johnston's agent Bill McMurdo standing in the vestibule and casually asked him if Johnston was going to Celtic and when told the deal had not yet been transacted, because of contractual discussions, simply replied, to the astonishment of McMurdo, 'We'll take him then!'

And so Souness slammed another door shut, this time on Rangers' controversial past. In a matter of seconds, you could say.

That instant pragmatism was reflected in a statement, quoted in the *Guardian,* on the day of the signing,

> I'm buying him because he is, first and foremost a fantastic player but I have to tell you this, if he signs for Rangers Football Club, Celtic won't recover for ten years.

A statement that has stood the test of time. Just after that signing, I met Walker in his office for a personal face-to-face showdown, after he had taken offence to something I had written about his protégé Andy Roxburgh but, inevitably, that sudden Souness manoeuvre came up and, not surprisingly, he was full of praise for the initiative. I also sensed that he was relieved that his former captain was receiving more favourable reviews, thus underlining what I always recognised as his much-tested, but durable respect for the man. Souness seemed no longer under the cosh. But it couldn't last.

THE EXIT

Why didn't we see it coming? Even though he gave the impression that he could swat off any criticism and that sustaining flak seemed simply to renew his mission in football, we should have known that an inducement to return to England was going to be difficult to reject. Underneath the imperturbable veneer, he was clearly feeling the effect of constantly being sniped at in the press, much of which was of his own doing, as Murray himself was eventually forced into admitting. But he had used Murray's financial backing wisely, with more to come, which is why we thought the relationship was impregnable. It had put him in total command of the Rangers culture, eventually winning four League championships, (although for the final title Walter Smith guided them over the line in the last few games) and four Scottish League Cups. And as a bonus he introduced exceptional European nights at Ibrox, like the evening they put paid to Dynamo Kiev 2–0 on 30 September 1987, which astonished Europe, not just by the victory, but by the audacious pre-match tactic of Souness in telling his groundsman to mark off the pitch to the narrowest allowable dimension to thwart the dazzling wide play of the great Oleg Blokhin. He shrunk the pitch and sent home a delirious crowd. He could do anything as far as they were concerned. You could be tempted to think that this affected his personal judgement, giving the impression that despite recurring success, he was on a mission of self-destruct, that I had to witness in some amazement at times.

In commentary on the Old Firm game in August 1987 at Celtic Park, I admit I almost stalled mid-sentence when he swept the legs from the man who had scored the only goal of the game, Billy Stark. The fact that the Celtic player was wearing only one boot at the time and had the other in his hand preparing to re-commence battle is still difficult for me to comprehend given my lack of understanding of what makes people self-harm. The subsequent expulsion and a five match ban, not only for the Stark tackle but for allegedly using obscenities to the referee, was merely the start of a sequence of indiscretions that demonstrated that Walker was in an unrelenting mood as legislator. For Souness, in February 1990, found himself banned from the touchline for a year and fined £ 2,500.

Those who enjoyed his discomfort weighed in eventually, in effective ways. I knew both the tea-lady Aggie at St Johnstone's Muirton Park, who acutely embarrassed him and the television producers at Scottish Television who, frankly, 'shopped' him. Decent, well-meaning people going about their separate businesses but bonded by a hatred of Souness and the club he managed. Aggie was a couthy soul. And, as a Celtic fan, was a gift to the media when she revealed her confrontations with Souness, describing him to Grampian Television as 'a plonker'. I recall watching him that day walking around Muirton Park on his own, well after the crowds had disappeared, like a man allowing himself to simmer down, having just learned that he had lost his expensive signing Oleg Kuznetsov to a serious knee injury in the game. Whatever Aggie had done to him, the Russian's calamity had done more. He bore a scunnered look and could not hide his anguish in front of our cameras about that. Then came the television pictures that caught him out. More sleekit than the forthright Aggie's sabotage though.

After a league game against Hearts at Ibrox, on 17 February 1990 STV provided evidence to the SFA that showed Souness peeping out from the tunnel at Ibrox shouting instructions to his players. By the strict interpretation of the law he shouldn't have been there. He should have known that. But these pictures were not provided to the SFA until weeks after the incident. It was as if the television producers had exacted a citizen's arrest. He actually fell out terminally with his first signing Terry Butcher for having dared to give a subsequent interview to that now despised channel, so enraged was he. Punishment was to follow. It was a kind of Doomsday scenario for Souness. At that time I knew little of what was going through his mind, although he was to reveal much to Rangers historian David Mason, in later years. He admitted to him that his marriage had gone wrong and that he was suffering continual headaches through high blood pressure, little realising they were related to his serious heart condition in later life.

He went on to tell him, 'I felt if people tackled me in a certain way, it was ok. But I got cards. I suppose it's in the Scottish mentality, the "I'll show you mentality" – I used to say to Phil Boersma as I took to the field, "Is the target straight on my back today?"'

But I had no inkling of what was really going through his mind when I interviewed him on 13 April 1991 after a comfortable 3–0 home win against St Johnstone. It was bland and forgettable. But, on reflection, I believe he couldn't get it over with quickly enough and there was none of the usual banter afterwards. Three days later I received a call asking me to attend a press conference at Ibrox.

There they sat, in the Meiklejohn Suite, funereally. David Murray, Walter Smith and Graeme Souness were the ones which eyes were concentrated on. The scene remains something of a blur, as what we were hearing was about a departure only weeks away from a possible league triumph again and it was difficult to grasp the reality of all this. I recall a few words from the chairman announcing that the manager was leaving for Liverpool, then Souness spoke briefly, mentioned Smith, referred to Murray and then walked out, briskly. I felt it was as if he had sucked the air out of the room and created a vacuum that left an almost gormless chairman trying to make sense of it all to us. Smith, on the verge of an illustrious managerial career, nevertheless was looking like had just been asked to go into the ring and face a bull, and the press corps were baffled, firstly by the suddenness of it all with the club nearing another title, but waking up to the reality that this man was never likely to have ended his career north of the border. The only real difference between Souness and Steven Gerrard and Brendan Rodgers, in later years, who deserted their Old Firm posts midstream at the first tempting offer from the south, was that these two men were gentle lambs compared to one of the great provocateurs of the age whose last act left behind an embittered support.

Years later, Ernie Walker, in retirement from his hugely influential role within FIFA where he had been chairman of the UEFA stadium committee and part of the triumvirate which awarded the 1994 World Cup to the USA, but by that stage suffering from the prostate cancer that prevented him from attending that tournament, sat with me at the St Andrews Sporting Club in Glasgow, where I acted as chairman. In the midst of a night of dining and boxing we talked at length about the Souness era. He was in good, optimistic form despite his affliction and said not a bad word about the former Scottish captain. But four little words stuck out. 'I told you so'. As I look back on that I recall a scene that summarised much of what had happened to Scottish football and the lasting effect Souness's presence in the land would have in the future, underlining the point Walker was making. It was a night in Belgrade on 2 March 1988 when Rangers had just lost 2–0 to Steaua Bucharest, inspired by the famous Gheorghe Hagi, whose son was to sign eventually for the Ibrox club. In the airport that night a distraught looking Souness, fully aware of the criticism of his foreign import trend, swept up to me and uttered almost a plea for clemency, in light of the increasing hostility to his policy.

'How can I win anything in Europe playing only 11 Jocks?'

It was crude, brutal and sounded almost like he was insulting the very breeding ground from which he had emerged himself. But, he was telling us a developing truth that offended our ears, although the facts were staring us in the face.

THE CONSEQUENCES

The parochial eras of Stein, Waddell and Ferguson were now far distant and Walker's 'I told you so' was linked to the fact that on 8 September 2001, Martin O'Neill fielded an entirely non-Scottish Celtic side – Rangers had accomplished that the year before – as other Scottish clubs began to recruit from further afield also provoking Andy Roxburgh to raise his voice to me in a discussion, 'What bloody good does any foreigner in Scottish football do for me as manager of the national side!' His market of choice was shrinking. The factor that might have helped, UEFA's three foreigner ruling in the 1990s, was blasted away by both the Bosman ruling and the EU freedom-of-movement statute. UEFA president Lennart Johansson, an intimate friend and fellow prostate cancer sufferer of Ernie Walker, was forced into compliance with a bitter reluctance, shared by his Scottish colleague. For from then on, each succeeding Scotland manager would be handicapped, not only by such limitations, but also by trends in society where electronic gadgetry was increasingly seducing young people away from getting their knees skint playing football which had been the natural breeding grounds of our greatest players.

Inevitably interest swung towards European club football, generated principally by the Old Firm and their eternal rivalry for supremacy, which would continue to play out on foreign fields, given that their respective histories told them they rightly belonged there. Although when Martin O'Neill assembled some of us around him at Celtic Park, along with Peter Lawwell, at the start of the season just after Seville 2003 and uttered, 'A Scottish side will never win a European trophy again', it came out as brutally as anything Souness ever uttered about his country and suggested the Old Firm in future would merely be playing out fantasy football in Europe. Not that it dulled the senses of their supporters who had turned away from the various underperforming national sides in great numbers, particularly the Rangers support, as club football began to dominate the news and foreigners continued to flow in. It had paid dividends for some. For within two years of Souness's arrival, attendances at Scottish football matches had increased from 2,446,262 to a staggering 3,874,079 on the back of foreign importation.

Walker represented the democratic nature of the game that was powerless in the face of commercial realities. He failed in his efforts to implement radical change to the Scottish game, with his Rinus Michels initiative of 1995, disappearing into a void. The Dutchman – like the former First Minister of Scotland Henry McLeish – painfully discovered that setting up investigations and offering solutions for reconstruction of our game would meet resistance based on blatant self-interest and inevitably require the blessing of the Old Firm who, although strong on cordial rhetoric about the Scottish football community, would support nothing which thwarted their lust for dominance. Walker had the clear foresight of a man who genuinely loved the game, but had no real weaponry to fend off the assault on the old ways. He was bound to lose. Although when he succumbed to cancer on 14 May 2011 there were loud lamentations throughout the various European bodies, regretting the loss of a man who bravely endured his encroaching disease, even as he still influenced the decisions that affected world football. But the dynamism Souness represented is no mere parochial footnote in Scottish history. It was global and unstoppable, reaching a crescendo in 2021 when a self-appointed elite proposed setting up a European Super League which, although temporarily rebuffed is only, in my view, in hibernation. For Scotland had been one of the first countries to sample the commercial convulsion world football was then to experience.

But one incident cries out to be seen as a neat precis of the clashes in that period between the establishment and this restless, foraging individual. It was when Souness was summoned to the disciplinary committee to be sanctioned for that illegitimate appearance at the tunnel in the Hearts game. He was accompanied by Rangers security officer, the former policeman Alistair Hood who certainly anticipated that the manager would have the book thrown at him. What he did not know is that Souness knew in advance precisely what the committee had in store for him, but had left Hood in the dark about it. Hood suspected afterwards that the person he thought might have alerted Souness was the inevitable figure of journalist Jim Rodger who had sniffed out the information from someone within the SFA and for which he had no equal. So when they arrived, Souness, dressed to kill as usual, objected to sitting in what he considered a broom-cupboard to wait for the committee to assemble. They decided to sit on the top of the stairs and had the uncanny experience of watching the committee troop up past them, all of whom cheerily acknowledged Hood, but ignored Souness. When they eventually faced each other and went through the rigmarole, the chairman announced that there would be a touchline ban for two years and that the Rangers manager would be fined £5,000. What then followed astonished the unexpecting Hood. Souness suddenly reached into his inside pocket and produced a stuffed envelope and proceeded to count out pound notes, 'One… two…three…' And so on. When he got to £4,999 he stopped, turned to Hood and asked him if could he lend him a pound as he had run out. Hood, barely recovering, obliged.

It was delicious effrontery. It was mockery of the kind that would have enraged those who disliked him of course. But to those of us who knew him it was the wholly personable Souness of the flamboyant style that, knowing he was for the high jump, was determined to create his own gilt-threaded parachute. Even Aggie might have laughed about his audacity. And assuredly Ernie Walker, who by then was travelling around Europe in his work for UEFA, would have had a quiet private chuckle about it as he sipped his malt by Lake Geneva or somewhere, perhaps aligning it to the word 'Class' Stein had used about his captain.

All this would never have happened had not a mild-mannered, thoroughly Scottish man, David Holmes, decided to invite a player from an Italian club to come and help him out, hoping for some sort of miracle. Because of that Holmes was once described by Jim Blair of the *Daily Record* as, 'The joiner from Falkirk who would be the carpenter from Nazareth'. In that sense Holmes would only have been disappointed that Souness failed to prove he could walk on water.

Many people believed the man sitting beside him now to complete the fantasy table, could achieve such a feat. Inevitably I have to put Jock Stein beside his former captain.

CHAPTER 13

The Coal Face

I LIVE ONLY a footbridge away from the village of Blantyre on the other side of the Clyde, where a football pitch still exists that I hold in as much reverence as the nearby David Livingstone Memorial Centre. That's just the way I am. During one of those days of research in a public library, trying to find some relevant information about football in that village, I began to feel I had as much chance of finding anything worthwhile as discovering the whereabouts of Shergar. But I then stumbled upon an item in the now defunct *Blantyre Gazette* newspaper that made me feel like disturbing the old men reading their newspapers around me, with a scream of 'Eureka'. I admit that the excitement I experienced made me feel like a fossil hunter who has to explain why this curious item he has found, which looks nothing special, is actually ammonite, a shell that definitely tells us something valuable about our distant past. Skimming through the microfilm of the archives of that local newspaper – a process that actually makes me feel dizzy and queasy – looking for any possible references to local football of the past – I stopped at one point when a name caught my eye in a column of the sports pages. Matt Busby. It was dated 1 August 1942. What was Matt Busby doing in Blantyre in 1942 that required an article in a newspaper? At that juncture in his career he was an established figure in the eyes of the Scottish public as a Hibernian player, but principally as a man who had established himself in English football, firstly with Manchester City, then Liverpool and won the devotion of people, like my grandfather. He had watched him playing in the wartime internationals for Scotland against England, and told me pointedly, 'Matt has the heart of a lion.' A quality that was to lead him eventually to Old Trafford. So why was I awakened so abruptly from the drowse of research?

The date gave me an initial clue. A world war was clearly still raging on. Busby was in the army, like many other players of that era.

As I read on it became clear that he was in Blantyre representing his battalion in a football challenge, with undoubtedly a supply of talent from senior football like himself, to hand. There was nothing grand about the day. Just a five-a-side competition organised by the junior club Blantyre Victoria at their small stadium. Reading on further, the article explained that a couple of teams were unable to attend because of a shortage of players and as the *Gazette* explained, 'The difficulty was overcome with Matt Busby (Hibs and Scotland) raising an Army five, bringing the contestants back to the original six teams.' And added almost casually, 'The Vics obligingly decided to play the Army five, beating them two goals to nil.' That in itself would have meant nothing, except for that other piece of information I had already gleaned. This is what made the difference to the day. For a gangly 19-year-old had signed for the Vics earlier in the 1940s and was a regular in their side. He was known to some as John, to others as Jock and his surname was Stein. The flute-playing Orange Order pal from his teens, Harry Steele, (although Stein had no association with the organisation) verified for me that the singularly left-footed defender did play for the Vics that day.

This is where the fossil hunter in me needed to explain why it meant so much to me. It was about the fact that a pre-season five-a-side match, of little apparent value, had brought together, for the first and only time as players, two men who in later years would go on to conquer European football as managers. To me it was like tracing football greatness to its origin. And I began to imagine that Castle Park in Blantyre could rival the playing fields of Eton, which supposedly supplied the indomitable spirit for Wellington to go on to his particular European triumphs. But there was a wider implication which sunk in later. For there would have been no stadium, no Blantyre indeed and little chance of either of these two men going anywhere in life, had it not been for what still lay, but in diminishing seams, under their feet, as they faced each other that day... coal. That fossil fuel, rightly demonised at the COP 26 conference in Glasgow in October/November 2021, only a few miles away from Blantyre, cannot be airbrushed out of the history of so much football in our country, nor from the grandeur of the success of these two men. For there in the various seams, hundreds of feet underground, were the vital sources of power for the industrialisation of Scotland in the 19th century and secured employment for many who rose from cramped working conditions to seek a sense of liberty in the open air of a football field. Sure, they were all glad to see the back of the mines there eventually, for the locals had paid a deadly price at times, as Blantyre still records the worst mining disaster in our history when, on 22 October 1877, 207 men were killed in a fire-damp explosion, the cause of which was never fully established. Heaping salt into the wounds of the grieving, within six months of the disaster 34 women, widowed by it, were evicted for not being able to pay their rent, offering us an insight into the master/slave relationship of a mining community then. It could be a brutal existence. Stein, and Busby, who knew nothing about the young man he was playing against that day, certainly went down their Lanarkshire mines in a more socially enlightened age but still had to endure similar hardships of working in appalling conditions. So those few words in a newspaper had encouraged me to believe that labouring at the coal face had produced men, sometimes flirting with disaster, as we shall see, who were well prepared to face whatever life threw at them. That working past was never forgotten by either of them, as I learned at first hand. For Stein never dropped his identity with the Blantyre mining stock, as he perilously revealed to me one night at the height of the miner's strike in 1984, a year before his death.

We were driving back from a public meeting I had chaired in Dumfries. As we approached North Lanarkshire, well past midnight, we could see an increase in traffic. There were lorries on the road employing nocturnal stealth to evade the miners' picket lines and transport coal to various depots. There was no mistaking that. We had known about that in advance. Stein twigged them immediately. 'Effing scabs,' he said and for the remainder of the trip, as we neared the traditional colliery areas, he would turn on his full-beam headlights to try and dazzle the drivers, completely disregarding what the serious consequences might have been for them in the dead of night. 'Bitch', was the kindest expression he used about Maggie Thatcher. At that time, about 18 months before his death, he was a successful manager with a global reputation and his large Mercedes, which he always drove like he was auditioning for Le Mans, was evidence of a standard of living well beyond the level of anybody standing in a picket line. And yet there was something in his DNA which alerted him to an attack on his kith and kin. But, being Stein, he would also offer a rationale that was more cerebral. For as we neared the end of our journey he began to lecture me about Arthur Scargill the English leader of the strike campaign.

'He's nothing but an egoist. He's just pulling them into the mire. If they had left all this to Mick McGahey (the NUM leader in Scotland) he would have had had the whole thing sorted by now.'

It was the pragmatic ex-miner speaking. A pragmatism that was central to his eventual footballing code. A man who admitted to me he would feed the rats with bread during his meal breaks 1,000 feet down in the Castle Colliery pit, which lay directly under where my home now stands in Bothwell. And, despite the efforts of the local historians to remind us of our village's mining background, that heritage is now largely forgotten, amidst the surface comfort of detached houses, neat lawns and privet hedges. Somewhere below our very foundations, Stein was involved in an incident that might have changed his career dramatically. This comes from a book by an anonymous miner in the archives of the Bothwell Historical Society and only surfaced for my attention in January 2022.

Big Jock was a footballer and a good one. He worked on the Pickrose, a small motor-driven winch used for hauling hutches to and from the lye. Jock had newly transferred from his local junior club to Albion Rovers and clearly had a great future ahead of him. One day we were waiting in the lye when an oncost laddie came rushing along, breathless and gasped and told us there had been an accident. A rake (a quantity of coal in a waggon) had run away and was off the road with big Jock under it. The way was blocked and only the smallest of men like me could squeeze through. We found the roadsman beside the agonised Jock and we managed to lift the hutch and pull Jock clear. The Fireman arrived and organised a stretcher party to lift him up the pit where it was found his leg was badly broken. That should have been the end of Jock's football career, but he was a determined chap.

That last sentence is a classic understatement. In all the time I knew him and talked over old times, Stein never once mentioned that incident. He did have a limp because of a chronic ankle problem that brought an end to his playing career but I have to wonder if his inability to use his right leg to effect, as a player, can be traced to that leg break. However, the entire passage is a reminder of the constant subterranean danger that was faced with consummate grit. So if you identified as an ex-miner in the football culture you had no need to expand on any other virtues you might possess. They were all fellow survivors. They were clannish in the very best sense of the word. That is why the ubiquitous journalist Jim Rodger was able to move around among the elite in the game and be on such familiar terms with the likes of these men from the coalfields – Jock Stein, Matt Busby, Bill Shankly and Willie Waddell – with impunity and no door ever being slammed in his face. He was another who had dug deep and triumphed in avoiding silicosis. He was proudly one of THEM, self-identifying regularly as the 'wee miner fae Shotts' and declared this to Jack Webster of the *Daily Express* in 1973:

'We worked against the hazards of water and reek and foul air, without toilet facilities and in an atmosphere which would likely bring you silicosis, howking towards some seam of coal which would bring warmth to people's homes. When I left the pits I found that I needed no taskmaster in my life. My taskmaster is the Davy lamp which still sits on my desk.'

Humphrey Davy's lamp, which detected low levels of oxygen and reduced the possibility of explosions, could stand as a symbol for those managers who came from the mines and whose decision-making, based simply on the need for survival, fortified them for what were certainly lesser challenges on the surface.

But, if ever there was a game in which a gold-plated Davy lamp should have been presented to a Scottish captain, it was the time Rangers captain Jock 'Tiger' Shaw, ex-miner from the Bedlay Colliery in North Lanarkshire, led his country to victory over England in the Victory International against England, at Hampden in 1946. It would have been a token of gratitude from a nation badly in need of spiritual regeneration after the rigours of the World War, even though this was supposedly an 'unofficial' international. In later years when the former Rangers captain talked to me over the counter of his newsagent's shop in the village of Glenboig he would, in effect, claim that it was the mining culture that won the day for us.

It was a game I had watched on tiptoe, because I had 139,468 for company inside Hampden Park that sunny afternoon, so different from that more sedate day of the Paterson fight later that year. On occasions before then, when we entered a huge crowd at Hampden, I would be lifted by my father and transported from the top of the terracing down to the track around the field, via a chain of compassionate Glaswegian hands, passing the weans over their heads to safety in the city's version of 'kindertransport', that pre-war mass rescue of kids from continental Europe. But I had come of age, wearing 'longies' and thus, disqualified, I was learning to rough it with the rest, when the stadium in those days gluttonously crammed us all in and where it was considered manly to stand up to rib-crushings and the challenge of dealing with the call of nature. But it was like watching the game from behind a battalion of Scots Guards who were reluctant to let you see anything. It was of no great concern, since it was the sense of occasion that mattered, more than a clear vision.

Clinging on, both physically and mentally, as the game nears its goalless 90th minute, I see a flurry of activity among players at the opposite end of the pitch, looking no bigger than Subbuteo pieces. I see the ball in the air, just. I see the giant English goalkeeper Frank Swift moving along his line. And then, suddenly, a man in a khaki uniform grabs me in a hug as my father falls on top of me as well. Scotland have scored. Blindsided by my position, this total stranger just back from the wars and my father and myself in this impromptu jig, is proof enough that Scotland in the last minute have won this totemic game by the prodding foot of Jimmy Delaney – Jimmy Delaney, from the mining community of Cleland in Lanarkshire, previously of Celtic Football Club, then with Manchester United. He and the other mining stock of that day lived long enough for me to catch up with them as the years unfolded.

The first was Shaw. He was popular in an area characterised by largely passive and genial sectarian division. Everybody went into his shop for their newspapers and the local gossip, regardless of team loyalties. He had lent status to the area by simply being the 'weel kent face' throughout Scotland. For me it was before the days of a professional broadcasting career and I was there merely as an outsider who had come to teach in the area and consequently date my Glenboig fiancée. But I remember him as a grizzly-looking, soft-spoken man who, like many warriors of his ilk, was reticent to talk too much about the event, as if he had a private pact with the memory of the day that he was not willing to release. You had to gradually coax events out of him. But what he did reveal was something of which I had then been totally ignorant – that the core of the Scottish defence that day, left full-back Jock, centre-half Frank Brennan and right-back, Jock's brother Davy Shaw, all had been drawn from a couple of miners' rows in his home village of Annathill, just a stone's throw way from Glenboig. All three of them had worked down the mine at Bedlay Colliery. This extraordinary fact began to obsess me.

So eventually I took myself up to Annathill almost with a sense of pilgrimage. There it was. Three miners' rows, grey, neat, uniform – a village minding its own business without any sense of the kind of importance I was trying to heap on it. I suppose I was in danger of romanticising its existence because of how much these three sons of the place had meant to me on that now distant day. I was later to bear in mind DH Lawrence's Walter Morel character in *Sons and Lovers* who summarised a miner's existence with stunning brevity. 'You get used to it. You live like mice and pop out at night to see what's going on.' That was a reflection on a stark daily routine enmeshed in harsh living conditions which Shaw, born on 29 November 1912, must have endured himself. For in that same year a Royal Commission was set up to report on housing conditions across Scotland's industrial belt. In one of its eventual 1918 summaries it stated:

The miners row of inferior class is often a dreary and featureless place with houses, dismal in themselves, arranged in monotonous lines or in a square. The open spaces are encumbered with washhouses, privies, etc, often out of repair and in wet weather get churned up into a morass of semi-liquid mud with little in the way of solidly constructed road or footpath – a fact which adds greatly to the burdens of the overwrought housewife...........If the pit is a wet one, the miners' soaking clothes must be left out at night by the kitchen fire; and as the kitchen is a sleeping apartment, even when there are one or two other rooms, the steam and gas which are given off as the pit clothes dry are highly injurious to the children who may be in one of the two beds nearby........the 'privvy midden' still unhappily retains its place in the mining villages.....and it is so impossible to keep clean, so foul-smelling and so littered with filth of all sorts, that no decent woman can use it, while if children do so, it is at grave risk to the health of their body and mind.

But, despite such widespread examples like that, whereas Walter Morel's character suggests negativity and capitulation, Annathill itself exemplified a more typical and positive reaction. For in that same year of 1912, Bedlay Junior Football Club was founded. It came straight from the bowels of the earth. It was fight back. It was about releasing themselves from the shackles of grim working conditions by attempting to shape something of their own destiny. Many activities would eventually flourish in mining communities around the land with the emergence of brass-bands, male voice choirs, the unique sport of quoiting, pigeon-fancying, all like a communal gasping for fresh air. But, above all, football established itself as the main respite from work and flourished in virtually every mining village in the land, but particularly in Ayrshire, Lanarkshire and Fife. Hugh Brown, the principal of the Scottish School of Physical Education at Jordanhill in Glasgow, used to tell his students, 'If you want to find out how a mining community is faring, go and have a look at the football ground. It if looks spick and span then life is on the up and up.' This was illustrated clearly by the history of the club which holds the record for the number of Junior Scottish Cup wins, Auchinleck Talbot of Ayrshire, whose stadium was surrounded by collieries. After opening their Beechwood Park in July 1909 they began a gradual dominance of local football and by 1916 had taken part in ten finals, winning five of them and then won the Ayrshire Cup for the first time in 1921. After which comes a sad reading of their club history when it states,

However due to the closing of the mines in the area and the closing of the miners row clubs like Glenbuck and Cronberry the football in the district was in decline. It hit Talbot hard and they went dormant during the 1928/29 period due to financial trouble.

In entirely changed circumstances and no longer so umbilically tied to the mines, on 21 May 1949, I was among a crowd of 68,000 watching them win the Scottish Junior Cup final at Hampden 3–2, against Petershill, in certainly the outstanding final of my generation.

One of the main reasons for the lift-off to such a growth of football in the communities was that it seemed to reflect the structures and behaviour established underground. Technique, hard graft, mutual dependency, order, discipline, bonding, basic teamwork which they lived out underground for the sake of survival, came naturally to them. Not for them the free-market philosophy of every man for himself. And there was barely an interval between work and play, as the annals of Twechar Rovers football club reveal in the words of a villager, Robert Douglas, before the introduction of pithead baths.

Twechar miners, nearly aw the miners, we seen them – they used tae come up the pit, straight doon the park – the park's doon by the canal. They came doon there. Up the pit, no even washed, oot in the park, black faces and everything, playing fitba.

My wife Jess recalls her schooldays in the early 1950s when she would take the Annathill bus.

'It was full of miners. They were all black with the coal dust, covered in it. They didn't have baths at work then. And they all smoked, like chimneys. And they talked fitba all the time.'

Such enthusiasm was channelled into organised leagues, particularly after the introduction of half-day Saturday working, and which would produce, over the years, many great players in a wide variety of positions. But the one I was interested in at that time was the miner from Annathill who had captured my imagination, 6ft3 Frank Brennan, a colossus at the heart of the Scottish defence in that famous victory, who had only come in at the last minute to replace the injured Rangers centre-half, George Young, and directly faced the vulturous English centre-forward Tommy Lawton who had scored more goals against us, by far, than any other of his colleagues. Brennan tamed him. So his success at Hampden was to take him from Airdrieonians to St James Park, Newcastle after that game. That move was home from home for him. He had gone to a club entwined with the mining industry and playing with men who didn't need to be told what a Davy lamp was. It was not just Newcastle United. It was working-class united. That is exactly how he was seen by the 'Toon' supporters who felt the border up there, further north, was meaningless to them. The paradox for me was, that despite all the efforts I made to meet and talk to Brennan while I worked in the south, I failed, but did meet his famed direct opponent of that day, the man they called the Hammer of the Scots, Tommy Lawton, whom I feared as a kid. I used to picture him as Bela Lugosi, the man who played Dracula on the Hollywood screen and quivered at mention of his name on radio.

'Matthews to Carter, on to Finney, there's the cross and there's Lawton with his head...'

Raymond Glendenning's commentating voice used to provoke terror in me mentioning these English players, particularly that last one. But there he was decades later, one night at Wembley inside one of the lounges after an England game, when he recognised me with my BBC London camera crew looking for interviews. He limped awkwardly towards me and pushed out his hand. I grasped it and was about to take some measure of revenge by asking him about that famous game at Hampden where a big ex-miner did not give him a kick at the ball. Except he couldn't talk properly. Unknown to me he had suffered a severe stroke and his few staggered words came out with extreme effort and completely threw me off balance. Nature had played a nasty trick on him and witnessing the awful state he was in almost made me feel guilty that I had harboured such youthful resentment against a great player who just happened to wear the white shirt of England.

None of those hazards of ageing seem to have been inflicted on Jimmy Delaney, the goal scorer, when I talked to him in his neat, tidy home in the mining neighbourhood of Cleland village around 1986. He never had much hair, so in that respect he looked remarkably little changed, for his whole manner was crisp and alert to my questions which were based on the 40th anniversary of the Victory Cup win. He had worked in the mines at a very young age but did not labour the point. So, principally, we analysed the game but could not fail to discuss his remarkable career which saw him win Cup medals in Scotland, England, Northern Ireland and Wales. And it said much of his personality that he talked more about the contribution of other players on that day rather than himself. What I do vividly recall is the tribute he paid to his great rival the Rangers player Willie Waddell. It was Waddell whose header across goal from a free-kick enabled him to make contact with the ball to score that famous goal. Of course, Delaney played at centre-forward that day, not as the renowned winger he was. These were the early days of conspiracy theories which gave rise to the suggestion that the selectors chose both the Rangers Waddell and the former Celt Delaney that day, to appease the factional Old Firm hordes. A world war had clearly not cleansed the city of its quaint sectarian ambience.

Waddell never worked at the coalface, although he was brought up in the mining community in Forth and could not have avoided being influenced by their work ethic. It was in his bone marrow, I believe, as Rangers manager, when the club could have imploded after the awful disaster on 2 January 1971 when 66 of their supporters died on Staircase 13. He controlled the consequences, over the heads of the directors and stabilised the club at a time when it was still in the shadow of Stein and went on to create the most modern stadium in Britain at the time, as well as winning the European Cup Winners final in Barcelona as manager, in 1972. These, together, constitute one of the great achievements in Scottish football in my lifetime. His great rival on the other side of the city though was working towards another colossal feat.

AS ONE DOOR CLOSES

Blantyre Ferme No 3 pit closed in August 1964. It was the last pit in the village. Seven months later on 9 March 1965 Jock Stein, who had worked there as a lad, became Celtic manager, fully aware that some traces of his past were being wiped out by the wind of change affecting Scottish industry. He was about to implement his own wind of change that, admittedly, to start with barely rose above that of a chilly draught, losing his first two home games to St Johnstone and then to his former managerial club, Hibernian, 1–0 and 4–2 respectively; then won only one of the four remaining home League matches and suffered heavy away defeats 2–6 at Falkirk and 1–5 at Dunfermline. But that whimper turned into a loud roar. The winning of the Scottish Cup 3–2 against Dunfermline on the 24 April 1965 redeemed him. In his early days, and thereafter, he would regularly remind the players of the sacrifices the working-man made to support the club. They owed the tillers of the soil a special effort. Even after that triumph in Lisbon when his players were increasingly thinking of their material welfare and the captain McNeill knocked on Stein's door to ask for a wage rise for the lads, he was sent packing with two abrupt words which I leave to the reader's imagination. McNeill was too embarrassed to go back so quickly to the dressing room and decided to spend about quarter of an hour in the toilet, then re-entered to announce that negotiations were on-going. McNeill's summary of that incident?

'He still had the miner's mentality. He never got anything easy in life, so why should we?'

Stein was not alone in never forgetting what the coalface was like. There were the other two major figures, close to him, who started life in the pits and whose futures would overlap with Stein – Matt Busby and Bill Shankly.

It is irresistible to compare these three men who had so much in common and who accomplished great feats in their time. But Stein's circumstances were unique. South of the border the other two did not have to contend with the sectarian issue, as managers in England, that plagued some social life and provoked factional hatreds around Stein. But all three came from 'howking' coal as Jim Rodger eloquently put it. They were all confirmed socialists in their working days. They were honest men who placed great stress on family life. They overrode lack of basic educational qualifications and could utter words of wisdom based on unimpeachable experience. Although, on that last aspect, Shankly outshone the other two when it came to philosophising and whose sayings could stop you in your tracks, wondering why you hadn't thought about that before – my favourite of which still is, 'A football team is like a piano. You need eight men to carry it, and three who can play the damn thing.'

But there were stark differences among the three. Stein and Shankly were Protestants and definitely Rangers-inclined as youths. Busby was a Catholic from Bellshill, rooted in his love of Celtic. This meant that when he had a trial for Rangers as a youth, he suffered the orthodox and inexcusable rejection when they discovered his religion, but to his dismay, also learned that Celtic had cooled on him because of his brief flirtation with the Ibrox club. That hurt him deeply and simply packaged him for export to the south, where fame and fortune eventually lay – winning, as a manager with Manchester United, five League titles, 2 FA Cups and the European Cup in 1968.

Shankly, like the other two, was knee deep in partisan hostilities in his Ayrshire mining village of Glenbuck in Ayrshire where the gravitational pull of the Old Firm could make the communities outposts of bitterness. When I brought that up with Ian St John, one of his great signings from Scotland, at one of his summer football schools, he made it clear about the Shanks.

'He would absolutely ban any mention of the Old Firm in the Liverpool dressing room. From his background he knew it would just cause arguments and division. He just hated that toxic nonsense.'

But in their mining days the sectarian division, with all its daily consequences, seemed as natural to the three of them as the air they breathed. However, the evidence seems clear enough that Stein did not identify with the rampant bigotry. Harry Steele, the former miner, who acted as my Homer in pursuit of Stein's life, emphasised that for me when he talked about the divisions that caused fights in Blantyre.

'There was plenty between Catholics and Protestants. There was a lot of drink taken. You should have seen the fights then. And of course when Blantyre Celtic played the Vics, the Protestant boys would come down from High Blantyre and the Catholics from Low Blantyre and some of the bloody mayhem that would go on after these games was unbelievable. Now, I was in the Orange Lodge myself and played the flute in the local band, but all the time I was with Jock I never heard him say anything about the Catholics and by God there was plenty said about that, for all his pals were Orange.'

That is what made Stein's progress in life so unique. He turned his back on all of that. His signing for Celtic as a player from minor league Welsh football in Llanelly on 4 December 1951, in any other society might have passed unnoticed. But it was a divided environment he had been brought up in and his decision could not fail to affect friends and family alike. He made me aware of that one evening in a hotel in the north of Scotland after an Aberdeen match. We had appeared in front of an audience which had peppered him with questions about his career. He was coming towards the end of his time at Parkhead, so he might have been conscious of the changing atmosphere around his club, which was segueing from triumphalism into doubts about his stewardship. For he became strangely melancholic. This was so different from the man who could put the fear of death into players, officials, journalists and cameramen and apparently had no room for sentimentality in his make-up. But for some reason he opened up. He told me of how his best pal from childhood ignored him for the rest of his life after that signing for Celtic and that his father George would never wish him well before his matches against Rangers because of his own Rangers loyalty.

But it is possible Stein derived his ferocious temper genetically. For the *Glasgow Weekly Mail* reported on a game on 24 May 1909 in the Burnbank and District League, between Earnock Rovers and Blantyre Victoria. It tells us that there was a rammy in the match when the Vics, the team Jock would eventually play for, were 2–0 up. George Stein, miner, struck an opponent who had fouled him. The newspaper goes on,

> Mr Orton the referee ordered him from the field whereupon there was great confusion, the crowd breaking in and stopping the game. After the resumption the accused challenged the referee and struck him a severe blow, knocked him down and rendered him unconscious.

George Stein ended up in the Burgh court where he was charged with assault and according to the *Mail*, 'was fined 30s or 21 days imprisonment'. Given that employment was hard to find I suspect he paid up. It was a background of passion in the game which Jock Stein clearly had running in his own veins and which could surface in earth-shaking outbursts at the height of his career. His record certainly refutes any chink of weakness in his character, winning ten League titles, six League Cups, nine Scottish Cups (including one with Dunfermline) and of course was the first British manager to lift the European Cup in 1967. Over and above that he initiated changes that would become the norm in Scottish football. He was the first Scottish manager I ever saw wearing a tracksuit, which normally was black and mud-splattered and conveyed the impression of the working-man in his dungarees. He initiated formal press-conferences, for he saw his job as a political one, which essentially was different from anything Busby and Shankly had to engage in. He felt that Rangers had too much influence in the media and set about correcting that with the gusto of a shooter on a grouse moor. He used the telephone to great effect, sometimes late at night to impress or intimidate some of the press whom he thought favoured Ibrox. He gradually amassed a corps of spies sympathetic to his cause who would pass on information to him, not only about the social conduct of his players but also any journalist who would utter any criticism of his players. This was all so new to the Scottish game which had been populated by managers like Scot Symon of Rangers and Tommy Walker of Hearts, whose gear at training sessions would also have suited Sunday church and who, although they might have had disagreements with the media, were not into the kind of Stein pursuits, with the whiff of blood in the nostrils.

It had all been so gentlemanly by comparison with the practices Stein brought into being. He rescued the Scottish game from orthodoxy, exhibiting both tactical brilliance, motivational genius, but also ruthless displays of power, at times, that could make men feel like they were about to face their Maker. The players were in awe of him. It was a mix of admiration and fear. He handed out laurels to those who worked hard for him, but understandably could not please everyone and left some with bitter resentments about how they were treated.

He was the genuine revolutionary who could not have failed to inspire spirited individuals like Ferguson and Souness to follow in his reforming footsteps, but in their own inimitable ways.

All of these lasting influences have been outshone and perhaps overlooked, by that one historic day in Lisbon on 25 May 1967. It was like an out-of-body experience to those of us who only a few months previously had associated Celtic with the Scottish season of rain, mud and aspirations of glory which seemed a mere figment of their imagination. Now here they were, under a burning orb in the heavens, set into an immaculate blue sky and within a marbled amphitheatre which looked as if it had been left behind by the Romans. And on the field of the Estadio Nacional, which had housed rallies for the Portuguese fascist dictator Dr Antonio Salazar, Celtic put to the sword another autocrat, the Argentine coach Helenio Herrera. He was the defensive guru who had appeared invincible as he masterminded Inter Milan to European supremacy. Much of Europe had slavishly adopted his tactics. But it is what occurred just before the players entered the field that caused a pause for reflection. For some reason both managers and players were held up for an agonisingly long period in the steps of a dark tunnel that led up to the pitch before being allowed forward. They fidgeted, naturally anxious to get on with it away from the gloom. For Stein this stance in the dark was a perfect reminder of how far he had come in life. He had admitted to Hugh McIlvanney of the *Observer* before the game that he would never forget what he had emerged from.

> There's nothing as dark as the darkness down a pit, the darkness closes down on you if your lamp goes out. You think you'd see some kind of shapes, but you can see nothing, nothing but the inside of your head. I think people should go down the pit at least once to see what it's like.

Rising from the dark tunnel in Lisbon to the glorious sunshine was a resurrection of the daily survival of his early days, this time with more than a pithead shower as comfort up above. Instead, a shower of adulation awaited him. For in fact the Italian champions were blown away, in front of 60,000, some of whom, outside the Celtic community itself, could scarcely believe their eyes. A youthful side had shattered the concept of *catenaccio* football – an Italian word that means 'door-bolt' and could be described as football's equivalent of a chastity belt – a defensive tactic to avoid penetration. But, after going behind to a Sandro Mazzola penalty, the two goals by Tommy Gemmell and Stevie Chalmers led to a jubilant pitch invasion at the final whistle and the momentous raising of the cup by Billy McNeill. Much of Europe celebrated these newcomers exploding the myth of the value of defensive football. It felt like that moment in the *Wizard of Oz* when Judy reveals the fraudulence of the Wizard and his whole edifice collapses. Herrera was no longer an omnipotent footballing czar but merely an Argentine in a neat Armani suit. So his peers did indeed shower Stein with praises, most notably Bill Shankly who was there to support his ex-miner friend.

I met the Shanks 13 years later in 1980, in the Orchard Park Hotel in the south-side of Glasgow. He was preparing to go to Hampden Park to be honoured by the SFA for his services to football, a year before his death. He had enjoyed a glorious career with Liverpool winning three English First Division titles, two FA Cups and one UEFA Cup in 1973. But now, in retirement, my interview with him lacked any of the old chirpiness and wit. He was a lost man, cut off from any football commitment. There was something of an uplift in the mood when Stein, now Scotland manager, came into the room. Shankly always called him John, as his mother and father had, and that name seemed like it was only permitted to those really close to him. But you could tell Stein was surprised at the downbeat nature of his old friend from Glenbuck. Shankly believed his life had become meaningless with barely any challenge left for him – a challenge which had been there from the day he went underground for the first time. So I wondered there and then about Stein. How would he cope with his retirement, this obsessive man whose active mind made sleeping a nightly problem for him?

My conjecture was short lived. He died pitchside in Cardiff as Scotland played out a World Cup qualifier with Wales on 10 September 1985 as complications from his heart condition caused his lungs to fill with water. He had effectively drowned. It was a death of self-sacrifice, for had he taken his prescribed water-pills he might have survived. But the effect they had on him would have interfered with his managerial duties, as it forced too many toilet breaks for his liking, so he had desisted. The public reaction to his death was as if people were acknowledging the fulfilling of the duties of a warrior on the battlefield.

Exactly 36 years on from that night, in a Glasgow conference hall, the COP 26 delegates, however compromised their conclusions might have appeared to be, sounded the death knell for coal-mining. Stein, Busby and Shankly, and those many others who sought release from the claustrophobia of that existence, by playing football, would have expressed no regrets. None of these men nursed nostalgia for that way of life. But, whatever their misgivings, the only way they ever talked about hacking at the coal face with a pickaxe, was with pride. For Stein knew it had equipped him to shoulder burdens that he carried successfully to the very pinnacle of the game. Which is why the former mining and cotton mill community of Blantyre can proudly boast of association with two famous quotations which arise from the presence of a memorial to an explorer and the existence of a small football stadium where the feet of the mighty once trod:

American journalist Henry Stanley to a hero on the shores of Lake Tanganyika in November 1871 and as quoted in the Encyclopaedia Brittanica in 1872, 'Dr Livingston, I presume?'

Ex-miner Bill Shankly to a hero in a stadium in Lisbon in May 1967, as quoted to me eventually by the man himself, 'John, you're immortal now!'

The words simply remind us that what that sportsman and the explorer shared over the centuries was a restless spirit that drove them on to defy convention and strike out beyond the limitations of their own parish and touch unprecedented heights.

* * *

The thought of immortality is perhaps the appropriate way to end the reveries of a fantasy dinner especially as it hopefully illustrates the breadth of Scottish achievement in vastly different fields. I have to thank the guests for allowing me to recall how I stuck a mic or a camera in their faces or phoned them at unearthly hours, in what is my eminently selfish profession. I can't say my odyssey was all fun. But much of it was. All of it though was inspirational, in manifold ways, which is why they were all around the table. Without them life would have been much poorer. However, although I have ended with stories about a famous manager who happened to be one of Scotland's most renowned teetotallers, I have to call for a toast, with whatever is to hand. It has to be for Miss Paton who brought sport into the classroom during a world war but could never have imagined what affect her story would have on a boy who immediately wanted to be another Eric Liddell. She never did complete Liddell's story because in 1944 there was little news about what was happening in China where, pre-war, he had gone as a missionary. We learned later that even when he was placed in an internment camp by the occupying Japanese, he still remained true to his principles and refused to organise sporting events there on a Sunday. Then, much later, we were to learn he had died of a brain tumour in that camp on 21 February 1945, thus ending a life of inspiration for us all. The least publicised of his achievements was in giving a boy, irritated by acne and waiting to have his tonsils taken out, a new lease of life, one Friday afternoon.